TEACHING STUDENTS WITH BEHAVIOR DISORDERS

TEACHING STUDENTS WITH BEHAVIOR DISORDERS:

TECHNIQUES FOR CLASSROOM INSTRUCTION

Patricia A. Gallagher,
University of Kansas Medical Center

LOVE PUBLISHING COMPANY
Denver · London

Copyright © 1979 Love Publishing Company
Printed in the U.S.A.
ISBN 0-89108-091-0
Library of Congress Catalog Card Number 78-78027
10 9 8 7 6 5 4 3 2

To the teachers who share themselves
by guiding students in stress
to successful accomplishments

ACKNOWLEDGMENTS

For Support and Encouragement

Paul Gallagher
Alice Kampsen

Pam Mauch
Linda Ross

For Teaching Activities

Anna Margaret McGuire
Sue Menke White
Mary Whitaker
Lyn Ann Zey
Kathy Jarvis
Dodie Nelson
Marie Mahoney
Nan Hoffman
Lupe Saman
Harold McGuire

Susan Fenner
Pam Mauch
Linda Ptacek
Mary Kierl
Sister Le Ann Probst
Connie Anderson
Diane Federman
Sue Norris
Patti Bishop
Skelly Larson

For Manuscript Typing

Phyllis Rogoff
Pam Hudson
Eleanor Abrams

For Manuscript Feedback

Alice Kampsen
Dick Whelan
Judy Freed

Herb Kampsen
Judy Wilson
Al Larson

For the Photography

Jerry Harkness

To the Adults in the Photographs

Anna Margaret McGuire
Lyn Ann Zey
Sue Menke White
Pat Weakley

Mary Whitaker
Marvin Fleming
Harold McGuire

To the Students in the Photographs

(A special thank you to the typical children who
generously gave their free time to portray the
students in the photographs.)

Katie Larson
Doug Chamblin
Jeff McGuire
Karla Rumsower
Dave Mahr
Joanne Larson
Tom Colgan
Hank Bednar
Cindy Walahaski
Paul Moylan
David Gill

Shelly Evanson
Tim Mahr
Kella Ward
Marirose Larson
Steve Colgan
Lorri Metzger
Carol Fitzpatrick
Dan Mahr
Nora Larson
Jim McGuire

CONTENTS

FIGURES

ONE

INTRODUCTION

- Organization of the Book
- What is Structure?
- Who are Students Labeled Emotionally Disturbed or Behaviorally Disordered?

INTRODUCTION

This text describes the *structured approach,* an educational intervention strategy teachers can use with students who are exhibiting maladaptive behavior patterns and are experiencing social and academic failures. The techniques described are practical for use in special or regular classrooms and as content for methods courses in special education teacher training and inservice training, and by other professionals who are less frequently exposed to students who exhibit these characteristics.

This work was influenced initially by a concept described by Haring and Phillips[1] and further developed by the author. The concept evolved within a special education teacher preparation program at the graduate level. The participants, in addition to the author, were university students, and teachers who had sustained contact with behavior disordered students in a variety of settings. Classroom interaction provided an exchange of thought and techniques used in working with special students. This mutual sharing and feedback was fundamental to development of the strategy and to reinforce its viability, since changes can be made easily as new ideas are developed.

Procedures, techniques, and activities are described in Chapters 2 through 8. The procedures and techniques remain constant across age groups. Because elementary and secondary teachers use the approach, however, the activities are a representative collection for ages six through eighteen. If the structured approach is used with sensitivity and consistency, it will benefit many "special" students.

---

[1] Norris Haring and E. L. Phillips, *Educating Emotionally Disturbed Children* (New York: McGraw-Hill, 1962).

ORGANIZATION OF THE BOOK

The information in the following chapter is addressed primarily to teachers and future teachers of behaviorally disordered or emotionally disturbed students. The self-contained classroom is used as a model for this book — which in no way suggests that this type of environment is the best or only educational setting feasible for behaviorally/emotionally disturbed youth. It is only one of several options in a continuum of education services. The self-contained room is, however, an ideal focus for a book of this nature because it provides for "pure" treatment without distractors, concentrating on the subject of this book — the behaviorally or emotionally disturbed student.

For this book, then, the hypothetical class is a special self-contained classroom, considered here to be the least restrictive environment at a specific time in the students' life. This type of class has an average of eight students, is the only class of its type in the building, and may or may not have a support system (a team of personnel from various disciplines such as social service, psychiatry, and administration who have a close working relationship with the teacher). Further, the hypothetical class is a new one, scheduled for a fall opening. This text relates only to school hours and does not suggest roles or strategies for other important adults in a student's life, nor does it negate their relevance.

The procedures are described in order of their occurrence, beginning with the teacher's employment interview, the initial meeting with the students, and ending with integrating the special student into a regular classroom. Appendices, each found at the end of the chapter, contain supplementary information of a practical nature to aid the teacher in carrying out the procedures suggested within that chapter.

WHAT IS STRUCTURE?

The term *structure* as it applies to education can have varied meanings. For some, it suggests a rigidly disciplined, highly organized environment managed by a teacher using a predetermined curriculum. For others, it refers to concepts proposed by the early educators. For teachers of emotionally disturbed students, it was defined by Hewett[2] as the *contingencies associated with school tasks,* and by Haring and Phillips[3] as the *clarification in the relationship between behavior and its consequences.*

In their landmark study, Haring and Phillips reported the use of a structured environment in which classroom variables were arranged for the purpose of interfering with the students' maladaptive behaviors; and opportunities for successful academic experiences were provided. Emotional, social, intellectual, and physical factors in the students' lives were not separated into categories for amelioration; therefore, emotions were not isolated for treatment. Education was conceived to be a treatment tool, and healthy emotions were considered the byproducts of successful academic achievements. Teachers utilized the learning process to guide students toward the realization of their potentialities. Clear expectations for every task assignment and follow-through on the the requirements were firmly established. Follow-through was achieved through the systematic application of consequences which were pleasant or unpleasant contingent upon the students' responses.

The educational strategy described in this text retains the Haring and Phillips concept of interference and structure, and is expanded to include a clarification in the relationship between stimuli such as curriculum materials, teacher instruction, and room furnishings, and the students' expected responses. The basic subject curriculum was extended to include art, music, physical education, and special activities on a non-contingent basis. Procedures were identified; they represent a combination of techniques reported by Haring and Phillips and elements of behavioral management, programming, administrative styles, teaching practices, and classroom experiences.

Eight procedures have been defined and arranged in progressive order so that the clarifications between stimulus and response, response and consequence are always present. The procedures are: pre-academic year planning, educational diagnosis, selection and adaptation of materials, programming, behavior modification, scheduling, maintenance, and phasing-out. They are dependent upon regular teacher skills and are designed to be used *in addition to* good teaching practices. Some procedures are emphasized when the structured approach is initially implemented; other procedures become prominent as the student achieves

---

[2] Frank Hewett, *The Emotionally Disturbed Child in the Classroom* (Boston: Allyn & Bacon, 1968).
[3] Haring and Phillips, *Educating Emotionally Disturbed Children.*

academic successes. All procedures are used in a special self-contained classroom. Portions of the procedures are used with students in resource and regular rooms. For example, provision of an individual daily schedule of assigned work may help a regular class special student who has difficulty organizing time and completing tasks. For a special student in the self-contained classroom, however, the daily schedule would include additional techniques such as immediate feedback, alteration of low and high probability tasks, reinforcement, and one-to-one adult contact.

The "special" student is approached as a learner who has inappropriate behaviors that interfere with social interaction and academic performance. The strategy concentrates on a student's present and future responses. A myriad of variables, past and present, can contribute to the student's inadequacies; but the teacher concentrates on the here and now. This does not diminish the influence of past behaviors on the present. The teacher uses information from the student's past to heighten sensitivity and understanding, then utilizes this knowledge for individualized application of the structured approach. For example, the case history of one student revealed a chaotic, tension-filled home environment, and the history for another indicated a life replete with fantasies. Each student had a daily schedule of assigned tasks. The former student needed time upon arrival at school to freshen up and unwind; this was done through a scheduled activity that brought about a degree of relaxation. The fantasizing student needed contact with reality; therefore, this student's schedule began with a task involving teacher-pupil interaction and the use of concrete materials. Thus, the students' histories gave clues for personalized planning.

The structured approach emphasizes that tasks and responsibilities must be commensurate with the student's current levels of performance. These vary between and within academic subjects. Social competencies associated with the student's chronological age also vary. Activities designed to challenge the students, encourage creativity (often disguised by the student's divergent behaviors), self-discovery, and abstract processes usually are introduced after the student has acquired basic skill success. Planned instruction helps students achieve short-term goals that are approximations of the long-range goals written in an individualized education program. Activities are presented sequentially and, in many cases, are broken down into incremental steps to maximize success. Feedback and reinforcement follow every task. Task completion is not done initially at a fixed pace. Students' behaviors are the teacher's main source of evaluative feedback; their responses are observed for subsequent selection of materials, instructions, expectations, and reinforcement.

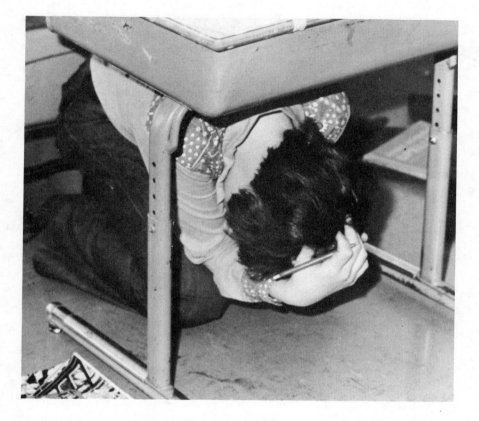

WHO ARE STUDENTS LABELED EMOTIONALLY DISTURBED OR BEHAVIORALLY DISORDERED?

Kauffman[4] has written about the factors associated with classifying children labeled "disturbed." The introductory paragraphs of his book succinctly introduce these children to his readers and are reprinted here because of their relevance to teachers.

[4] J. M. Kauffman, *Characteristics of Children's Behavioral Disorders* (Columbus, OH: Charles E. Merrill, 1977).

This book is about children who arouse negative feelings and induce negative behaviors in others. These children are not typically popular among or leaders of their classmates and playmates. They usually experience both social and academic failure at school. Most of the adults in their environment would choose to avoid them if they could. Their behavior is so persistently irritating to authority figures that they seem to invite punishment or rebuke. Even in their own eyes these children are usually failures, obtaining little gratification from life and chronically falling short of their own aspirations. They are handicapped children — not limited by diseased or crippled bodies but by behaviors that are discordant with their social and interpersonal contexts.

Some of the behaviors that handicapped children exhibit are recognized as abnormal in nearly every cultural group and social stratum. Muteness at age ten, self-injurious behavior, and eating of feces, for example, are seldom considered culture-specific or socially determined problems. Such disorders are most likely to be viewed as discrepancies from universally applicable psychological or biological developmental norms. On the other hand, many behaviors handicap children because they violate standards peculiar to their culture or the social institutions in their environment. Academic achievement, types of aggression, moral behavior, sexual responses, language patterns, and so on will be judged as normal or disordered depending on the prevailing attitudes in the child's ethnic and religious group, family, and school. For example, failure to read, hitting other children, taking the belongings of others, masturbating, and swearing are evaluated according to the standards of the child's community. Thus, a given behavior may be considered disordered in one situation or context and not in another simply because of differences in the behavior that is expected by the people the child lives with . . .

It is important to recognize the fact that many behavior disorders are situation-specific for reasons other than social norms. Social contexts and social interactions, through the ubiquitous learning processes of modeling, reinforcement, extinction, and punishment, produce and maintain human behavior. Adults and other children in the youngster's environment, then, may inadvertently arrange conditions that develop and support his undesirable or inappropriate responses. Ironically, it may be these very adults who then initiate action to have the child labeled *disturbed* or his behavior labeled *disordered*. Were these adults to change their own behavior in relation to the child's, or were the child to be placed in a different environment, he would behave quite differently. The locus of the problem in these cases may be as much in the child's caretakers or peers as in the child himself — the child may be as "disturbing" as he is "disturbed." Children's behavior influences the actions of their parents, teachers, and others who interact with them. Children "teach" their parents and teachers how to behave toward them as surely as they are taught by these adults. Teaching and learning are mutually interactive processes in which teacher and learner frequently and often subtly exchange roles. When a child is having difficulty with his teacher, parents, or peers, it is as important to consider their responses to his behavior as it is to evaluate his reactions to their behavior. It is not surprising, therefore, that an ecological perspective, which posits a complex interaction of the disturbed child with many environmental factors, is gaining popularity.[5]

---

[5] Reprinted from *Characteristics of Children's Behavioral Disorders* by J. M. Kauffman, pp 5-6, by permission. Copyright 1977, Charles E. Merrill Publishing Co.

Kauffman's work is a welcome addition to the literature written about characteristics of "disturbed" children. The literature and the experiences of teachers strongly suggest vast differences among the special children labeled emotionally disturbed or behaviorally disordered. These children are presented in the following chapters as they have been seen in the classrooms.

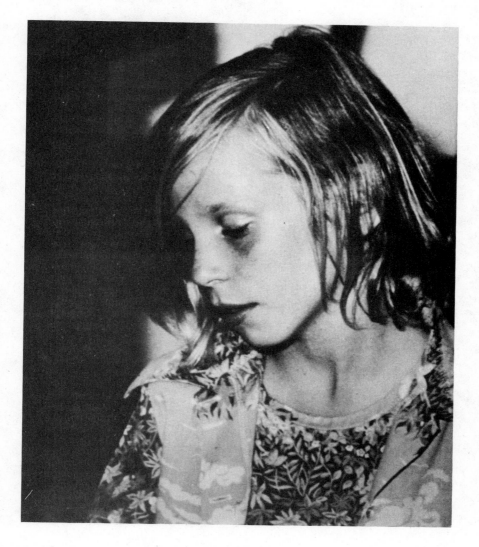

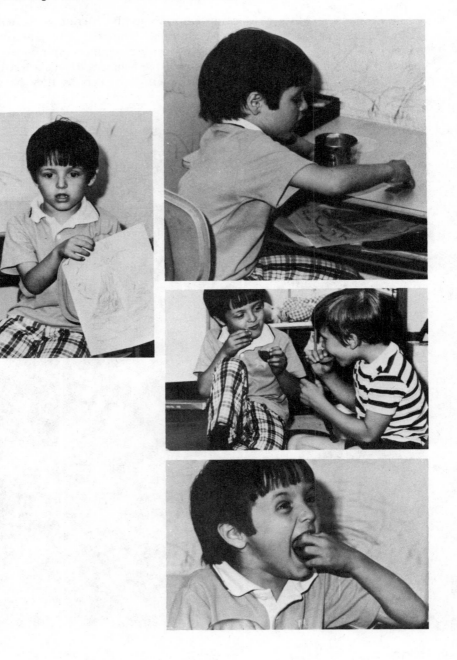

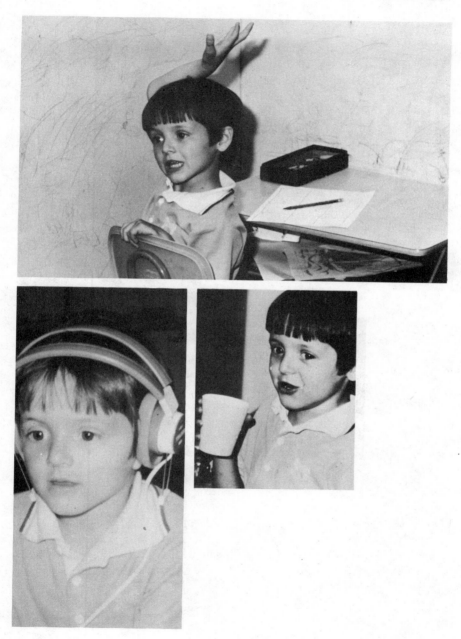

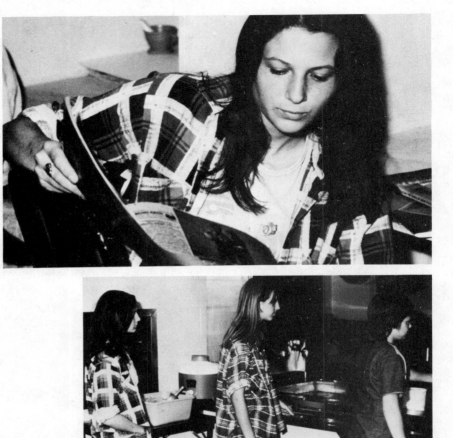

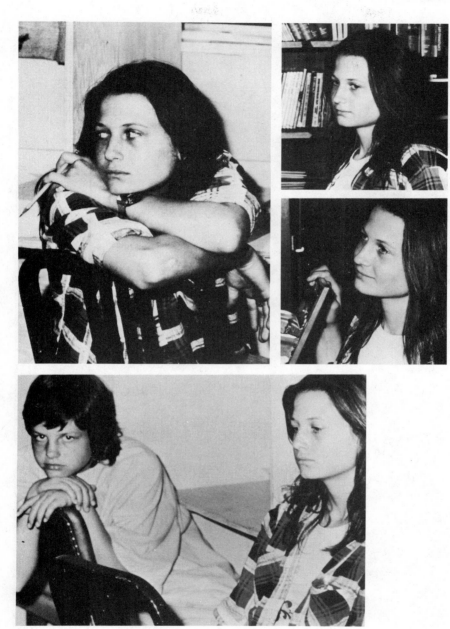

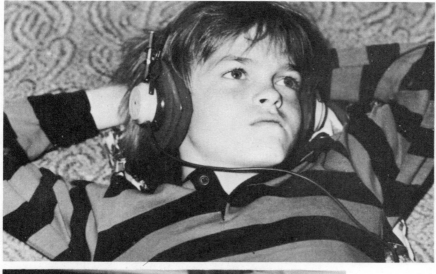

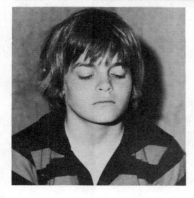

TWO

PRE-ACADEMIC YEAR PLANNING

- The Job Interview
- Planning Days
- Ordering Classroom Materials
- Arranging the Classroom Environment
- Appendix to Chapter 2
  - Inexpensive Items for Use in Storing and Organizing Materials
  - Items to Collect for the Classroom
  - Sources of Free or Inexpensive Materials
  - Resources for Classroom Materials

PRE-ACADEMIC YEAR PLANNING

Pre-academic year planning is a feature of the structured approach which the teacher uses before the students begin their first day in the classroom. The teacher who does advance planning is prepared to meet many of the emotionally disturbed students' needs. Since these students frequently exhibit unpredictable behavior, the teacher will not be able to anticipate all their needs; however, advanced planning can result in a collection of materials, a backlog of ideas, prepared activities, and an organized classroom, thus contributing significantly to a healthy, positive learning environment. Conscientious planning also can extend the teacher's tolerance for stress, heighten sensitivity to student behaviors, and enhance openness to new techniques. Planning conveys an important non-verbal message to the students: "I care"; "I've been thinking about you and getting ready for you"; "Welcome." Student anxiety can be reduced by visible and tangible evidence to indicate the teacher's understanding, concern, and behavior expectations.

For purposes of this book, it is assumed that the teacher is not already "on the job." The pre-academic year procedure is subdivided into four major activities: a) the job interview, b) planning days, c) ordering of classroom materials, and d) arranging the classroom's physical environment.

THE JOB INTERVIEW

The interview provides the teacher with an opportunity to explore personal expectations and those of the employer relevant to the special classroom teaching position. Information accrued from the interview, along with job market opportunities, geographic locations, and family considerations, are important variables which can affect a teacher's commitment to a contract. The teacher who signs a contract should be fully aware of the consequences resulting from the commitment.

Work conditions can influence a teacher's performance; therefore, a conscientious effort should be made to determine the conditions. If conditions are unfavorable, unhappiness, stress, conflict, and anxiety can develop. Many effects, including inconsistent behavior, can result. Students with behavioral disorders need stable, consistent support. They quickly recognize adults in stress and react inappropriately. A teacher whose actions are inconsistent and unpredictable will be ineffective with the students, often times without realizing how it happened. Favorable job conditions contribute to the teacher's performance, including the ability to be consistent in teacher/pupil relationships. Emotionally disturbed youth benefit from predictable and consistent expectations.

The job interview is a pre-employment experience which the teacher should enter into with a degree of preparedness. The interview may be any length, may involve more than one staff member at one interview, or more than one interview. For example, the public school applicant initially may be screened by a district personnel director, then interviewed by the special education director and supervisor of teachers who work with behaviorally disordered students; or the residential school applicant may be interviewed by the medical director of the children's division and the school's administrator or head teacher. The applicant should request a meeting with the building principal if that individual has not been included in interviews. Persons who have been involved in the interviewing process include superintendents, special education directors, building principals, supervisors, boards of education, school advisory boards, nurses, teachers, residential directors, personnel directors, psychiatrists, psychologists, and special project directors.

If the applicant's acceptance of a contract is contingent upon specific work conditions which he or she believes are necessary to effective teaching, these should be discussed during the interview. Not only should the teacher inquire about specific conditions, but should be prepared to explain their importance. These clarifications are important for the interviewer who is considering opening a new classroom for students with behavioral disorders, or is replacing a teacher in a situation described as "disastrous," or is concerned about hiring a teacher whose educational procedures are acceptable to the staff. An understanding of the teacher's and administrator's philosophical approaches to educating youth with behavioral disorders should emerge in the exchange of information which occurs during the interview. Work conditions and their significance which the teachers may want to discuss are:

1. *Flexibility of school day.* A flexible school day — one in which the teacher can arrange the blocks of time needed for individual and group instruction, to be free from instruction, and to be away from the classroom — is desirable for:

    a) *Preparation of materials.* Even though a large number and great variety of educational materials are available on the market, the teacher will spend a considerable amount of time adapting and selecting materials to meet individual needs of the students.

    b) *Attendance at meetings and conferences.* Public school special education teachers frequently are required to attend meetings of the special service personnel, as well as building, committee, and district meetings. Residential teachers attend team meetings. Teams of personnel including the special teacher also are involved in the students' intake, review, and exit conferences. Time for participation and travel to the meetings is needed.

    c) *Assistance to other teachers.* With a flexible day, the special class teacher can be a resource to other teachers who may seek help for special students mainstreamed into regular classes, or for regular class students experiencing learning/behavioral problems. The regular class and special class teachers can benefit mutually from such interactions: The regular education teacher receives assistance for students, and the special education teacher has the opportunity to keep current with regular class activities and in touch with "normal" behavior. He or she also gains a better perspective and frame of reference for the students' phasing out of the special classroom.

    d) *Conferences with parents.* Meetings should be held as often as possible and necessary to keep parents or child care workers informed of the students' progress; to solicit their help in creating a total milieu environment; to respond to questions and concerns; and to listen to suggestions that could benefit the student in the classroom. Conferences usually are held before the school day begins, after school, or during evening hours. If the day is flexible and even shortened on occasion, the teacher will have more time options to spend with parents and others concerned with the students' development.

e) *Mainstreaming contacts.* Special education teachers need time to contact teachers in their building, community, and/or the students' home school to establish the proper communication network for mainstreaming. From time to time, teachers also need to contact support personnel. For example, a teacher may need to be in frequent contact with the bus driver as a result of a student's notorious bus behavior.

f) *Individual tutoring.* A flexible day allows additional blocks of time for individual counseling to students who may be in a crisis situation or experiencing growing pains, and additional tutoring to students who may be blocking on a specific academic concept. Time also may be needed to help students who have been phased into some of the regular class activities. For example, a special student may be reading with a sixth grade class which plans to produce a play based on a story in the reader, and the special student may need coaching for a role in the play.

g) *Assessment of new students.* Before new students are placed in a special class, the teacher needs a block of time to conduct informal educational diagnoses. Results of the diagnoses are used to determine specific academic strengths and weaknesses, instructional levels, types of materials, amount of support needed, and other information considered necessary for the individualized education program conference. (The informal educational diagnosis procedure is described in Chapter 3.)

h) *Planning time.* Lesson planning consumes an inordinate amount of time. Each student might engage in from 5 to 15 activities per day. Thus, if the class has eight students, the teacher might plan from 40 to 120 separate activities, many of which are different from each other. Teachers also need to plan the proportionate amount of time they and their aides are to spend with each student. During a student's initial weeks in the class, the teacher cannot plan the lessons a week in advance because each daily activity must be reviewed and analyzed before the next day's activity is planned.

A teacher's daily lesson planning can be fully or partially undone by a student's unpredictable behavior. This unpredictability is more common during a student's initial months of enrollment. For example, a student may be scheduled for a math lesson wherein the teacher introduces a new concept. The student is upset about a recess incident, however, and his thoughts are not on the academic task. He destroys his paper, throws the math counters into the air, and promotes a fight with another student. The carefully considered lesson plan did not materialize, and if the teacher had planned a week's activities, all remaining plans would need alteration — a time consuming task — whereas, in daily planning, only one day's activities need be readjusted when necessary. Although daily lesson planning requires a sizeable block of planning time, it is a more efficient technique than weekly planning, especially during the early months of a student's enrollment in a special classroom.

i) *Preparation of reports and record keeping.* In addition to the myriad of forms normally kept by teachers, special education teachers frequently are required to prepare reports for staff members, parents, child care workers; and to record student behaviors and academic progress for accountability purposes.

2. *Preparation time.* During the job interview, the teacher should inquire about access to the school building before the academic year begins. The teacher needs one or two weeks to prepare the classroom and plan educational activities for the students. This time is additional to the inservice time required by most educational settings before the opening of classes. (Details regarding preparation activities are given in the subsequent planning sections of this chapter.)

3. *Phasing-in.* This is a technique by which students are enrolled in the special class, one at a time. This approach is recommended so teacher and student can become acquainted and begin to establish rapport. The student needs individualized time to develop awareness and exhibit appropriate responses to classroom expectations. As one student begins to adjust to the classroom activities, another student is introduced to the class. The phasing-in continues until all students scheduled for the special class stay the full school day. In residential settings some teachers use certain time periods to teach a student on the ward before the student begins work in the

classroom. No specific length of time can be recommended for an individual student to become ready for a full day — this is almost impossible to predict.

Teachers are urged to use the phasing-in technique; however, many school settings have administrative or philosophical reasons for not allowing the phasing-in technique as described. Some may permit a short phasing-in period, such as one week. If this is the only option, a teacher must adjust the technique accordingly. In any event, teachers are not encouraged to begin the academic year with all students entering on the same day, nor are the teachers encouraged to accept a student before an informal educational diagnosis and educational plan have been done (as discussed elsewhere in this book).

4. *Teacher aides.* First, will the classroom have an aide? This is an important consideration, because a good aide is a teacher's right arm. The aide can prepare materials, provide immediate feedback, work with students, supervise lunch, be a supportive adult during crisis situations, be the guide and partner for a substitute teacher, and serve as a model for behavior. Frequently, students with emotional problems have not had sufficient or sustained contact with well adjusted adults. Students' observations of the aide's positive interactions with the teacher can lead to many incidental learnings of appropriate social behaviors. A salaried aide who has regular working hours usually is preferred over volunteer aides. Some volunteers are prone to report to the classroom at their convenience, and these times may be in direct conflict with their original time commitment. Hence, the students and teacher who rely on the aide's assistance do not receive the planned benefits.

Can the teacher interview the candidates if aides are available for special classrooms? Some potential aides are filled with missionary zeal and are desirous to "reform the sinners." Others have deep personal convictions that disturbed youth are "born trouble makers" and need strong discipline; still others do little more than offer sympathy. Obviously, these individuals will not have positive effects on the students' behavior, because of their extreme conceptions of deviant behavior. Sources for aides include sorority alumni, college students in psychology classes, high school students in honor programs, homemakers, Junior League, and unemployed teachers, among others.

5. *Lunch break.* Is a lunch break included in the schedule? Some schools have no lunch programs because the regular students return home for lunch. But most educational settings have lunch rooms, dining rooms or cafeterias. Behaviorally disordered students can find many opportunities for inappropriate behaviors during lunchtime in a large setting for which they have not been prepared. Some need guidance in eating skills and table manners.

The public school special teacher sometimes is the only staff member who has daily lunch supervision responsibility. If the school has not anticipated the teacher's need for a lunch break, the interview can reveal this. One suggestion would be to hire a lunch supervisor if the teacher does not have an aide. At this point, the teacher should indicate that the lunch period actually is part of the academic program and the students will be taught the skills necessary to participate in the cafeteria or lunch room setting. The teacher would assume responsibility for this instruction, with the supervisor assisting, after which the supervisor can maintain the program. A lunch break is recommended highly, especially for teachers who have a full school day with their students, for the following reasons:

a) *Moral support.* A teacher needs time to revitalize and become ready to resume the day's remaining activities. This is especially crucial for teachers who have sustained contact with their students, without an aide, and a non-flexible day.

b) *Communication.* Frequently, a special education teacher is confined to the classroom beyond academic hours because of sporadic transportation, early arrivals, and late departures. The teacher has little or no opportunity to get away from the classroom. The lunch break offers the teacher an informal opportunity to meet the staff, acquaint others with the special education program, and establish communication. If this occurs, the special education teacher becomes a more effective member of the total teaching staff. Furthermore, the teacher has an opportunity to discern which teachers would be accepting of a special education student for mainstreaming.

c) *Attitude.* The special education teacher needs to convey to other teachers that he or she is first a teacher and that the "special" refers to the specialized needs of students. If negative attitudes toward special education exist, they must be dispelled by the

25

special teacher and the building principal. The informal atmosphere surrounding a lunch break is a logical place to begin developing positive attitudes toward special education.

6. *Budget allowance.* Has a budget been provided for the class? If so, the teacher should explore details regarding the amount and its disbursement. If a budget has not been allocated, the teacher should determine if the classroom has been supplied adequately. (Details on budget considerations and basic classroom equipment are described in the third section of this chapter.)

7. *Use of reinforcers.* If a teacher believes that extrinsic reinforcers may be necessary in the classroom, he or she should inquire if their use is permissible. Although a teacher may be knowledgeable in the use of behavior modification techniques, especially the fading technique necessary to reduce extrinsic reinforcers, use of such reinforcement may not be compatible with the school's philosophy.

8. *Availability of substitute teachers.* If a teacher cannot report to the classroom, will a stubstitute teacher be available? What are the procedures for obtaining a substitute? Will the substitute have experience with special education students? Will the substitute have had experience with emotionally disturbed students?

9. *Student teachers.* Some schools accept student teachers from colleges and universities. Should the special education class be selected for that purpose by the university, will the teacher have an opportunity to express personal views regarding the placement arrangement of a student teacher? Will the university supervisor have frequent and sustained contacts with the student teacher and special education teacher? Will the university supervisor delineate responsibilities and expectations, provide feedback, and be supportive if difficulties arise?

10. *Visitors.* Special education classrooms frequently are visited by high school and college students, school personnel, members of charitable organizations, and sororities. Are visitors screened before they visit the classroom? Who does the screening? Will the teacher receive advance notice of the visitations? Can the number of visits and the amount of time for each be regulated?

11. *Supportive personnel.* The teacher should inquire if at least one non-teaching professional will be available for consultation on a regular basis and emergencies. Back-up support also will be needed if a student becomes violent in the classroom.

Some administrators do not understand the needs of students with behavioral disorders and, therefore, may not be amenable to the 11 major variables described. Other administrators may agree basically to the teachers' requests, but certain factors may preclude or delay affirmative, committed answers. For example, an administrator may agree to the phasing-in technique but may respond "no" to its implementation because (a) reimbursement might be reduced because it is determined by the number of students' full attendance days, (b) transportation costs would increase during the time when the vehicles are only partially filled, and (c) no class placements for the students are made while they are waiting to enter the special education classroom.

Assuming that the above considerations are resolved to the satisfaction of all, and that the teacher signs a contract, the teacher should anticipate a period of time described here as "planning days."

PLANNING DAYS

The time the teacher spends working in the classroom before the students' arrival is designated here as *planning days.* The teacher needs one to two weeks to complete educational diagnoses, order materials, plan student activities, and arrange the physical environment. If the class is scheduled to open in August or September, the teacher may be required to attend inservice activities before the school year begins. Therefore, the teacher must add the planning period to the required reporting time.

The teacher should ask the administrator when classroom planning activities can be done. Special arrangements may need to be made because some school buildings normally are not available for use until inservice sessions are held. The teacher will not likely receive pay for the planning work but, paid or unpaid, benefits of a planning period cannot be overemphasized. During this time, the teacher engages in the following activities:

1. *Report reading.* A student's placement in a special classroom will have been a decision resulting from a planning conference attended

by the parents, school personnel, and other appropriate individuals. Evaluation data, school reports, and records may be available to the teacher. All authorized reports relevant to educational interests should be read prior to the student's entrance into the classroom. Careful attention should be given to the medical aspects. The teacher should be cognizant of students' special physical needs. For example, a student with a bladder problem may need frequent toilet breaks; a diabetic student would not be given sweets; and a low vision student may need special media and materials considerations.

The teacher can also glean from the reports ideas to be used as possible reinforcers and become more aware of the students' special interests and needs. Report reading should give the teacher a "feel" for the students, initiating the development of sensitivity to each one. For example, one report revealed that a thirteen-year-old female student had suffered repeated physical abuse, and another that a seven-year-old student had witnessed the agonizing death of his mother in an automobile accident. This information would give the teacher some insight into the student's behaviors and provide clues for educational and social planning. With the thirteen-year-old girl, the teacher might avoid physical contact such as wrapping an arm around the student's waist or placing a hand on her shoulder until determining how gentle physical contact is interpreted by this girl. For the seven-year-old, the teacher might decide to not use reading materials that have illustrations of happy, smiling mothers until the current effect of the child's trauma is determined.

Some teachers prefer to read reports in detail before they meet their students; others believe they may be biased by reading reports before meeting their students. Teachers should develop the ability to be nonjudgmental when reading these reports. The detailed reading or non-reading of reports before the students enter the class should be a decision based on the benefits it will have for the students' growth. Regardless of the preference, teachers must go through reports to obtain information on the physical and emotional needs of the students, and telephone numbers of parents, guardians, or child care workers, including emergency ones.

2. *Conferences and contacts.* The teacher is strongly encouraged to meet the students individually before their first day in class. A half-day conference should be planned for each student to allow ample time for the student and teacher to become acquainted, and to

accomplish the educational diagnosis. The teacher also needs this time to orient the student to the classroom routine and the physical environment, and to explain to the student his or her placement in the special class (Details pertaining to the diagnosis conference are given in Chapter 3.)

A get-acquainted conference with the student's parents also should take place. Some teachers prefer doing this the same day as the informal diagnosis if the parents are available. Other teachers prefer a brief visit or telephone call to the home, ward, or residence room; school policy in regard to home visits and phone calls should be reviewed before following this practice.

Some special education teachers seek out school personnel who have had prior interactions with the students, to gain added insight and to procure ideas which could be built into a support system. For example, a male staff member may have been available to an adolescent boy for weekly "man-to-man" rap sessions. If the sessions were beneficial, perhaps they could be continued. A discussion with a student's former teacher may reveal specific curriculum techniques. For example, a student may need the teacher's support and encouragement to undertake the first item on any worksheet; this student may desperately require reassurance before attempting written assignments.

3. *Communication channels.* Each school has specific formal means for communication, which usually is explained during the inservice days. The channels include procedures for requesting materials, substitute teachers, counselors, and first aid, for obtaining audiovisual equipment, and for reserving rooms. The special education teacher should be aware of additional channels — for example, how to request a conference or meeting, how to report child abuse, drug abuse, or truancy, and how to contact back-up personnel (e.g., child care workers). The teacher also needs to know the administrative hierarchy relating specifically to the special education class.

Some communication channels are informal; these channels can enhance a teacher's program if he or she recognizes them. Frequently, the custodian, a most knowledgeable person in many school buildings, can be the teacher's and students' loyal friend. Custodians can repair broken shades, locate needed desks, save broken crayons, salvage discarded workbooks, tell the mood of the school, and be a "counselor" and model for students. In one junior high school, three emotionally disturbed boys frequently sought out the custodian for advice, for a crying shoulder, and for sharing special happenings. Cafeteria personnel often are "forgotten heroines" except during lunch hour when demands are heavy. They can save materials (for example, gallon glass containers for terrariums or five-pound coffee cans for drums). They can put a little extra food on a tray for a child whose only balanced meal is the noonday one, or they can give an extra spoonful of favorite food to a student who has had a "super" day, or to a student who needs some extra tangible attention. They also can be supportive of special class programs by asking questions, making comments, or verbally reinforcing improvement in a student's academic and social behaviors. Their kitchen also can be a marvelous learning environment. School secretaries can be a source of information for items which haven't been included in the school policy handbook, such as where a teacher can have a cup of coffee or a cigarette. Secretaries also can tell how to expedite requests, procure needed forms, "screen" phone calls, and teach selected students office skills.

ORDERING CLASSROOM MATERIALS

Special education teachers frequently have the opportunity to order classroom materials. Before teachers decide on the orders, they should obtain answers to the following questions.

What is the budgeted amount? Is this the full amount for the entire school year? Will subsequent years have a comparable budget? The budget for a new class might be considerably higher than the following year's budget. Public school teachers may be eligible for two budgets — one from special education funds and the other from the regular building fund. The teacher should ask about this. Is the budget amount to be divided according to specific categories such as equipment and/or instructional materials; consumable and/or permanent items? Can a small amount be used for a petty cash fund? Some schools provide consumable items to students, so teachers will not need to order these items and will have more money for purchasing permanent materials. The consumable supplies may be given directly to the students and/or be made available to the teacher upon request. Some school districts require teachers to complete requisitions for supplies housed in a central facility. A few schools have their own supply rooms where teachers can take the materials as needed.

What about deadlines? Some schools set deadline dates, when all purchase orders are sent. Other schools have a set deadline date for budget expenditures but allow orders to be sent out any time up to that date. The latter arrangement is advantageous to the teacher because materials can be ordered as the needs of the students indicate.

What firms are used for material purchases? Many schools limit purchases to specific firms; however, the teacher may be able to order some items from other firms by using special requisition forms.

Is there a curriculum center? Some school districts have a center at which instructional materials are on display. The teacher can check to see if these materials are available on loan. Sometimes, single copies of materials are needed for short terms. If the materials can be borrowed, their purchase is not necessary and, thus, the budget is stretched.

A teacher should keep a list of items wanted for the classroom, within a broad price range. The teacher then is prepared if an organization would like to purchase items or donate funds for specific classroom materials. Frequently, organizations want quick responses, and some of them prefer the purchase of a single large item rather than a collection of small items.

Ordering materials for a classroom, especially an empty one, is not easy. The budget amount is an obvious consideration. The teacher might begin by making a list of wanted materials or going through several catalogs, marking items with A (need to have), B (nice to have) and C (can be teacher-made or scrounged). Before the teacher orders permanent items, their durability and multi-purpose use should be considered. Catalogs can be obtained of the firms approved by the school for purchases. Usually, the school has these catalogs on hand. Some basic purchase considerations for a special self-contained classroom include:

1. *Furniture.*
   a) *Desk and chair for each student.* The teacher should select desks and chairs that have adjustable heights. Double desks are recommended for primary and intermediate aged students; these allow the students to spread out materials, especially when workbook, paper, pencil, and manipulative aids are needed for one activity. These desks also allow space for another pupil, aide, or teacher to work with the student. Several extra desks and chairs are suggested if the budget allows, to anticipate the increased number of students that may appear in a class.

b) *Teacher's desk or work table and a swivel chair.* Many teachers of children with behavioral disorders constantly are moving in and around individual students and groups. They seldom use a desk during the school day; however, they do need a work surface for planning and materials preparation. Some teachers prefer to have a conference table in lieu of a desk because it offers a larger surface which can accommodate a lesson plan book, daily lesson and schedule sheets, books, student papers, resource materials, etc.

On the rare occasion when the teacher has time to sit in a chair, he or she should be comfortable; therefore, a chair should be selected carefully — possibly one with a contour back, rounded arms, and mounted on casters. The latter feature has the advantage of allowing the seated teacher to move freely from student to student — teachers of primary aged children particularly need this respite. Figure 2.1 illustrates these considerations.

c) *Tables.* Tables should be available for group activities, project displays, arts and crafts construction, interest centers, and manipulative materials. Table designs vary. Many teachers prefer round tables because they invite discussion; others select rectangular tables because round tables have lost space. A U-shaped table, as shown in Figure 2.2, frequently is selected by teachers of primary children. The table can accommodate the entire class or small groups for instruction and/or discussion. Several children or small groups can work at the U-shaped table simultaneously. Many teachers also have discovered that tables are useful for students who are learning how to work in groups. When these students sit at tables, they do not engage in as much pinching, slapping, kicking, or wrestling as when they are sitting next to each other on chairs. The table surfaces seem to act as a boundary.

d) *Study carrels.* Individual study carrel "offices" are useful for many students. A study carrel can be created by placing a portable tri-fold screen, or a three-sided large cardboard carton around the desk. Screen and space dividers can be positioned between desks to create individual study areas. Study carrels also can be made with a three-sided wooden screen attached to the desk or a three-sided cardboard partition placed on the student's desk. If a room is exceptionally small, a rectangular conference table with multiple learning stations can give each student his or her own work space. Study carrels with removable partitions are more

Fig. 2.1. Options, teacher's desks and chair.

Fig. 2.2. Options, tables for group instruction or activities.

desirable than permanent ones. Dividers that are affixed permanently to the floor and ceiling do not allow flexibility in the physical rearrangement of the room. Figure 2.3 shows some different types of carrels.

e) *Chalkboards.* If the classroom doesn't have a stationary chalkboard, portable ones can be purchased. They also can serve as space dividers. Instruction in regular classrooms frequently includes use of a chalkboard; a special classroom should also make use of this form of instruction since the students are being prepared for eventual instruction in the regular class and familiarity with typical instructional methods aids the transition.

f) *Storage space organizers.* If the classroom does not have sufficient built-in shelves, a teacher can order portable shelves, portable cabinets with sliding doors, stackable cubes with drawers, and similar structures. These also can serve as room dividers. Open shelves, which sometimes are distracting to students who are overstimulated by visual stimuli, can be enclosed by curtains, as shown in Figure 2.4.

g) *Clock and timers.* An electric wall clock with arabic numerals 1 to 12 and several kitchen timers are needed. The clock should have well-defined minute markings, a *long* minute hand, and *not too short* hour hand; clock hands that are too short can confuse students who are learning to tell time. Kitchen timers are used for activities that have time limits, as well as for implementing the daily schedule. These are illustrated in Figure 2.5.

h) *File cabinet.* A file cabinet with provisions for locking is needed if the teacher keeps confidential records in the room. The cabinet is also useful for storage of tangible reinforcers, answer keys, and special surprises for students.

i) *Mirror.* A full-length mirror is needed, especially for some self-image activities, personal appearance awareness, and clothing-sewing lessons.

2. *Equipment*
   a) *Physical education equipment.* The room should have at least a minimum amount of physical education equipment for outdoor and indoor recesses, especially if the teacher is responsible for the

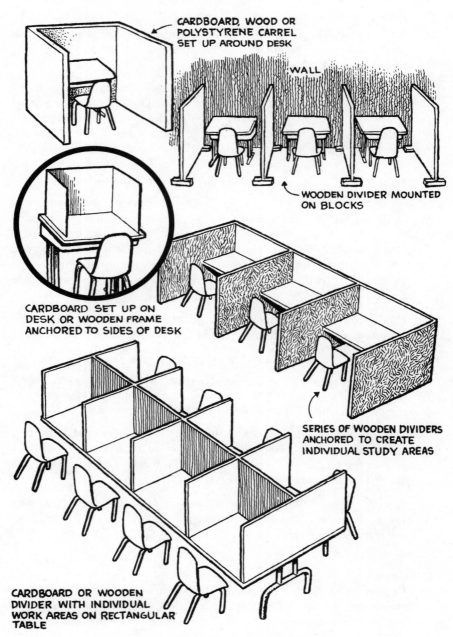

CARDBOARD, WOOD OR
POLYSTYRENE CARREL
SET UP AROUND DESK

WALL

WOODEN DIVIDER MOUNTED
ON BLOCKS

CARDBOARD SET UP ON
DESK OR WOODEN FRAME
ANCHORED TO SIDES OF DESK

SERIES OF WOODEN DIVIDERS
ANCHORED TO CREATE
INDIVIDUAL STUDY AREAS

CARDBOARD OR WOODEN
DIVIDER WITH INDIVIDUAL
WORK AREAS ON RECTANGULAR
TABLE

Fig. 2.3.   Options, study carrels.

Fig. 2.4. Options, storage arrangements.

students' lunch recess. Jump ropes, utility balls, basketballs, footballs, whiffle balls, and old tires are good for outdoor activities; nerf balls, safety type darts and boards, indoor horseshoe sets, chinning bars, slant boards, tension hand grips, and punching bags can be used for indoor classroom activities. All these items can be used in a gymnasium if the teacher has access to it. If the teacher is responsible for the students' physical education program, gym equipment such as tumbling mats and scooter boards are needed.

b) *Playtime equipment.* Playtime equipment such as building blocks, Tinkertoys, Legos, construction straws, magic trick materials, picture puzzles, dolls, spirographs, board games, toy trucks, and marbles frequently are enjoyed by elementary aged students.

Fig. 2.5. Clock and timer.

c) *Instructional aids.* A wall or table map of the United States, an individual state map, and a globe should be included in every room. Additional maps will be needed for students studying specific geographic regions. Science equipment appropriate to the student's age, interest, and study area should be provided. This equipment might include science kits, magnets, microscopes, slides, test tubes, terrariums, aquariums, and cages for animals. Additional instructional aids include mathematical devices such as a ruler, yardstick, meter stick, abacus, and counters; charts showing proper handwriting strokes, mathematical concepts, punctuation marks and phonics, illustrations; posters displaying "Great Master" reproductions, ecology, and safety themes; and flannelboards, pocket charts, and pegboards.

d) *Audio-visual equipment.* A phonograph, tape recorder, Language Master, and sound filmstrip projector have many uses. Several sets of earphones for the phonograph and filmstrip projector and blank tapes and blank Language Master cards also should be ordered.

e) *Games.* Games for short activities of 5-, 10-, or 15-minute duration and games for longer periods should be ordered. Instructional games such as Spin and Spell, Dominoes, Bingo, Concentration, Four Score, and Scrabble can be used by groups or adapted to individual use. Leisure time games include chess, checkers, Battleship, and Monopoly. Also, teachers and students can make educational games. The open-ended game format is great; it allows for several different games to be played on one game board.

f) *Music.* Teachers should select a variety of records for music appreciation, for story telling, for square, folk, disco, or modern dance and mood settings.

g) *Art supplies.* Each room should have a minimum of art supplies such as water, oil, and finger paints; colored chalk, pencils, pens, and crayons; construction, drawing, and finger paint paper. Paper should be ordered in a variety of colors, and sizes ranging from 9" x 12" to 24" x 26". Art tapes (rolls or pre-gummed paper) are available in many bright colors, including fluorescent ones. Posterboard, paint brushes, oaktag, clay, popsicle sticks, yarn, and burlap are other useful art materials. If a teacher is responsible for the students' art instruction, additional materials are needed.

h) *Desk trays.* Two-tiered desk trays, of wood, metal, cardboard or plastic, are useful for "in" (work materials) and "out" (completed assignments) of students. Some of the different types of desk trays are illustrated in Figure 2.6.

3. *Books.* Before ordering books, the teacher should determine which curriculum laboratory (if there is one) materials are available for long- and short-term loan. Furthermore, the teacher could check to see if any classrooms have extra books. If, after a teacher reads a catalog description, he or she wishes to order a book, an examiner's copy should be requested before the order is placed. Catalog descriptions can be misleading.

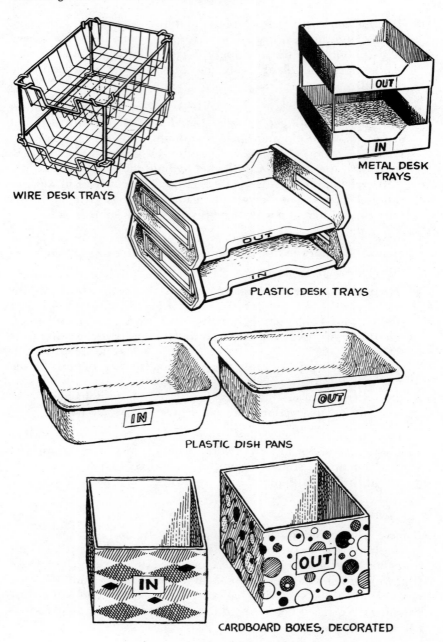

WIRE DESK TRAYS

METAL DESK TRAYS

PLASTIC DESK TRAYS

PLASTIC DISH PANS

CARDBOARD BOXES, DECORATED

Fig. 2.6.   Options, desk trays.

a) *Textbooks.* Textbook materials should include basic and supplementary series; high interest, low vocabulary materials; and, above all, materials that are motivating to the students.

b) *Teacher manuals.* Teachers' manuals should be procured for as many texts as possible. Manuals contain a myriad of teaching activities in addition to information regarding the developmental strategy used in the texts.

c) *Workbooks.* A variety of workbooks should be available in the classroom to meet individual needs. Specify in the purchase order that you want answer keys included.

d) *References.* Adult and children's dictionaries and a good set of encyclopedias should be available.

e) *Magazines and library books.* These materials can be borrowed but should be readily available to the special class.

f) *Resource books.* Every teacher should have some resource books. These could include an anthology of poems, a collection of short stories, a novel, a book of finger (puppet) plays, and a book of nursery rhymes, all age-appropriate, to be used during unplanned free time — for example, while students are waiting for a delayed bus arrival.

g) *Grading aids.* Teachers can obtain a series of cardboard grader cards for speed and facility in calculating numerical grades.

4. *Teacher supplies.* One of the easiest methods for ordering teacher supplies is to secure a comprehensive education company catalog or office supply catalog, and go through it page by page, listing needed items. In this manner, items such as stapler, thumbtacks, scissors, felt pens, index cards, masking tape, and similar essentials will not be forgotten. Also needed are items such as a hammer, screwdrivers (flat one and a Phillips), rags, flashlight, needle and thread, plastic bucket, and possibly a transistor radio, which can be used for current events, special news items, and weather reports and warnings.

5. *Consumable items.* Consumable items often are overlooked until they are used up. Every classroom has items that need replacement: writing paper, file folders, spirit masters, paper toweling, facial tissue, and soap, for example.

6. *Student materials.* Teachers may want the students to bring specific items to school. These could include notebook, scissors, glue, ruler, smock, crayons, pencils, compass.

ARRANGING THE CLASSROOM ENVIRONMENT

The classroom arrangement depends upon room dimensions and proportions, amount of furniture, source of lighting, number of students, location of shelves, doorways, and windows. Since each teacher must consider these physical variables in addition to student needs, a model floor-plan cannot be described; however, basic considerations are suggested:

1. *Classroom arrangement.* The classroom should be arranged before the students begin their first day; major changes should be avoided until the students become acquainted with the first setting. A student's familiarity with the physical environment can aid in development of independent mobility. If students know the location of their desks, work folders, paper, pencil sharpener, art supplies, science equipment, and where these materials can be used, they do not have to depend upon the teacher for that information. Some severely emotionally disturbed students become easily upset and frustrated if the environment is out of order, and some do not recognize people or objects when they are not in their familiar settings. Room rearrangements, however, can be made judiciously when the students' needs change.

   The door leading into the classroom should be identified conspicuously. The identification can be decorative even though its primary purpose is to help students who have space and physical orientation problems. Figure 2.7 gives some examples.

2. *Designation of room areas.* During the initial months of the students' enrollment, the room should be divided into areas marked according to their activities, such as work area, game table, free time, and exploration. Frequently, emotionally disturbed students do not know which behaviors are appropriate for different environments; designation of physical areas can assist in establishing boundaries and selecting behaviors. Posters, signs, and mobiles serve the dual function of being attractive room decorations as well as identifying the

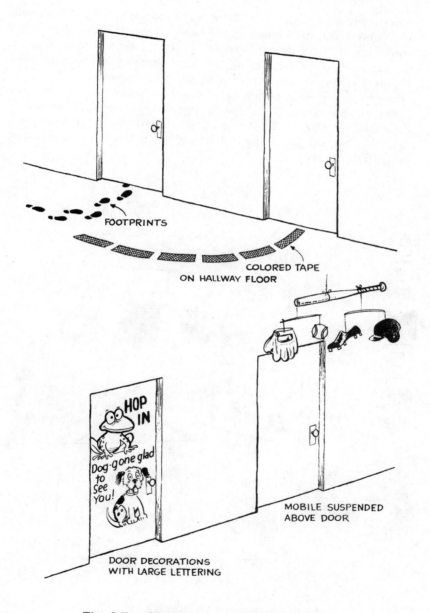

Fig. 2.7. Classroom identification aids.

specific areas for different activities. For example, the area in which students' desks are located could be designated "work area." If a student was "goofing off," he or she could be reminded that the behavior is acceptable during free time but not in the work area. Figure 2.8 illustrates some possible area designations. As the school year progresses, area designations can be changed to indicate new room arrangements. Teachers having large classrooms should be especially cognizant of the need for small space arrangements, desirable because large space invites gross motor actions and loud verbalizations.

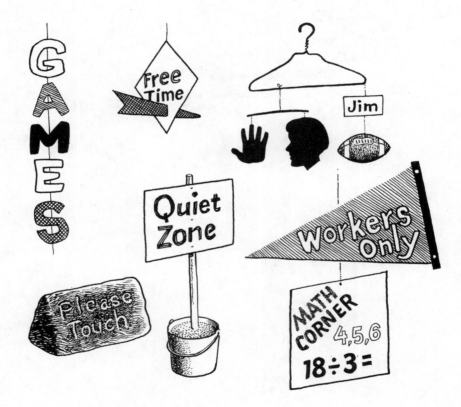

Fig. 2.8.   Designation of classroom areas.

The individuality of a student also can be identified. Each student's study area could have a mobile suspended above it, with each mobile having the students' name, handprint, silhouette, or picture of a favorite activity.

3. *Teacher's view.* During the initial months of the program, the teacher should determine a vantage view — a location where he or she can see the most students at any one time. By employing this technique, the teacher can see and move to students who request assistance, who need help in academic work, or who need emotional support. Resolution of arguments, fights, and harassments can be aided if the teacher has witnessed the incident. Figure 2.9 shows two different arrangements possible using the same furnishings.

4. *Study carrels.* Some or all the students may need individual work areas for certain or all instructional activities during the initial months of a program. The carrels are physical boundaries for students who cannot discern boundaries of self and space. Carrels frequently referred to as "offices" can provide the students with areas for retreat, for thinking, for decorating, for responsibility, or for independent study and privacy. Carrels also can be used to reduce visual disturbances. (Auditory disturbances could be reduced by having the student wear a set of earphones.)

Study carrels created by removable partitions are advantageous for minor and major room arrangements. For example, two students may be ready to interact for a short activity such as introduction of new words for a literature assignment. The floor or portable desk partitions could be removed, allowing the two students, seated at their desks, to participate in the beginning segment of the literature lesson. The partitions can be replaced when the students finish the introductory activity and are ready to individually pursue the silent reading portion of the assignment.

Some rooms may need one or two desks with anchored wooden partitions. These study carrels are more difficult for students to destroy. Later, they can be used for other purposes such as a hobby area or listening station. Synthetic arrangements (those not usually found in regular classrooms) are used to help students in stress. These arrangements are removed gradually as students learn to internalize boundaries and exhibit self-control. Figure 2.10 gives an example.

Fig. 2.9.   Vantage views.

Fig. 2.9. Vantage views (continued).

PARTITION REMOVED TO
FACILITATE INTERACTION

Fig. 2.10. Removable partitions to facilitate interaction.

5. *Clocks.* A clock with clear arabic numerals 1 through 12 should be placed where all the students can see it easily. Students frequently repeat their anxieties such as, "When is lunch?" "When will my bus come?" "When do I go to my sixth hour?" Also, students with behavioral disorders frequently have time orientation problems. Their time-associated anxieties can be reduced if they have a visible clue. If a student wants to know when lunch will be, the teacher can state the time and physically point to the clock hands to show the lunch time. Attractive cardboard clocks for group and individual special times can be posted near the electric clock for comparison to the actual time, as shown in Figure 2.11.

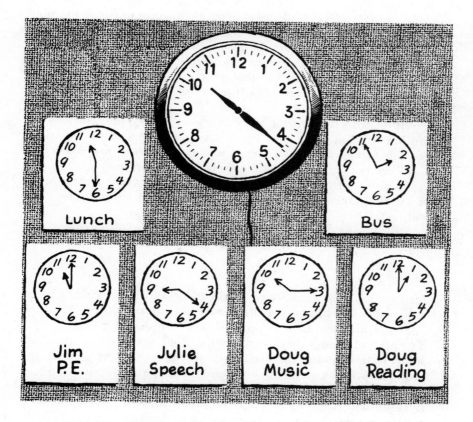

Fig. 2.11. Alleviating time concerns by use of clock displays.

6. *Desk trays.* Many behaviorally disordered students are overwhelmed by the physical presence of books (especially hardbacked ones), workbooks, papers, and pencils in their desks. Also, these items can invite inappropriate physical manipulation. Student materials do not need to be located in the student's desk. If each student would have an "in" and "out" work arrangement, his or her view of schoolwork could be made less threatening. Two-tiered desk trays can be used for each day's materials. Materials are placed in the "in" tray, where students remove only the items needed for one assignment. When the student completes the assignment, the materials are placed in the "out" tray. Teachers and aides pick up the completed materials from the "out" tray for grading. The top tray is best for "out" work, where students can see their accomplishments more easily.

Location of these trays should be given some thought. They can be placed on the floor near each student's desk, on bookshelves, or on window counters. If the desk trays are located away from the desks, students are given opportunities to legitimately move about the room.

If students can tolerate work materials in their desk, the teacher can have an "in" and "out" work tray placed in a central location. For this arrangement, "in" refers to completed students' work, and "out" refers to graded materials ready for students' pickup.

These systems should not be mixed for the same student or he or she could become confused about the different meanings for "in" and "out."

7. *Identification of possessions.* Students' desks, chairs, study carrels, coathooks, lunchbags, pencils, notebooks, and so forth should be labeled with their names. Some of these are shown in Figure 2.12. Teachers of junior high and senior high emotionally disturbed students have found this technique just as important to their age group as primary grade teachers have. Labeling items with students' names is another aid toward self-identification. Name labels also can eliminate haggling and fighting over propery ownership. Possession of an item can be a serious concern to the student. Furthermore, students who have not learned to share, as a result of deprivation,

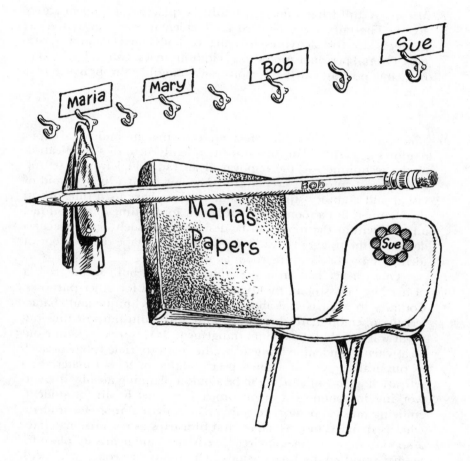

Fig. 2.12.   Identification of possessions.

over-indulgence, or inexperience, need to feel secure with some physical properties before they can learn to share.

8. *Mirror.* A full-length mirror should be placed for students' easy access. The mirror can be used for incidental learning, as well as planned affective activities to enhance body imagery and awareness. Overall personal appearance, clothing styles, hair styles, grooming, and posture can be demonstrated tangibly through use of a mirror.

9. *Time-out area.* Time-out refers to removing an individual from reinforcing events. The literature frequently describes application of the technique as "the removal of an individual from a setting which has reinforcing events to a time-out room which is void of visual and auditory stimuli." Some teachers have used time-out in this manner. But a room is not a requisite for the time-out technique; an area within the room can be designated as such. Some teachers designate the time-out area by laying masking tape on the floor or identifying a corner of the room as such.

One teacher had an 8′ × 8′ time-out room built in one corner of her large classroom; the room was also used for other purposes. Contrary to what is said about the time-out technique and characteristics of emotionally disturbed youth, this multi-purpose time-out room was a viable classroom arrangement. It was used as a time-out area when a student exhibited specific inappropriate behavior such as physical aggression against peers, adults, or school materials; a retreat for a student desiring to be alone; a planning area by students working in committees or on projects; a quiet booth for students enjoying musical or story records; an audio-visual room for students who used slides, movies, tapes, and filmstrips as resource materials; a special area for "magic circle" activities; and a private place for teacher-pupil counseling sessions. The room was constructed with beaver boards on two sides against a plastered wall and a permanent chalkboard wall. The room was decorated with posters, a rug (discarded carpet), and floor pillows. Furniture and audio-visual equipment were taken into the room as needed. Outside walls of the room were used for bulletin boards. Figure 2.13 illustrates such a multi-purpose time-out room.

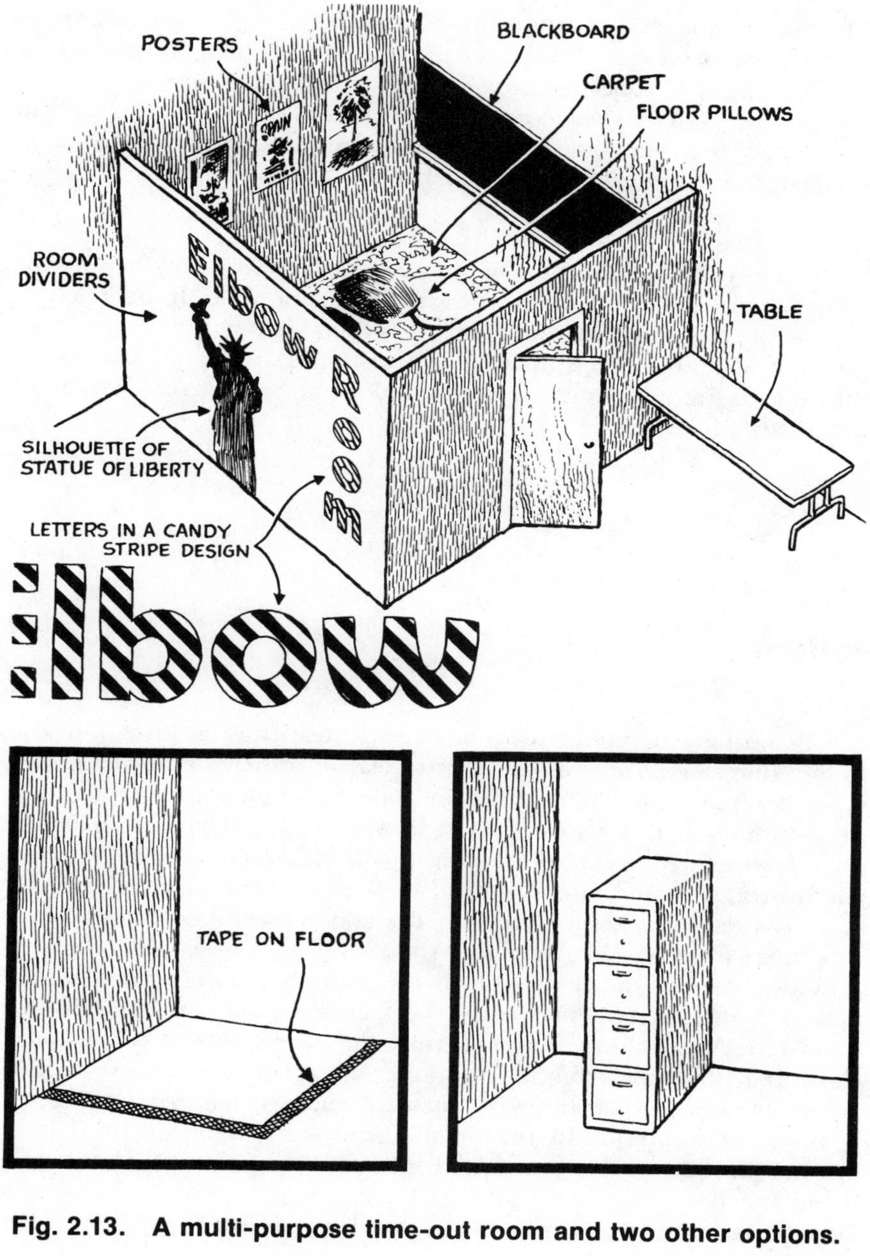
POSTERS
BLACKBOARD
CARPET
FLOOR PILLOWS
ROOM DIVIDERS
Elbow Room
TABLE
SILHOUETTE OF STATUE OF LIBERTY
LETTERS IN A CANDY STRIPE DESIGN
TAPE ON FLOOR

Fig. 2.13. A multi-purpose time-out room and two other options.

10. *Bulletin boards.* Bulletin boards should be arranged advantageously for several reasons: They can be used for displaying students' work, teaching new concepts, providing extra credit activities, expanding students' interests, or as a source for student expression. Boards can be designed and completed by the teachers or students. Figure 2.14 gives some ideas for bulletin boards.

If the room contains an abundance of materials, the teacher may be wise in not having all of them available at one time. If students are exposed to all the "goodies," they may become saturated. Students probably will enjoy each item more if materials are gradually brought into the classroom. Some could be saved for a "rainy day" or brought out at strategic times.

SUMMARY

Planning is a prerequisite to effective teaching. It gives purpose to the educational program and helps a teacher anticipate student needs. Good teaching doesn't just happen. The pre-academic year planning procedure includes a series of sequential events that lay the foundation for the *structured approach.* During the job interview, the teacher and administrator should discuss critical work conditions such as flexibility of school day, lunch supervision, aides and substitute teachers. Before actual teaching, the teachers also should engage in certain planning activities. Assessment of the students' educational strengths and weaknesses, record reviews, and conferences also are accomplished during these days. After information is accrued, the teacher will be able to order classroom furniture, equipment, books, and other supplies. Arranging an environment that conveys a structured and personalized atmosphere is the final technique of the pre-academic year planning procedure. Some techniques of this procedure continue throughout the school year; therefore, they function to support the continued growth of students, along with the teacher's emotional control and satisfaction.

I'm Glad to Be Me

PHOTOS OF STUDENTS

Good work is in the bag

Ken Paul Karen Randy

PAPER FLOWER POTS WITH EACH STUDENT'S NAME ON A FLOWER POT AND PLACED ON THE BOARD. THE FLOWER STEM IS IN VARIOUS LENGTHS. STUDENT HELPS THE FLOWER GROW BY ADDING PORTIONS OF THE STEM AND PETALS OF THE FLOWER AS AWARDED FOR APPROPRIATE ACTIVITIES.

Tim

A THREE DIMENSIONAL SCARECROW IS PLACED ON A BLUE DENIM BACKGROUND. PUMPKINS ARE SCATTERED AT THE BASE OF THE SCARECROW AND BOARD. EXTRA CREDIT ACTIVITIES ARE WRITTEN ON THE REVERSE SIDE OF THE PUMPKINS.

Start the day on the right foot

A PAIR OF LARGE PAPER LEGS IS ATTACHED TO THE BOARD. ONE FOOT IS PLACED AHEAD OF THE OTHER TO GIVE THE EFFECT OF WALKING

Fig. 2.14. Motivational bulletin board ideas.

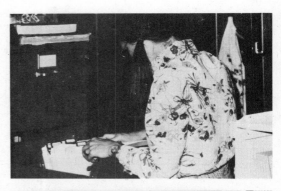

APPENDIX TO CHAPTER TWO

INEXPENSIVE ITEMS FOR USE
IN STORING AND ORGANIZING MATERIALS

For Students:

Three-gallon ice cream cartons
Mailboxes
Oatmeal boxes (stacked sideways and glued together)
Cloth sacks
"Portable" plastic buckets or dishpans (stackable)
Shoeboxes
Cigar boxes
Manila folders
Accordion-type folder with fold top and string
Three- and five-pound tin cans with plastic lids

For Teachers:

Large artist's portfolios
Suitcases
Footlockers and trunks
Large cardboard storage boxes (collapsible when not in use)
Large cardboard mailing tubes
Bags with drawstrings (to be hung on closet hooks)
Shoe bags (for scissors, paint brushes)
Spindles
Pegboards
Recipe boxes
Multiple skirt hangers (for hanging charts)

For Classroom Materials:

Stacks of cardboard file cabinets
Cloth shoe holders (for scissors, paint brushes)
Wire baskets (stackable)
1/2-gallon milk cartons hung on a pegboard
Large tin cans
Scrapbooks
Carts (on wheels)
Small buckets or baskets with handles (for crayons, scissors, pencils, brushes, etc.)
Hosiery boxes
Bleach bottles (plastic) with necks cut off, handles left on
Baby food jars/cottage cheese containers (for pins, staples, clips, stickers, etc.)

ITEMS TO COLLECT FOR THE CLASSROOM

Baskets	Plastic Margarine	Kites
Bricks	Containers	Bread Wrappers
Hats	Concrete Blocks	Trunks
Masks	Paper Doilies	Milk Cartons
Maps	Styrofoam	Dried Flowers, Weeds,
Bottle Cutting Kit	String, Twine	and Moss
Coffee Cans	Egg Cartons	Orange Crates
Balsa Wood	Wood Dowels	Plastic Wrap (e.g., Saran)
Wood Burning Set	Wood and Plastic Spoons	Plastic Eggs (L'Eggs
Macaroni and Other Pasta	Plastic Containers	hosiery containers)
Plastic Containers	Bleach Bottles	Hangers
Plastic Trash Bags	Cotton (balls & loose)	Pastry Brush
Potato Chip Cans or	Bottles	Clothespins
Tennis Ball Cans	Buttons	Broom
Soda Bottle Cartons	Foam Rubber	Boxes - all shapes
(wood and cardboard)	Hosiery Boxes	and sizes
Milk Cartons	Baby Food Jars	Box Tops & Can Tops
Photo Albums	Straws	Butcher Paper
Catalogs	Waxed Paper	Newspapers
Sand	Tin Cans - all sizes	Feathers
Old Photographs	Egg Shells	Jars
Leather Scraps	Bicycle Boxes	Plastic Glasses and Cups
Old Suitcases	Toothpicks	Word Scraps
Window Shades	Nutshells	Old Textbooks and
Pizza Boards	Laundry Basket	Workbooks (to cut apart)
Pop Tabs (from aluminum	Packing Materials	Plastic Bags
cans)	(styrofoam "peanuts")	Cardboard Tubes

Paper Sacks
Record Album Covers
Curtain Rods
Tongue Depressors
Shoeboxes
Mattress Boxes
Can Opener
Beans, Beads
Trays
Jokes and Riddles
Paper Punch
Ideas (kept in a file,
  notebook, on tape or film)
Shoe Polish
Empty Window Cleaner
  Spray Bottles
Felt, Burlap, or Vinyl
Florist Tape
Sectioned Boxes (liquor
  store is a good source)
Foam Rubber Pieces
Magnets, all sizes
Scrapbook
Sequins, Glitter
Cookie Cutters
Old TV without parts

Old Calendars
Paraffin
Cereal Boxes
Wallpaper
Bottle Caps
Tools
Cloth of all kinds
Old Clothing
Wire Cutters
Puzzles
Mixing Bowls
Old Slides
Flashlight
Magazines
Travel Brochures
Pictures
Plastic Utensils
Carpet Scraps
Old Sheet (for dyeing)
Old Checks
Plastic Tablecloth
Aluminum Foil
Comic Books
Old Film Canisters
Mirrors
Tape

Travel Posters
Wire
Pipe Cleaners
Greeting Cards
Gift Wrapping Paper
Paper Plates
Cord
Recipes
Plastic Pail
Rocks
Rice and Popcorn
Tile Squares
Clay Pots
Used Light Bulbs
Pegboards
Recipe Boxes
Pillows
Rugs
Yarn, Thread, Jute
Contact Paper
Used Paper for Recycling
Flour and Salt
Label Maker
Hamburger and Other
  Cartons (from "fast
  food" places)

SOURCES OF FREE OR INEXPENSIVE MATERIALS

Garage/Yard Sales
Teachers, Grandparents, Parents, Friends
Auctions
Estate Sales
Sidewalk Sales
Book Sales
Second-Hand Book Shop
  (exchange a coveted best seller for some
  children's paperback books)
National Merchandise Shows
  (Home Show, Boat, Sports and Travel
  Show, Hot Rod Show — these often give
  away free pamphlets, posters, and items
  during display and show times)
Sororities (donations and volunteers)
Print Shop (paper scraps)
Appliance Stores (large appliance cartons)
Carpet Stores (samples and upholstery fabric)
Radio Stations (records from disc jockeys)
Pizza Restaurants (cardboard circles)

Montgomery Ward, Sears & Roebuck, and
  other department chain stores (slides of
  items that appear in their catalogs, often
  discarded; old catalogs)
Bakeries (charts, coated sacks, day-old
  doughnuts)
Municipal Offices (charts on safety)
Grocery Stores (posters, standups, displays,
  racks, fruit crates)
Airlines (posters, pamphlets, flight
  attendants' "wings" for children)
R. F. Kennedy Foundation (for pamphlets)
Chambers of Commerce (city maps, list of
  places to visit, places offering tours)
Nurseries (small plants often discarded)
Telephone Company (teaching materials,
  phone books, excess colored wires)
Armed Forces Recruiting Stations (posters)
Army/Navy Surplus Stores (used and
  recycled items)

Construction Companies (cable spools)

Newspaper Publishers (newsprint paper left on rolls)

Instructor Magazine (many free items available from monthly list)

Avon (free samples)

Knit shops, craft stores, construction sites (odds and ends that they will give away)

Paint Stores (discarded acoustical tile)

Publisher's Exhibits (curriculum materials and samples; sometimes you can field-test materials and thereby get a free copy)

Pet Shops (leaky aquariums frequently are sold at a much reduced price, and they can be used for many other purposes)

School Districts (a source for old textbooks)

Goodwill Industries/Salvation Army (inexpensive recycled items)

Dinner Playhouses and Playhouses (sometimes will offer free matinees)

Publishing Companies (often will send free posters advertising a series)

Wallpaper Shops

Banks (frequently have pamphlets and sometimes media such as transparencies on how to use checking accounts, savings accounts)

Cleaning Shops and Carpet Shops (heavy duty cardboard rolls)

Cleaning Establishments (some have unclaimed clothing)

Radio and TV Service Shops (discarded appliances and parts)

Department Stores (window displays)

Bread Discount Stores (wrappers, snack discounts)

Ice Cream Stores (cartons)

Police and Fire Stations (information and safety pamphlets)

Police (auctions on unclaimed merchandise)

U.S. Department of Agriculture (pamphlets, homemaking ideas, demonstrations)

"Help" Letters to Newspapers, Parents, etc., describing needed good and services)

School Cafeteria (cans, boxes, egg cartons, etc.)

School Lunchrooms (milk cartons and empty dixie cups)

Friends, Relatives, In-laws, Clubs, Organizations, Sororities, etc., as "Junk Bankers" (supply with a list of needed items)

Stores (leave your name and phone number at stores having large, colorful advertising displays that eventually might be discarded)

Dentists-Doctors (inquire about old magazines from the waiting room)

A "Junk" Drive

Treasure Hunt with a list of needs; check:
Drawers (especially kitchen)
Wastebaskets
Recycling centers
Back rooms of grocery stores
Attics, basements
Alleys behind stores
School storage rooms
"Give Away" sections of newspapers

Foreign Embassies (posters, information, and speakers representing their countries)

Train-Bus-Airline Terminals (timetables)

Florist Shops (containers, ribbon)

Car Dealers (posters, advertising pamphlets)

Restaurants (paper placemats, balloons, plastic utensils, paper coasters, cartons, corks)

Gas Stations (maps, pamphlets)

U. S. Government Printing Office (free pamphlets)

Animal Shelters, Humane Societies (pamphlets on animal care)

Telephone Books (white section usually has concise but interesting history of the city or area, with a list of points of interest)

Motels/Hotels (stationery, guest soaps, sewing kits, etc., if requested)

Hair Styling/Barber Schools (free or discount shampoos, haircuts, styles — good as reinforcers)

Lumberyards (scrap wood, sawdust, wood curls)

Junkyards (gears and movable parts from clocks, radios, wheels, etc.)

Merle Norman Cosmetics/Mary Kay Cosmetics (free samples and makeup demonstrations)

Mental Health Associations (pamphlets; films — often loaned)

Each city or area has its own unique sources. These are worth investigating.

RESOURCES FOR CLASSROOM MATERIALS

Abbey Press Produces cards, gifts, posters, banners, plaques, and books, many of which are appropriate for classroom use. Most of the products are "feelings"-oriented, useful in self-concept discussion and activities. The company has an outstanding selection of posters. St. Meinard, IN 47577.

Beacon Press: *The Seed Catalog* (Jeffrey Schrank) A collection of ideas or "learning seeds" for use with adolescents and adults. Books, films, tapes, records, games, and publications are listed on a wide variety of topics and issues. The philosophy is that "learning takes place through involvement with a variety of viewpoints and opinions." Jeffrey Schrank also is author of *Teaching Human Beings: 101 Subversive Activities for the Classroom* (Beacon Press), which contains ideas to stimulate teenagers and includes units on racism, drugs, violence, sense education, and death. 25 Beacon St., Boston, MA 02108.

Celestial Arts A source of inexpensive posters for room decorating or reinforcers for students of all ages. Emphasis on feelings and love. Dept. P 1172, 231 Adrian Rd., Millbrae, CA 94030.

Center for Applied Research in Education: *Teacher's Almanac* (Dana Newmann) A book containing hundreds of ideas for elementary teachers; most could be adapted for use with adolescents. Includes games, formulas, recipes, riddles, experiments, bulletin board ideas, lists of free materials, word etymologies, pen pal addresses, historical anecdotes, and others. Also includes a ready-to-use student interest inventory, a guide to printmaking, and ideas for plants from the kitchen. 521 Fifth Ave., New York, NY 10017.

Constructive Playthings Specializes in materials for special education and early childhood education. One such item is self-sticking felt tape, sold in 1" x 15-yard roll; helpful in flannelboard activities. Catalogs available free to teachers who write request on school letterhead. 1040 E. 85th St., Kansas City, MO 64131.

Dell Publishing: *Big Rock Candy Mountain* A resourceful book listing ideas, books, and materials (many of them free) that can be ordered for classroom use. 750 Third Ave., New York City.

Developmental Learning Materials DLM has a catalog presenting its materials which the company describes as "designed for success experiences for children." Includes materials for language, communication, math, fine and gross motor development, body aware-

63

ness, self-concept, visual perception, career awareness, auditory perception, social awareness, and eye-hand activities. Also has Easy-Grip Scissors, softly spring-loaded plastic continuous loop handles, requiring only light finger or palm pressure. 7440 Natchez Ave., Niles, IL 60648.

Educational Service, Inc.: *Display* (Lucy Laurain) A handbook of elementary classroom ideas for creating of bulletin boards; one of the *Spice* series, which includes hundreds of classroom activities for topics such as science, language arts, health, black studies, ecology. P.O. Box 219, Stearnsville, MI 49127.

E-Z Grader Products are hand-size cardboard slide charts that can be used by teachers and students to calculate grades. Charts available for calculating percentages, letter grades, averages, chronological ages, and various phonic skills. P.O. Box 24040, Cleveland, OH 44124.

Fidelity Products Company A business supply firm with numerous items for classroom use, including cardboard storage files, drawers and organizers of all sizes, plastic storage bins. Catalog available upon request. Building 2873, 705 Pennsylvania Ave. S., Minneapolis, MN 55426.

Giant Photo Posters range in size from 16″ × 20″ to 24″ × 36″ on topics including patriotic, world neighbors, social concerns, sports, travel. Art prints available in two sizes, 16″ × 20″ and 8″ × 10″, full-color reproductions of famous paintings and scenic photographs. Catalog available upon request. Box 406, Rockford, IL 61105.

Good Apple Publishes a giant newspaper five times during the school year, packed with creative ideas. Good Apple also produces records, individualized learning center kits, and items that lend themselves to self-concept awareness activities, including a poster series entitled "My Very Own Posters," and note pads called "Happy Grams" and "Warm Fuzzies," which can be sent to students, their parents, or other teachers. Box 299, Carthage, IL 63231.

Hook 'N Loop — Charles Mayer Studios, Inc. A nylon, velvet-like fabric available in 30 colors. Hook 'N Loop tape is available with various pre-coatings of adhesive or with plain backing to be used with various adhesives. Can be used to create bulletin boards; the tape is used by attaching it to objects which are then hung on the bulletin board. Three-D objects such as telephones and tools, as well as graphs, charts, and papers, can hang securely. The tape has a bonding strength which allows repeated removal and replacement of objects. 140 E. Market St., Akron, OH 44308.

Huff & Company Offers portable study carrels that can be used for single and double desks and floor space arrangements. Constructed of vinyl laminated polystyrene; can be folded into three sections. Wood carrels of four or six sections also are available. P.O. Box 3675, Stanford, CA 94305.

Incentive Publications Produces the "Kids' Stuff" series, a child-centered presentation of many basic concepts in math, language arts, science, and creative writing. A popular book, *Nooks, Crannies and Corners*, describes various learning centers for creative classrooms. A companion book is *Center Stuff*, containing many activity sheets which can be clipped out and reproduced. Box 12522, Nashville, TN 37212.

Learning — **The Magazine for Creative Teaching** Published nine times a year. Each issue has an abundance of unique and challenging teaching ideas. A must for elementary and junior high teachers. Subscription Department, 1255 Portland Pl., Boulder, CO 80302.

Lectro-Stik Corporation Produces the "E-Z Up" clip, a white plastic clip approximately an inch long with a wax adhesive back. These clips adhere to metal, glass, wood, tile, concrete, and other surfaces. Papers can be easily added or removed from the clips. A special discount may be given to schools which order a certain amount of boxes. 3721 Broadway, Chicago, IL 60613.

Love Publishing Company Publishes books for teachers of exceptional children. Topics include teaching methods and techniques, communication with parents, educational assessment, games, music, art, bulletin board ideas for special education students. The company also produces math, science, reading and language materials for exceptional children. *Focus on Exceptional Children* is a single-article journal published 9 times a year. 6635 E. Villanova Place, Denver, CO 80222.

Merrill (Charles E.) Publishing Co.: *Structuring the Classroom for Success* (Cara Volkmar, Anne Langstaff, & Marilyn Higgins, 1974) "Creating Activity Centers" is a topic well covered in this book. Columbus, Ohio.

Milton Bradley A school supply firm. Catalog containing school furniture and equipment sections available upon request. Springfield, MA 01101.

Peabody College: *Free and Inexpensive Learning Materials* This guide lists 2,800 learning resources available to teachers. Entries are indexed and organized under 96 headings, with descriptions, prices, and ordering information given for each. Division of Surveys and Field Services, Nashville, TN 37203.

Printery House A catalog is available illustrating a selection of inexpensive, colorful posters. These posters (14″ × 21″) are suitable for decorating the room or for special gifts to the students. Each poster has a message related to feelings, life, friendship, and other affective topics. Conception, MO 64433.

School Days A company that produces instructional materials, many appropriate for use in special education classrooms. One item is "Post-It Strips" (Scotch brand), mounting tape with adhesive on both sides for displaying papers, etc. without damaging the wall surface or display material. Catalogs available to teachers who write request on school letterhead stationery. 973 N. Main St., Los Angeles, CA 90012.

Tri-Wall Containers The company's "Tri-Wall Pak" sheet is of sturdy, lightweight cardboard for use in "cardboard carpentry" — building creative classroom projects. Can be used by teachers and students to build learning centers, toys, models, classroom equipment, mobiles, etc. Boards available in the following sizes: 42″ × 54″, 4′ × 5′, 4′ × 6′, and 4′ × 8′. 100 Crossways Park West, Woodbury, NY 11797. (Cardboard carpentry tools, workshops, and information available from: Workshop for Learning Things, P.O. Box 321, Watertown, MA 02172.)

United Nations — Social Studies Materials Embassies, consulates, missions, and information bureaus established by foreign governments. Materials include illustrated brochures, pamphlets, maps, and films. A complete listing of the information services and embassies in the United States of all United Nations members is available by writing. Public Inquiries Unit, United Nations, New York, NY 10017.

Whole Earth Catalog Welcome addition to junior high or senior high school classrooms. Provides a variety of interesting information on current issues, organizations, crafts, etc. Addresses are provided for requesting literature on each topic. *The Whole Earth Catalog* can be found in bookstores.

GENERAL RESOURCES

Carrels (see **Huff & Company**)
Color Coding Self-adhesive office aid labels and self-adhesive color

coding labels, for color coding a series of cards. Available under various brand names at most office supply stores.

Magnetic Rubber Strips Provide a convenient method for displaying students' papers, artwork, etc. Available with adhesive or plain back; may be cut with scissors to desired size. Various brands, available in hardware and dime stores.

Placemats Some fast food or chain restaurants have printed activities which can be used during free time periods. Some placemats invite cartooning; others suggest travel routes to be traced; others give riddles and answers, etc. Perhaps copies could be purchased. Or ideas gained from a mat could be translated into classroom activities.

Scissors (See **Developmental Learning Materials**)

Tape, double-sided adhesive (see **School Days**)

Tape, felt (see **Constructive Playthings**)

THREE

EDUCATIONAL DIAGNOSIS

- Diagnostic Conference Organization
- Academic Subjects Assessment
- Academic Skills Assessment
- Assessment of Environmental Conditions
- Assessment of Teaching Techniques
- Assessment of Student Interests
- Ongoing Diagnosis

EDUCATIONAL DIAGNOSIS

Diagnosis, in the structured approach, is a procedure the teacher uses to obtain specific information pertinent to the student's academic program. The procedure is implemented during a conference held before or after a placement planning meeting and is continued throughout the student's enrollment. The diagnosis is primarily an informal educational one, and is designed to identify specific academic strengths and weaknesses by focusing on the student's current levels of performance. Results of the diagnosis can provide information directly applicable to teaching, such as levels of instruction and socialization, selection and adaptation of materials, provision of favorable learning conditions, and utilization of specific teaching techniques.

When a student's needs for special services are under consideration, a multidisciplinary team participates in a planning meeting. This group must include persons who are knowledgeable about the specific student and the evaluation data. The special classroom teacher may be a participant and may have been asked to contribute evaluation data. If the teacher has been asked to bring information, he or she should implement the diagnosis procedure prior to the planning conference.

Should placement in a special class for students with behavioral disorders be the team's decision, an individualized education program (IEP) will be designed. The program must contain annual goals and short-term instructional objectives. The special teacher is intimately associated with the implementation of the program; therefore, if the teacher had not carried out an informal educational diagnosis before the placement decision, he or she should do so before the first day of school if possible. Specific information is needed for the minute-by-minute and hour-by-hour instruction and activities.

71

The teacher should take a functional approach when conducting an educational diagnosis; that is, direct observations of behavior. If the teacher is to evaluate the student's ability to write, he or she requests that behavior. Further, the behavior will be broken into component parts. For example, to diagnose the handwriting of a seven-year-old boy, Merrill, who was described as, "He can't write," the special education teacher did the following to assess his writing skills:

1. Asked him to say the alphabet.
2. Asked him to read single alphabet letters when presented in alphabetical order — first the capital letters, then the small letters.
3. Asked him to read alphabet letters when presented in random order.
4. Asked him to write letters in order.
5. Asked him to write letters when dictated orally.
6. Asked him to copy single letters on a sheet of paper when they were presented in different positions as follows:

    a) on the chalkboard,
    b) on another sheet of paper,
    c) on a writing line immediately next to space where Merrill would write, and
    d) above the writing line where Merrill would write.

Merrill was successful on items 1, 2, and 3. On item 4 he wrote all the letters in sequence, but he intermixed the capital and small letters and reversed /b/ and /d/. On item 5 he experienced difficulty; he was able to write 14 letters independently but required assistance to write 12 letters (by asking to see the letters). When he copied letters as described in item 6, a, b, and c, he had difficulty in stroke formation and reversed some letters. When letters were written above his writing space, however, his writing was accurate. Merrill was given the opportunity to use various writing tools, including regular size 2 and 3 lead pencils, a primary pencil, felt tip pen, and various types of writing paper to determine if any of the materials affected his performance. Merrill's writing was enhanced when he used a regular size 2 lead pencil and close-ruled paper.

The teacher's functional assessment, as described, revealed that Merrill had certain handwriting skills, contrary to the statement that "he could not write." Specific handwriting strengths and weaknesses and a subsequent teaching approach were identified.

If a report reveals "ballpark" clues relevant to a student's academic abilities, these clues can provide a starting point for the teacher's educational diagnostic procedure. For example, David, a nine-year-old student, was reported as being able to (a) read at the fourth grade level; (b) do math at the second grade level; (c) write using manuscript letters; and (d) spell at the sixth grade level. The report provided information which did give the teacher a point of reference regarding academic levels, but the teacher also needed to know David's strengths and weaknesses within each basic skill area.

The teacher began assessing David's oral reading at the fourth grade level; however, by using additional levels of materials, it was determined that: (a) David's oral reading was at the fourth grade level; (b) but he could not read silently; (c) he learned new sight vocabulary if presented with a basal reading approach; (d) his word attack skills were on the first grade level; (e) his comprehension of factual questions was 90 percent; (f) his comprehension for vocabulary type questions was 40 percent; (g) he was unable to answer inferential questions; (h) he refused to read any stories which contained illustrations of people's faces; and (i) he had a strong preference for materials containing factual information and pictures of dinosaurs. A clinical report had revealed information relevant to David's avoidance of people's faces and his obsession for dinosaurs, but the teacher's diagnosis revealed specific reading strengths and weaknesses.

Diagnosis and teaching go hand-in-hand. The combination is a reevaluation and cyclic process. The teacher diagnoses, plans, prepares the learning environment, and teaches; then the student and teacher interact. These responses are evaluated and the cycle is repeated. This cycle is illustrated in Figure 3.1. The teacher who is having sustained contacts with the students is in an advantageous position to use diagnosis as an ongoing procedure because assessments can be repeated over a period of time. Behavior also can be observed directly in a variety of settings and situations. The reevaluations can result in more definitive descriptions of the students' strengths, weaknesses, and needs, and can contribute to current recordings of progress and growth. The teacher can use this information to continue and/or change the student's individualized education program.

The initial diagnosis may be carried out when a student is being considered for placement. If the placement conference decision was a special class assignment and if the teacher was not one of the evaluators, the teacher should carry out the informal diagnosis prior to the student's entering the special class so that the first presentation of materials in the

73

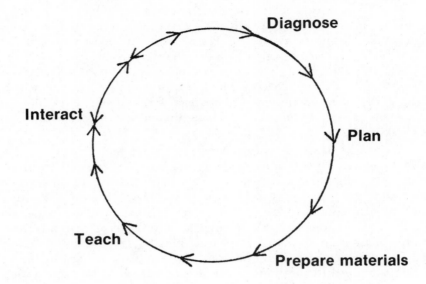

Fig. 3.1.   Cyclic reevaluation process.

classroom is as meaningful as subsequent ones. If the student is scheduled to enter class in September, the diagnosis can be done during the pre-academic year planning period. If the student is to enter during the academic year, the teacher can conduct the diagnosis during school hours if he or she has a flexible school day.

A teacher preparing for the diagnostic session should be fully aware of its goals. What information is *specifically* needed to carry out the student's program? Although the diagnostic session requires a considerable amount of preparation, the time and energy are not wasted. During the diagnosis, the teacher assesses academic strengths and weaknesses, conditions under which these occur, teaching techniques, and material modifications. A myriad of diagnostic materials is available; some that teachers of emotionally disturbed students might find particularly useful are given in this chapter's reference section.

No model diagnostic conference plan is provided here because a great amount of flexibility is needed with the procedure, but some general and specific considerations the teacher may want to keep in mind when preparing for the diagnostic conference are given as stimuli to further thinking on a more specific level.

DIAGNOSTIC CONFERENCE ORGANIZATION

If the conference is held during the planning days, the physical environment of the classroom should be organized to resemble the setting of the first weeks of class. Rearranging can be done after the diagnostic conferences, when the teacher has more knowledge of the students. If the room organization resembles that which the student will see when class begins, the teacher can discuss features such as the students having their own desk, chair, and study carrel; room areas designed for specific purposes and location of individual assignment schedules. The orientation offers students some familiarity with the classroom so they will not feel like strangers to the setting on their first day.

With prior knowledge of the students' interests, the teacher can display pictures, drawings, narrative passages, or symbols on the wall of the hall leading to the classroom. Paper lines and arrows in the students' favorite colors can be added. Such an effort can present a welcome and caring message. Figure 3.2 gives an example of one possible hall arrangement.

Many teachers prefer to set aside two to three hours for the diagnostic conference, breaking the session into segments; for example:

- Welcome (room orientation)
- Diagnosis
- Break Time (food is available)
- Diagnosis
- Break Time (explore the room)
- Diagnosis
- Break Time (explore the building)
- Get acquainted conference with parents or child care workers.

This schedule has the same basic format the student will have in class — that is, each classroom schedule will consist of a series of work activities interspersed with pleasurable activites. The conference routine, then, is a subtle orientation to the student's future classroom environment.

Each session should include the following elements:

- An introduction by the teacher, including a brief description of the role as special education teacher.
- An explanation of the purpose of the conference.

75

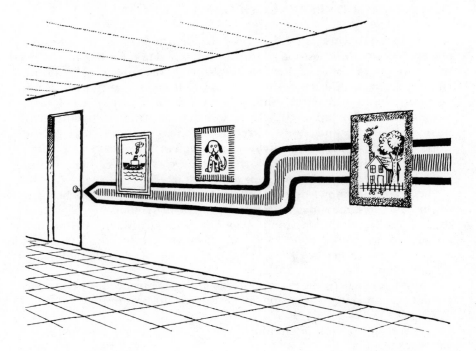

Fig. 3.2.   Suggestion for hall arrangement.

- A description of the classroom as it relates to the student's program goals (if placement has been decided).
- An ice-breaker to begin the session; for example, by exchanging riddles; discussing rock tunes or a recent sports event.
- Beginning at a success level — Choosing items in each subject area that the student is capable of doing before advancing to higher levels.
- Ending on a success level — As the student approaches a frustration level, several items from the success level should be added so the assessment of each academic area ends on a positive note. Frequently, testing brings students to a frustration or ceiling level — the level at which a student is missing all or a majority of the items — and testing then is terminated; this is a poor approach.

ACADEMIC SUBJECTS ASSESSMENT

Teachers can establish their own informal tests, combining original items with others selected from curriculum materials. Many teachers review the diagnostic tests found in most reading, math, spelling, and English series, then select or adapt items. The basic concepts taught at each grade level can be found in curriculum guides or scope and sequence charts which are published by textbook companies. These charts usually accompany basic series and are found frequently in a school's curriculum center. Tables of content in textbooks and teacher's manuals also provide this information for their respective grade levels. These sources can be highly useful in helping the teacher select test items relevant to their hierarchy of difficulty.

The teacher must have a wide range of materials available for the subject area to be assessed. Academic materials at least three grade levels below and above the assumed level of functioning should be gathered. If

the teacher has a range of materials on hand, any one of them may be used during the session. This range of materials not only will contribute to a flexible and efficient diagnostic session, but will convey to the student that working at a grade level different from the expected one (the level commensurate with the student's chronological age) is acceptable. For students working below grade level, the absence of a last-minute search for appropriate materials can prevent embarrassment, self-deprecation, hostility, or other negative feelings students may experience when a teacher has to scurry around to find something they can do.

The teacher should be aware that the presented material can create a student deficit. For example, a student could fail New Math problems because he or she has learned only "old" math. A myriad of variables can be considered in developing test items; only a few suggestions are offered here.

Math

1. Present computation problems without words and in various formats; for example:

   $$9 + 3 =$$

   $$9 + 3 = \qquad \begin{array}{r} 9 \\ +3 \\ \hline \end{array} \qquad \begin{array}{r} 3 \\ +9 \\ \hline \end{array} \qquad 3 + 9 = \qquad 9 + \_ = 12 \qquad \begin{array}{r} 9 \\ + \_ \\ \hline 12 \end{array}$$

2. Use both the new and old math symbols.
3. Include story problems which the student is asked to read. If the student has difficulty with the vocabulary, the teacher can read the problem. The reading level, not the math, may be the difficulty. Before introducing story problems, check to see if the vocabulary in the problems is clear and understandable — the student may be able to compute successfully but is confused by the verbiage.
4. Include time, money value, linear, metric, and liquid measurement problems.
5. Have manipulative aids available. Students' responses may differ if tangible items are used for calculations. The inclusion of concrete

and abstract test items in all subject areas should be considered carefully.

6. Determine the process the student uses to obtain wrong responses. Sometimes a student is able to share this information if asked. A teacher's assessment of a math worksheet revealed the process used by one student to obtain his erroneous addition answers. Figure 3.3 reveals that the student's responses to the first two rows of problems were correct, and incorrect throughout the third row. When the teacher evaluated the third row problems and the student's responses, she noted that the student coupled digits, added and placed the answer to each couple in the sum.

Reading

An informal reading inventory contains features that can yield useful information regarding the student's needs for a reading program. Sources for developing an informal reading inventory are given in the Bibliography, and teachers are encouraged strongly to develop one. The informal reading inventory has passages to be read orally and silently, and it will reveal:

1. *Reading levels.* It should be noted that calculations for the following levels vary slightly among reading experts.

   a. *Independent level.* Student reads comfortably and without help. Supplementary materials and library books are selected at this level. (99% word recognition; 90% comprehension)

   b. *Instructional level.* Student textbook is selected at this level. (95% word recognition; 75% comprehension)

   c. *Frustration level.* Material is too difficult. This level need not be assessed when the other two levels have been determined. (90% word recognition; 50% to 75% comprehension)

   d. *Listening level.* This is the highest readability level which the student is able to understand when someone else is reading. Materials can be audio-taped at this level. This is the student's probable capacity level. (75% comprehension)

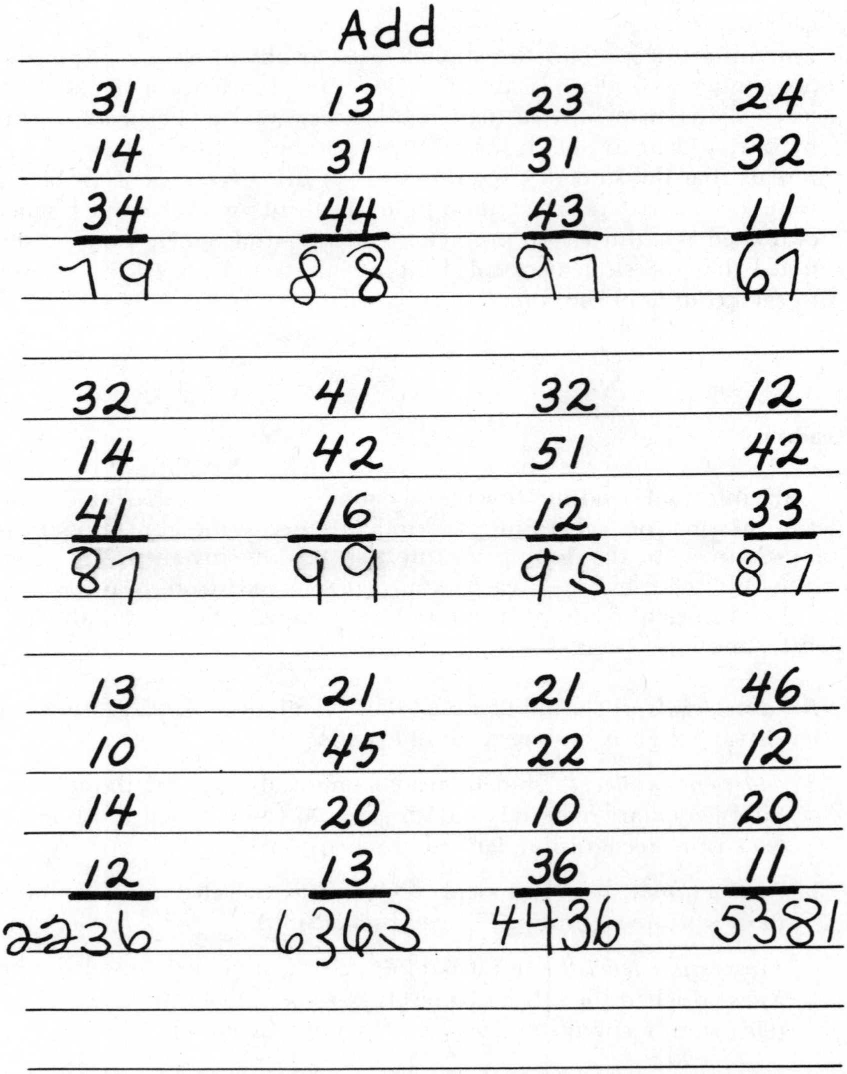

Add

31	13	23	24
14	31	31	32
34	44	43	11
79	8 8	97	67

32	41	32	12
14	42	51	42
41	16	12	33
87	99	95	87

13	21	21	46
10	45	22	12
14	20	10	20
12	13	36	11
2236	6363	4436	5381

Fig. 3.3. Sample math worksheet showing incorrect processes and responses in third row problems.

2. *Comprehension.* Each reading passage should be followed by at least five questions and should include questions requiring three different types of answers:

   a. Factual

   b. Vocabulary

   c. Inferential

3. *Reading errors.* The oral reading errors can be observed and recorded. Errors include:

   a. Omissions

   b. Substitutions

   c. Insertions

   d. Distortions

   e. Hesitancies

   f. Repetitions

   g. Needs assistance

   David, the nine-year-old introduced earlier, had a high percentage of "needs assistance" errors. He did not attempt to analyze words on sight; therefore, activities for learning word attack skills would be scheduled into his program.

4. *Format preferences.* Some teachers use actual pages from printed materials, selected before the inventory is given. Other teachers type or write passages on a series of single sheets of paper. For the former, the teacher should be aware that format can affect a student's performance; the student may respond better if the reading passage is limited to a single sheet rather than presented on a double-page card in a softbacked or hardbacked book.

5. *Content interests.* The teacher should include reading passages with different themes because, in addition to skills, a student's interests and prior experiences are factors that influence responses. Content can focus on topics such as city, suburban, or rural locations; social values; historical or contemporary events; ethnic or cultural factors; and fact or fiction subjects.

Strengths and weaknesses in reading and comprehension, level of instruction, content, and format preferences can result in a profile which will help the teacher select materials for the student. Subsequent assessment involving learning conditions, adaptations, and teaching techniques will add data to this profile.

Spelling

Students can be asked to write words from dictation. Dictate at a pace normally used in a regular class. If the student experiences difficulty, slow the pace. If the student demonstrates handwriting difficulties, ask the student to spell the words verbally. The student's responses may also reveal letter substitutions indicating an auditory deficit, such as "fork" for "forth"; letter substitutions indicating an error in rules, such as "familys" for "families"; or words indicating recall of known words that are revisualized, such as "feeonsay" for "fiancee."

Language

Oral and written expression can be sampled in a variety of ways. Students can be asked to tell a story; if the student needs encouragement, the teacher could provide stimulus pictures or story starter phrases. Younger students could be presented with a series of picture sequence cards and asked to place the pictures in order, then asked to relate a story about them. Older students could be asked to write a business letter. Student responses can be assessed relevant to vocabulary, sentence structure, syntax, sequencing, creativity, fluency, use of grammar, etc. Written language can reveal these factors in addition to the student's knowledge of punctuation marks, spelling, and capital letters.

ACADEMIC SKILLS ASSESSMENT

The teacher will continue the functional approach to the informal diagnostic session by evaluating skills associated with classroom activities. The teacher should determine which skills are needed by each student to proceed on the program plan. Three skills needed by almost all students are described in the following paragraphs.

Copying

Many academic subjects require copying skills such as copying from a textbook, workbook, or chalkboard. The student may experience difficulty in the copying process itself rather than in understanding the primary purpose of a lesson. One adolescent was asked to "write these sentences and insert the correct punctuation marks." The result was a paper containing sentences with poor letter, word, and line spacing; however, 11 of the possible 12 punctuation marks were placed correctly.

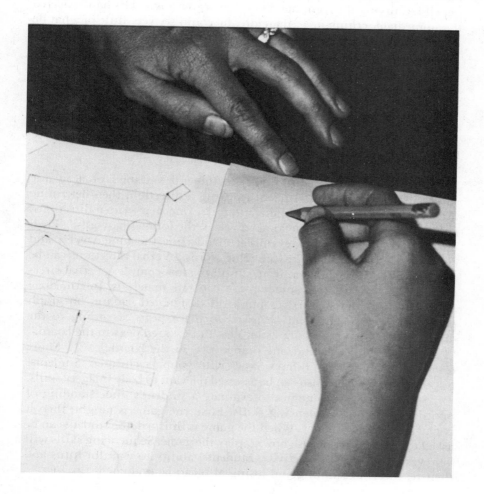

Assessment of copying skills can be separated from content knowledge, and these activities could be subdivided into the following steps.

1. Ask the student to copy from the chalkboard to writing paper.
2. Ask the student to copy from the book to writing paper.

Note the position of the book: Is it to the left, right, or above the student's writing paper? Is it on the student's lap? Note how the student holds the pencil. Merrill, the seven-year-old student referred to earlier, held his pencil by curving the right hand to a 180 degree angle. His hand covered the immediate writing area; therefore, he could see very little of what he was printing.

3. Ask the student to copy print which is on his or her own writing paper.

Merrill had the most success when the letters to be copied were written directly above his writing line.

Following Directions

Verbal and written directions are integral variables of academic subjects. Determine if the student can read a direction, then determine if the student understands the direction. Use one-step written directions; for example: "Underline the long vowels in the following words." Then increase the difficulty; for example: "Underline the long vowels and circle the short vowels in the following words." Verbal directions can be assessed in the same manner, from simple to more complex. Verbal directions can be given while students use concrete materials. Intermediate aged students can be asked to mark off designated squares on graph paper. Young students can be asked to place pegs, according to the directions, in a peg board; for example: "Put two red pegs in the board." "Put three green pegs and one orange peg in the board.". . . . Many teachers use the game "Simon Says" with younger children. Students' responses to the game also can be assessed relevant to body imagery skills.

Some teachers use games to evaluate a student's understanding of oral directions and sequencing skills. First, the game is taught; then it is played with the student. When the game is finished, the student can be asked to teach someone else how to play the game. Sequencing skills will be revealed in the latter activity. Students' ability to wait for turns and their reactions to winning and losing also can be evaluated.

Using Daily Living Skills

In assessing this area, teachers have asked students to arrange books and materials in a desk, sharpen pencils, erase a marking; to find the rest-room, or fire extinguisher; to use a drinking fountain, and to dial a telephone. Some secondary teachers include the completion of forms in their diagnostic sessions; students are asked to complete school enroll-ment forms, class cards, and social security and job applications. In addition to the teacher's using these means to assess student responses to these tasks, the students can become familiar with these forms. Com-pletion of the enrollment form also requires a commitment from the student to attend school.

In these sessions, teachers should be acutely aware of their termi-nology. Terminology during the academic assessment may create a prob-lem or response deficit; for example, one teacher confused a student by using the word "root" instead of the word "base." Another teacher used "rhyming words" when the student was familiar with "word families." In both of these examples the students understood the concept but they had not been exposed to more than one expression of it.

ASSESSMENT OF ENVIRONMENTAL CONDITIONS

Variables associated with the physical environment can affect students' performance. Each room has its unique features, but some conditions are common to most classrooms, and these can be assessed, as follows.

Assess Background Noise

Determine which types of noise distract or enhance performance. Assessment could be conducted when the student is working:

1. In a study carrel. (The use of headphones could be an option.)
2. In the presence of room noise from conversations between adult and students, students typing, students reading, students in a free time area, and while teacher is writing on chalkboard.

3. In the presence of hall noise.
4. With background radio sound. Determine possible performance differences among commentaries, stimulative and sedative music sounds. One teacher used a tape recording of various noises because the diagnostic conferences usually occurred when noise levels were minimal.

Assess Visual Arrangements

Determine whether visual materials are distracting or not. Assess a student when he or she is working:

1. In a visual free study carrel with only one material available, then when other materials are in close proximity.
2. At a worktable with only one material available, and when other materials are in close proximity.

Students' performance also can be assessed while they are facing various room features including bulletin boards, windows, student desks, door, and so forth.

Assess Audio and Visual Environmental Conditions

Discern if specific combinations of stimuli as described in the above items are distracting or favorable; for example, one student was able to work efficiently at a group table if there were no vocal noises.

Assess Teacher's Proximity

Evaluate the effects of teacher presence when:

1. Immediately next to the student.
2. Across the table from the student.
3. At a nearby desk.
4. Across the room.

Assess Time Conditions

Determine if time variables affect a student's performance.

1. What is the student's speed and accuracy under no time limits?
2. What is the student's speed and accuracy when a specific time is set for task completion?

3. How does the student perform when mini-breaks are interspersed with the work?

Assess Student's Approach to a Task

In approaching the work, does the student:

1. Try it?
2. Respond thoughtfully or impulsively?
3. Need coaxing?
4. Give up easily?
5. Become frustrated but keep trying?
6. Verbalize to "wiggle out" of a situation?
7. Refuse to engage in a task?
8. Destroy the materials?

9. Act hostile or belligerent?
10. Appear anxious or relaxed?

ASSESSMENT OF TEACHING TECHNIQUES

During the diagnostic conference, the teacher can use various teaching techniques with test items to evaluate possible differences in student performance. The student's responses to teaching techniques can give the teacher specific clues for instructional planning. Some of these techniques are described below.

Provide Reinforcement

Many behaviorally disordered students have "had it" with school. Their love for learning, intrinsic satisfaction from school activities, and internal locus of evaluation frequently are limited or nonexistent. Teachers may want to provide reinforcers to see if they can effect some performance changes. A variety of potential reinforcers could be used, including verbal or written approval, social interaction, body contact, free time awards, privileges, tokens or other tangible items. (Specific items that can be used as reinforcers are listed in Chapter 6.) The teacher can observe the student's responses to different reinforcers and assess if work increased or decreased, attitude changed, interest was shown, or additional skills were used.

The technique of providing reinforcement during a diagnostic session was obtained from a psychologist who shared the following experience: He gave a standardized IQ test to a recalcitrant ten-year-old boy. During the first testing session, the psychologist felt that the boy wasn't really interested and wasn't trying to give correct responses. After the testing was completed, he asked the boy to return the following week. During the second session, the psychologist administered an alternate form of the IQ test. This time he told the boy that for each correct response he would receive a nickel. The student's IQ score was 15 points higher on the second evaluation.

If a teacher uses reinforcers for some diagnostic items, a measure of the effects of reinforcement may be made. If a strong, positive reinforcer were used and the student's performance significantly improved, this certainly would provide insight about the student's potential level. Level of expectation can be a critical variable in the teaching and learning process. Since performances by emotionally disturbed students frequently are hindered by their defense mechanisms, a teacher may have more confidence in selecting teaching techniques if the diagnostic session reveals correct observations of a student's potential. The teacher also may want to use schedules of reinforcement as described in Chapter 6.

Provide Feedback

Note the student's reactions and levels of performance when various forms of feedback are given. Feedback could include:

1. Verbal responses, "Right" or "Wrong."
2. Written responses, "C" or " ✔ ."
3. Different tones of voice.
4. Variations of the same feedback such as:
   a. "3 right, 10 wrong."
   b. "You have 3 right but had trouble on the others."
   c. "Nice try; it's hard work, but you were able to get 3 right."
5. Immediate and delayed responses. In the diagnostic session the feedback could be immediate by sharing it with the student after each response, or delayed by giving it when a section(s) of the test has been completed.
6. Student self-checking. Answer keys can be available so students can evaluate their own responses. Some teachers have provided hand calculators for math self-checks.

Heighten the Interest of Materials

Observe if the student's performance changes when format alterations are made; for example:

1. A single worksheet with colorful outlines enclosing the work items.
2. Words such as *10-speed bike, jeans, patches, motorcycle, stereo tapes,* and *skateboards* replacing words like apples, balls, wagons, squirrels, and airplanes in math problems.

Provide a Variety of Working Tools

Various types of writing papers were available during the handwriting diagnosis of seven-year-old Merrill, introduced earlier. These included primary paper with alternating dark and light lines, primary paper with alternating broken and straight lines, primary paper with alternating red and green lines, and close-ruled paper. He also was given a primary pencil, standard size 2 and size 3 lead pencils, a felt pen, and a crayon. Merrill's letter formations were best when he used close-ruled paper with alternating broken and straight lines and a size 2 lead pencil. His spacing between letters improved when vertical red lines were added to his paper.

ASSESSMENT OF STUDENT INTERESTS

The diagnostic conference can be divided into work and break sessions, as mentioned previously. This format provides the opportunity to observe the student in supervised and nonsupervised situations. If the diagnostic conference should extend over two or three hours, at least three major breaks can be included. The breaks could be accomplished as follows.

First Break

During the first break, the teacher can make an honest statement regarding the student's work behavior, followed by, "Let's take a 10-minute break." The teacher could have on hand some edible treats such as milk, juice, lemonade, coke, coffee, raisins, cookies, doughnuts, or fruit. During the break the student may feel more at ease; the diagnosis, however, does not stop — the teacher unobtrusively continues to observe. Answers to the following questions could be used in planning a student's program:

1. Does the student interact with or avoid the teacher while eating?
2. Can the student converse with the teacher?

3. What type of language patterns does the student have?
4. What are the topics of conversation? Who initiated the conversations?
5. What are the student's food preferences?
6. What are the student's eating habits?
7. Was the student aware when the 10-minute break period was over?
8. When time was up, was the student willing to resume work?

Second Break

During the second break, the student can be given an opportunity to explore the room. Again, feedback should be given regarding the work, followed by, "Why don't you take a 15-minute break and look around the classroom? You can use any of the materials that you want to." Prior to the student's arrival, the teacher would have arranged the materials and equipment within invisible boundaries. Contrary to the comment in Chapter 2, suggesting storage of new materials until a rainy day, all items should be on temporary display during the diagnostic conference. The invisible boundaries and category of items within them are marked on a sheet of paper which the teacher uses to record the student's interests and preferences. A sample recording sheet is shown in Figure 3.4.

A frequency count of the number of times the student engages with an item, the number of times he or she goes to an area, or the amount spent with an item may be recorded. Perhaps the student will select one item — for example, a microscope — and use it during the entire break; the student may explore each area except the academic one; the student may flit from area to area; the student may find water to be a seductive object and have the water faucet running while licking the water constantly; or the student may withdraw by staring out the window.

Generally, students do not have their defenses up when they explore the room; thus, they give unguarded clues to their interests. The teacher can use these interests for topics of study, for room arrangements, and for reinforcers. Further, the teacher becomes aware of the student's social skills: Did Tom attempt contact? Did he look for approval? Did he ask questions? Did he tease? Did he withdraw?

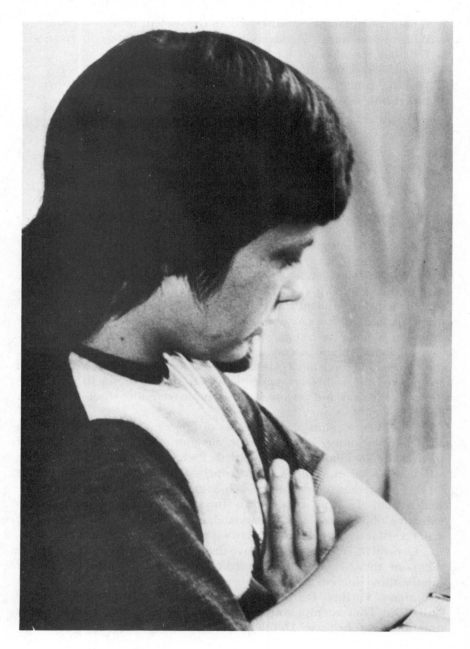

Expressive	Audio - Visual
threw darts - 2 min. asked T. to be "beat". T. won. S. was angry and stomped away - 4 min.	Used film strip projector 3 min.
Exploratory	**Academic**
Used Morse Code equipment. 5 min. Looked at Indian sand paintings 30 sec.	No contact. No physical contact with materials. Threatened to throw books through window.
Social	**Comments**
Asked how many "guys" would be in room. Any girls?	Flat affect while using materials. Moods varied - anger, interested, aggressive, passive.

Fig. 3.4. Sample recording sheet.

Third Break

During the third break, the teacher and student could explore the school building. The teacher can answer questions the student may have about the building and point to specific places the student will need to recognize, such as location of a restroom, lockers, and exits to the playground and main doors. The teacher also can point out the specific identification of the special classroom and take the route between the classroom and the building exits. Perhaps several "dry run" trips along the major routes will be necessary to familiarize the student with the physical environment. These activities also provide the teacher with information about the student's physical orientation abilities.

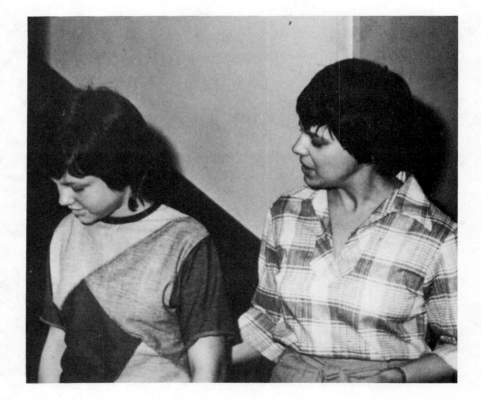

ONGOING DIAGNOSIS

After a student is placed in a special classroom, the diagnosis does not end. Results of the student's work are assessed continually before new activities are introduced. Some emotionally disturbed youth are unpredictable; others have extreme high and low levels of accomplishments regularly during their initial weeks and months in a program. Therefore, the teacher must incorporate day-by-day diagnoses and planning. Furthermore, weaknesses and strengths not observed in a diagnostic conference often will be observed during a school day. Two classroom incidents are described to highlight the importance of ongoing diagnosis.

Incident 1

A teacher assessed one student's English paper and the variables associated with the assignment. The assignment followed several class discussions regarding correct use of punctuation marks. The student was asked to copy five sentences from the English book and insert the correct punctuation marks. The teacher's analysis of the student's completed paper revealed that: (a) she correctly inserted 11 of the possible 12 punctuation marks, and it was assumed that she did not have space to insert the one missing punctuation mark; (b) she had between-word and between-lines spacing problems; and (c) letter formations were readable but her handwriting needed improvement, as seen in Figure 3.5.

Incident 2

Jeff was fighting back tears as he struggled with a spelling assignment requiring crossword puzzle skills — an activity he liked. A discussion with Jeff revealed why he was having difficulty: He did not know how to write letters when two boxes were provided for each letter ("I'm leaving blanks!"). If he wrote all capital letters, he would be wrong because "words aren't written that way," especially ones that are "in the middle" of a word. The simple diagnosis Jeff had made revealed that the puzzle format was wrong — it was causing wrong responses.

The teacher readjusted the assignment to reduce Jeff's frustration. The discussion concluded with his understanding that the error was made by the book's printer and that the immediate solution was to write

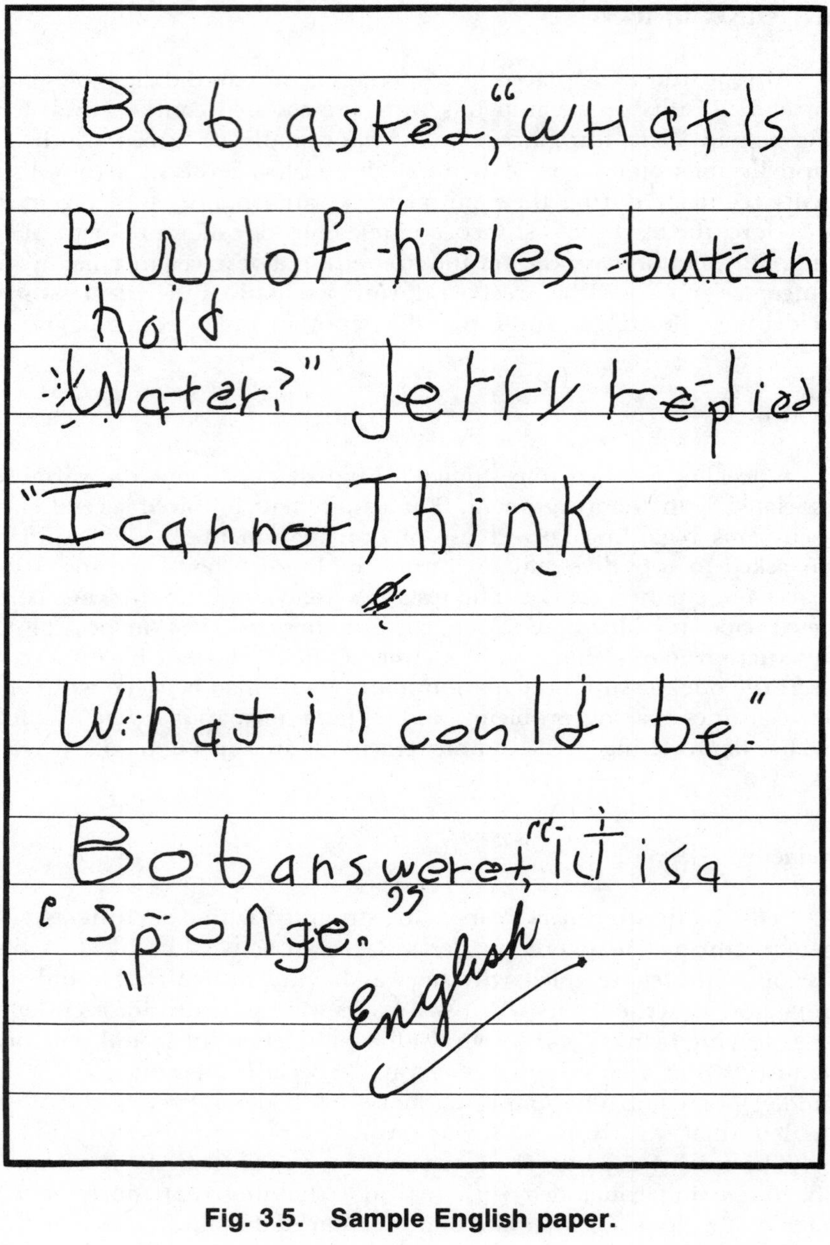

Bob asked, "WHat is
FUll of holes but can
hold
Water?" Jerry replied
"I cannot Think
What i l could be."
Bob answeret, "It is a
sponge."
English

Fig. 3.5. Sample English paper.

all capital letters. The latter was a compromise because the teacher did not have time to make a new puzzle format and Jeff insisted on finishing the page. When similar puzzle formats were found in the spelling book, the teacher designed a different format. Figure 3.6 is the sample of Jeff's completed crossword puzzle.

```
Here is a puzzle.
Write spelling words in place of the underlined words.


Down

1.  Set the book on the table
2.  He walked behind the parade.

Across

1.  Bring the dish here.
3.  Look for the taxi.
```

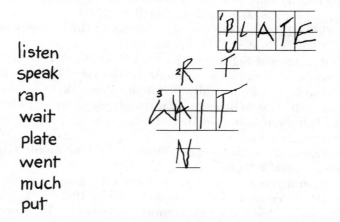

Fig. 3.6. Sample word puzzle with format confusing to student.

SUMMARY

Educational diagnosis can reveal specific behavior relevant to a student's strengths and weaknesses, thereby giving the teacher definite variables to consider in planning and implementing each student's program. Educational diagnostic skills include the teacher's ability to observe, to attend to detail, to know curriculum content, to know developmental growth patterns, and to discern effective teaching techniques.

The diagnostic procedure interrelates with the procedures of pre-academic year planning, curriculum adaptations, programming, scheduling, and behavior modification. It is not isolated to a single session; it is an ongoing procedure.

BIBLIOGRAPHY

Beery, Keith. *Remedial Diagnosis.* San Rafael, CA: Dimensions Publishing, 1968.

Brown, Louis, "Evaluation: Some Informative Techniques for Classroom Use." In *Strategies for Teaching Exceptional Children*, edited by Edward Meyen, Glenn Vergason, and Richard Whelan. Denver: Love Publishing Company, 1972.

Dale, Edgar and Chall, Jeanne. "A Formula for Predicting Readability." *Educational Research Bulletin* 27 (1948): 37-54.

Ekwall, Eldon. *Locating and Correcting Reading Difficulties.* Columbus, OH: Charles E. Merrill Company, 1970.

Farrald, Robert, and Schamber, Richard. *Handbook I: A Mainstream Approach to Identification, Assessments and Amelioration of Learning Disabilities.* Sioux Falls, SD: Adapt Press, 1973.

Gearheart, Bill, and Willenberg, Ernest. *Application of Pupil Assessment Information for the Special Education Teacher.* Denver: Love Publishing Company, 1970.

Hewett, Frank. *The Emotionally Disturbed Child in the Classroom.* Boston: Allyn & Bacon, 1968.

Kress, Roy, and Johnson, Marjorie. *Informal Reading Inventories.* Newark, DE: International Reading Association, 1965.

Lane, Pauline. "Individual Academic Evaluation." In *Strategies for Teaching Exceptional Children*, edited by Edward Meyen, Glenn Vergason, and Richard Whelan. Denver: Love Publishing Company, 1972.

Mann, Philip, and Suiter, Patricia. *Handbook in Diagnostic Teaching: A Learning Disabilities Approach.* Boston: Allyn & Bacon, 1974.

Miller, Wilma. *Reading Diagnosis Kit.* New York: Center for Applied Research in Education, Inc., 1974.

Moran, Mary. "Nine Steps to the Diagnostic Prescriptive Process in the Classroom." *Focus on Exceptional Children* 6 (1975): 1-14.

Moran, Mary. *Assessment of the Exceptional Learner in the Regular Classroom.* Denver: Love Publishing Company, 1978.

Otto, Wayne, and McMeneny, Richard. *Corrective and Remedial Teaching Principles and Practices.* New York: Houghton Mifflin Company, 1966.

Silvaroli, Nicholas. *Teachers' Manual and Classroom Reading Inventory.* Dubuque, IA: Wm. C. Brown Company, 1965.

Spache, George, and Spache, Evelyn. "Using the Individual Conference for Diagnoses." In *Reading in the Elementary School,* edited by George Spache and Evelyn Spache. Boston; Allyn & Bacon, 1969.

Valett, Robert. *The Remediation of Learning Disabilities.* Palo Alto, CA: Fearon Publishers, 1967.

Wallace, Gerald, and Larsen, Stephen. *Educational Assessment of Learning Problems: Testing for Teaching.* Boston: Allyn & Bacon, 1978.

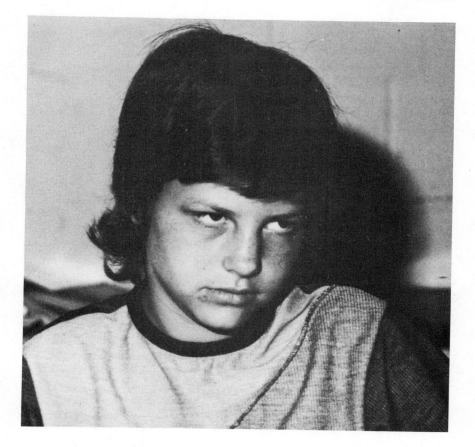

FOUR

EDUCATIONAL MATERIALS

- Selecting Educational Materials
- Adapting Educational Materials
- Making Curriculum Materials
- Creating Learning Centers
- Appendix to Chapter 4
  Resources for Classroom Materials

EDUCATIONAL MATERIALS

After the teacher has accumulated specific information regarding each student's educational strengths and weaknesses and style of learning, the process of selecting, adapting, and making classroom instructional materials — another procedure in the structured approach — can be initiated. The individuality and uniqueness of each student precludes the selection of predetermined materials per se. The teacher may be able to find commercial materials that can satisfy some of the student's needs, but most of the selected materials will require revision or supplementation.

Teachers should have a wide variety of curriculum ideas to meet the myriad of learning experiences needed by emotionally disturbed youth. The curriculum materials, ideas, and teaching techniques described in this chapter have been used with emotionally disturbed students and are offered to lure teachers into trying some of them, and embellishing, expanding, or deleting others. These suggestions may encourage teachers to explore the market of print and non-print educational materials and to stimulate teachers in the creation and design of materials which can give disturbed students success, independence, and feelings of self-worth.

SELECTING EDUCATIONAL MATERIALS

Selecting materials from the large number and variety available on the market can be overwhelming. Two major factors — budget and the student's specific needs — must enter into the selection process. A profile of each student's strengths and weaknesses obtained during the diagnostic session is an invaluable guide. Some general questions the teacher may want to consider when looking for materials are:

1. What do the materials do? Instruct? Enrich? Review? Motivate?
2. Will additional materials be needed at grade levels above and below the materials under consideration?
3. Should mediated materials such as audio reel-to-reel tapes, cassette tapes, records, filmstrips, flash cards, slides, and transparencies be considered?
4. Is the equipment necessary for the audio and visual media available?
5. Is there ample storage space for these materials?
6. Should materials encourage transfer of knowledge to a real environment? Some materials include activities for the students to do in their own environments; for example, reading mterial might include an easy-to-cook recipe, or a math section might include metric measurements in the home.
7. Do the students need materials that include practice and repetition exercises?
8. Should a basic text be accompanied by additional supplementary materials for followup — such as worksheets, projects, games, experiments?
9. Can consumable and non-consumable materials be bought separately?
10. Is a teacher's manual available?
11. If materials require students' written response, is the format appropriate and understandable? One popular reading series had appeal for adolescents but the worksheet format was confusing and frustrating to some. A single worksheet required four different responses: (a) fill in the blank with words; (b) draw a line to the correct answer; (c) circle the correct answer; and (d) fill in the blank with a single letter.
12. Will the physical aspects of the material be interesting to the student? If not, is the material amenable to physical adaptation? For example, the reading level of a certain text was appropriate for a student's instruction but the book had a plain, hardbacked cover. The teacher disassembled the text into smaller segments and designed a contemporary cover for each part.
13. Do comprehension questions include factual, vocabulary, and inferential ones?
14. Do comprehension questions lead to thoughtful responses or do they lead to ambiguous answers?

15. Do materials require the teacher's assistance while they are used by the students?
16. Does the material call for physical responses that the student can manage comfortably? For example, coloring within designated small areas can be difficult for some young children, and pushing a machine lever can be difficult for others.
17. Dn the materials specify the prerequisite entry skills?
18. Is it necessary that the materials be reusable?
19. Is it necessary that the materials be durable?
20. Will the materials have emotionally laden aspects? For example, a student who had witnessed the murder of his stepfather, the only person the student loved, was unable to respond appropriately to reading material with the father images as main characters.
21. Do the materials have illustrations which will enhance the student's progress? Some materials have illustrations which are artistically pleasing, yet busy and distracting. Some illustrations are located on the pages in a manner that can lead to confusion rather than interest. Figure 4.1 shows some different types of formats.
22. Do materials focus on a divergent or convergent thinking approach?
23. Is the material culturally appropriate?
24. Can materials be examined for a trial period prior to possible purchase?

ADAPTING EDUCATIONAL MATERIALS

Sometimes, teachers receive criticism for adapting materials — frequently referred to as "sugar-coating." Comments not uncommonly made to teachers include: "He isn't always going to have you around," or "Why do you spend so much time on materials when her other teachers won't be doing this for her?" Teachers of emotionally disturbed students are fully aware that one of the program goals is to prepare students for return to the mainstream of education, but they also must be sensitive to each student's current needs and levels of performance and often have to provide "crutches" until the students are able to proceed without them. Some of the adaptation techniques teachers have found useful are given below. (Any special materials used in the adaptations are described, with sources, in the appendix to this chapter.)

107

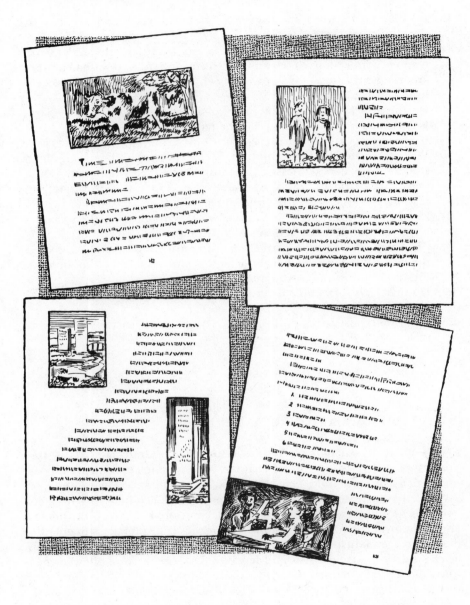

Fig. 4.1.   Example formats affecting interest and readability.

Altering Materials

1. *Clarify written directions.* Directions on worksheets often are written in paragraph form, frequently specifying several tasks. The series of directions can be overwhelming. The teacher could underline each direction with a different color to alert and assist the student in following the sequence of directions. Figure 4.2 provides an example.

Write your name at the top of this worksheet.

This exercise will show how well you can find pronouns.

Read each sentence. Look for the part of the sentence

that has the pronoun. Choose the pronoun listed under

the sentence. Then circle the number of your answer in

the answer column.

Fig. 4.2. Clarifying a series of directions.

2. *Camouflage materials.* If students enjoy reading lower grade level books but are sensitive about others responding negatively, a book disguise could discourage peer or sibling teasing. Make colorful book jackets. If students are uncomfortable about taking books home, provide carriers such as large brown business envelopes or envelopes made from construction paper.
3. *Present work in small amounts.* Tear pages from workbooks, hard-backed and softbacked books, and present them in small increments to students who become anxious about a full page or more of work presented at one time.
4. *Invent a workbook.* For a student who performs better when worksheets are presented one at a time rather than within a workbook, either: (a) remove all workbook pages and place only the daily

worksheets in the empty workbook; or (b) tear out workbook pages and give the papers to the student on a daily basis; when the papers are completed and graded, save them within the workbook covers to show the student at different times, making favorable comments about the number of completed pages.

5. *Make Language Master cards.* Cut paper no larger than the upper half of a Language Master card. Write desired information on the paper and attach it with a paper clip to the Language Master card; then audio record. A set of blank Language Master cards can be used repeatedly if visual information is presented in this way.

6. *Reuse printed materials.* If the supply of workbooks or worksheets is limited, the materials can be preserved and used repeatedly if clear acetate is placed over the worksheets. The student can use a water base felt pen or crayon to make the necessary responses. After the pages have been graded, the sheets can be cleaned with a moistened cloth. Be sure to have an ample supply of acetate sheets; students would have no evidence of their work if the sheets had to be cleaned immediately after each use. Acetate can be purchased in 9″ x 10″ sheets or by the yard in office supply stores.

Acetate also can be used to make a folder which includes a piece of lightweight cardboard; the student slips a worksheet into the folder and responds. After the student receives verbal feedback, the teacher writes his or her name, date, and comments on the cardboard, then cleans the acetate.

7. *Locate the pages easily.* If a student is proceeding sequentially in a workbook, diagonally cut the lower righthand corners of the pages after they have been completed. The teacher then can easily locate the pages that need grading, and the student can easily determine the next assignment page.

8. *Block out print.* If a student is distracted easily by working on a full worksheet, provide various sizes of oaktag so the student can cover portions of the page not being worked on. Students also can use pieces of oaktag as line markers for reading.

9. *Secure materials to desk.* Students who are frustrated by materials sliding around on their desks could have corners or sides of the material secured to the desk with masking tape.

10. *Reuse drill cards.* Index cards can be used for individual math practice. Multiplication, addition, subtraction, and division and fraction problems, clock faces, and so forth can be printed on cards which then are covered with clear, self-adhesive paper. Students can

use water-base felt pens for writing their answers. After the answers are checked, cards can be erased with a cloth or moist tissue; then they can be reused.

11. *Have students repeat directions.* Frequently, students are confused by or omit portions of verbal directions. Teachers can ascertain if a student has comprehended a direction by asking the student to repeat it. This technique helps students avoid possible errors resulting from not understanding the directions.

12. *Change response mode.* If a student has handwriting difficulties, provide multiple choice responses to questions. Students can mark, underline, or circle answers rather than write them.

13. *Change amount of work.* If a student has a work page containing numerous practice items, such as a long series of sentences requiring correct use of *was* or *were,* reduce the number of required items. The student could do every other problem, or draw a predetermined amount of bingo numbers that correspond with the item numbers to be completed, or the teacher can star (*) the items to be completed.

14. *Highlight materials.* Drab worksheets can be made more visually attractive by backing them with construction paper or wallpaper. Teachers also can add illustrations or make colored borders around work items.

15. *Relocate student materials.* The presence of a variety of educational materials, workbooks, pencils, and books in a student's desk sometimes can be overwhelming and threatening. To relieve this stressful situation, materials can be placed in containers located in other parts of the room, such as on a bookshelf, in stacked cartons, or in "in" and "out" trays; the student can take only those materials needed for one assignment and return them to their location when the assignment is finished.

16. *Make adjustments for physically handicapping conditions.* If a student is visually impaired, be fully cognizant of necessary adaptations — for example, the size of print which can be read by the student; the best viewing distance and angle for reading print materials; the best lighting sources and locations; and the use of eyeglasses. If the student has a hearing impairment, be aware of the best location to facilitate hearing — for example, seeing the face of a person who is speaking, being away from background noise if it masks conversations, and the use of amplification aids.

17. *Highlight essential information.* If a junior or senior high student is able to read a regular textbook at grade level but cannot tolerate

a full assignment, draw yellow felt pen lines through essential parts of the printed text before giving it to the student.

Adding Motivational Aspects

1. *Writing tools.* From time to time, give students an opportunity to select a different writing tool. Tools can include crayons, colored pencils, fountain pens, felt pens, chalk, or special pencils such as the extra large ones marked "think big."
2. *Bonus box.* Provide students with opportunities to earn extra credit. A bonus box can be filled with worksheets or task cards with directions for projects and activities. A suggested amount of credit should accompany each material, but the credit amount could be negotiable.
3. *Teacher's notes.* The teacher can write a note or letter and attach it to a student assignment. The note, for example, could give directions for an interesting activity elsewhere in the room, as a substitute for a routine assignment.
4. *Word hunt.* Encourage students to go on a hunt through their environment, looking for words such as *men, women, exit, stop, ped x.* Students also could hunt for reading or spelling words in newspapers, magazines, cereal boxes, model kits, and so on.
5. *Fishbowl.* On pieces of colored paper, write descriptions for unique fun and creative assignments or art projects. Put the papers in a fishbowl and occasionally allow the students to choose their own assignment.
6. *Clever cartoons.* Library card pockets attached to a chart or bulletin board can be used to hold cartoon character illustrations with gimmicky sayings, such as "First rate worker," "Dig up the facts," "Be a busy beaver," or "Press on." From time to time, the teacher can indicate, on a student's daily schedule, that he or she may select an item from the library pockets. These mini-breaks add variety to the routine.
7. *Art displays.* Arrange displays of the students' art work in the school library or hall display cases. This not only gives special education students an opportunity to be part of the school activities, but it offers other students and teachers an increased awareness of special classes.
8. *Publications.* If a student is pleased with a story, poem, or book report he or she has written, make spirit master copies for wider

distribution. If the student is pleased with an English, math, or social studies paper, it could be made into a transparency which the student could show to the class, using the overhead projector.

9. *Picture taking.* Take pictures of the students while they are working on assignments, projects, or interacting appropriately with their peers. Pictures can be displayed on bulletin boards and/or given to the students to share with others. Photographs can be great boosters of self-image. "Instant picture" cameras are best for immediate feedback, of course, but simple instamatic cameras are less expensive and easy to operate.

10. *Invisible message.* Write the student a personalized note using a special pen that writes invisibly (see Resource Section in the appendix to this chapter). Provide the student with the developer pen, which is used to make the markings visible.

11. *Beat the clock.* When a student is assigned a timed activity, give him or her a stopwatch to operate, and explain how to set it. Students also can use a stopwatch to time their assignments if they are trying to improve their records of task completion.

MAKING CURRICULUM MATERIALS

Frequently, teachers follow the manuals to determine scope and sequence of concepts presented in the textbooks, but teachers should feel free to create their own materials to replace the commercially prepared ones, if this will improve instruction. Lessons from commercial materials can be used in conjunction with teacher-developed materials, many of which will be created to acknowledge and respond to specific student interests or feelings. If materials for these personalized lessons do not exist, the teacher should design them.

Some of the curriculum materials used and made by teachers of behaviorally disturbed students are described in the following sections. These suggestions are representative; some are for primary-aged students and others for adolescents; some encourage exploration, others do not; some involve concrete materials and tasks; others entail abstract activities; they vary in the input and output modalities. They are intended to encourage teachers to explore the vast possibilities for curriculum materials.

113

Math

1. *Math board.* Glue library pockets on a large posterboard. Cover the outside portion of the pocket with transparent self-adhesive paper. Use water-base felt pens to write problems on the pockets. Provide a set of 1½″ × 2½″ cards with the corresponding answers for the student to sort through and place in the correct pockets. The problems can be cleaned with a cloth, allowing reuse of the math board. Figure 4.3 shows a teacher-made math board.

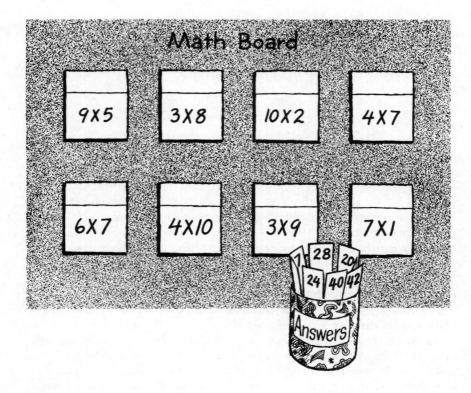

Fig. 4.3. Teacher-made math activity.

2. *Bingo cards.* Use bingo cards for practice in number recognition. Homemade bingo-type cards and alphabet letters can be used for letter recognition. Social studies player cards could be printed with the names of states; draw cards would contain names of their capitals. Then the game is played in the usual way.

3. *Dominoes.* A unique adaptation of the Domino game requires making a set of cardboard dominoes for math practice. Sets can be made with clock faces and matching time figures, as shown in Figure 4.4; or fraction numerals and matching illustrations.

Fig. 4.4. Cardboard domino game for math practice.

4. *Regrouping.* Tinkertoys can be used to teach early math concepts. The round pieces have 10 holes, which are helpful in teaching regrouping.

5. *Math circles.* Outline circles of approximate silver dollar size or larger with a black felt pen on a piece of one-color vinyl of approximate desk size. Write a numeral in each circle, and write the corresponding problems on paper or lightweight cardboard circles of the same size as those on vinyl. Give the student a set of the paper circles to place on the appropriate answers. The paper circles could contain simple story problems, basic or algebraic equations.

6. *Living skills.* If a secondary student is considering leaving school at the age of sixteen, certain math activities may help the student face some realities of adult living. One such activity is: The student first

locates a job in the newspaper want ads; using the salary quoted in the ad, the student computes net pay, as well as living expenses. Newspaper grocery ads, apartment rental ads, catalogs containing prices of clothing and household items, and brochures showing utility and insurance rates can help provide information about living expenses.

English

1. *Adopt a Ship Plan.* The U.S. Coast Guard will provide the name of a captain and his ship for correspondence with a class (see appendix to this chapter for address). The captain sends the ship's picture and a map of the ship's voyage. Individual crew members write letters in response to students' letters. This offers a good experience in handwriting, composition, social studies, and interpersonal relationship skills.
2. *Creative writing.* Give students an opportunity to play Ann Landers or Dear Abby for a day. Duplicate several letters from a newspaper advice column and glue each to a sheet of writing paper; do not include the printed reply. The student becomes the advice-giver by inventing and writing responses to the letters, which can be compared later to the real one, if desired.
3. *Newspaper day.* A school day could be set aside to emphasize learning from the newspaper. Plan all the day's subjects in relation to the newspaper; bring the local newspaper to class and explain and explore all sections. In math, for instance, grocery ads can be used for shopping problems. Also, give students opportunities to write and prepare their own news articles, headlines, and scoops. Serve doughnuts and coffee to create a newsroom atmosphere.

    Discuss reporting and provide reporting experiences. To reinforce the idea of correct reporting of facts, prearrange to have a person run into the classroom and briefly act out a situation. After that person leaves, ask the students to write their objective version of the incident — the resulting story variations are interesting and widely divergent.
4. *Travel brochures.* Students can make travel brochures of places they have visited or would like to visit. Sample brochures should be available for content and format ideas. Water colors, felt pens, 18″ × 24″ drawing paper, rulers, pencils, and magazines containing outdoor pictures are the materials essential to this activity. Reference books,

textbooks, and an atlas also would be helpful. Students design, write, and make their brochures, which can be displayed in the room.

5. *Student books.* Have the students write a short book or compile a collection of their creative writings. If the student can type, the final product will look "professional." If a spirit master is used for the handwritten or typed copy, duplicates can be made for others to read. One copy of the book could be bound; arrange this with a book-binder or locate spiral binding equipment. Abbey Press (see appendix to this chapter) sells books with contemporary design covers and blank pages. Whatever the materials and process, students' special book writing can be most satisfying.

6. *Comic book reports.* Provide comic books for students to use in a book report. Each student can convert his or her report into dialogue, writing it on blank paper that has been cut to fit over the original balloons of the comic strip. When the students are pleased with their revised comics, they can paste their dialogues over the original balloons to make permanent comic book reports.

   Another version results in a single captioned character with balloon. A comic character, a picture of a sports hero, or drawing of a fictional person is pasted near the lower edge of large oaktag sheet. A balloon is drawn to occupy the major portion of the paper, which then is covered with lamin or transparent self-adhesive material. The student can write a phrase, sentence, or paragraph in the balloon space, using a grease pencil or water-based felt pen; the writing then can be cleaned off with a cloth and replaced with another written passage.

7. *Shoebox reports.* Ask students to prepare a book report to be accompanied by a three-dimensional scene in a shoebox. A peephole in the side of the covered box or transparent wrap laced over the open top side will allow the scene to be viewed. (Larger boxes also could be used.)

8. *Re-created menus.* Ask students to suggest unique words for a lunch menu. For example, one Halloween menu was written as: Witches Brew, Ghost Flakes, Brown Sticks, Shaky Shimmering Salad, Trick or Treat Goblin Drink.

9. *Snoopy's prepositions.* A picture of Snoopy is pasted to a piece of lightweight cardboard and cut out; rebus drawings of a table, chair, tree, and/or doghouse are outlined on the cardboard cut out, and a piece of velcro or felt attached to the back of each piece. The objects are placed on a flannelboard or on the stage of an overhead projector,

117

and Snoopy is moved by the teacher and students into various positions to illustrate prepositions (above, under, beside, near, etc.).

Spelling

1. *Pegboard spelling.* A pegboard is placed on a wooden stand or propped against a solid surface. Letter cards one-inch square, each with a punched hole, are placed with the pegs on the board. These cards can be used for spelling practice, as well as for an interesting spelling test format. Pegboards from lumber companies can be used with golf tees as pegs. Extra-large pegs can be purchased from school supply stores.

2. *Spelling points.* Each letter of the alphabet is assigned a number — for example, 1 to 26 or 10 to 260, so that A = 1 or 10; b = 2 or 20; c = 3 or 30; etc. Ask each student to write the spelling words and give each letter its number value. Then students answer questions such as, "What is your most expensive word?" "What is the cheapest word?" "What is the total value of your list?" "How many words are worth 100 points or more?"

3. *Hidden words.* Use a hidden word format for spelling word practice, as illustrated in Figure 4.5. Provide a spelling list and the word puzzle. The student is to draw a ring around each located spelling word. Bonus points can be given if the student locates additional words.

4. *Personal touch.* For spelling or writing practice, include personal references — for example, "Paul's aunt is coming to visit next week." (*Coming, visit,* and *next* are three of Paul's spelling words.)

5. *Yarn spelling.* Yarn spelling can be a way for students either to take a spelling test in a fun way or to individually practice spelling words. Figure 4.6 illustrates the activity, in which one end of the yarn is attached to a popsicle stick and the other is threaded through a tapestry needle or wrapped with a piece of masking tape. On small squares cut from construction paper or oaktag, with a hole punched near the top of each square, consonants are written in blue and vowels in red, one letter per square. The student strings the yarn through the holes of the letter squares to spell. (Make 20 or 30 of each letter, and store all materials in a small box or other container.)

6. *Spelling code.* Present a weekly spelling list in a code of a type that has a symbol for each letter of the alphabet. Each student is given a copy of the code to translate the spelling lists.

Word list

civil
social
rights
strife
concern
individual

h	s	c	c	o	n	c	e	r	n	r
s	t	o	l	e	j	a	i	l	s	i
g	r	g	c	v	o	b	l	t	e	g
m	i	n	d	i	l	m	u	l	t	h
a	f	l	a	w	a	l	o	n	e	t
b	e	i	n	g	b	l	a	c	p	s
r	i	n	d	i	v	i	d	u	a	l

Can you find other words?

Fig. 4.5.   Hidden word format for spelling.

POPSICLE STICK

TAPESTRY NEEDLE

YARN

Fig. 4.6.   Spelling activity using yarn.

Social Studies

1. *Stamp collection.* Collect domestic and foreign stamps and mount each on a 3″ × 5″ index card. Using information from the stamp's picture, write questions on the card, such as, "Can you find the country that this stamp is from? Indicate the atlas page number on your answer sheet." "Who is the man in the picture? List some of his major contributions to society." "How much did the stamp cost? How much is that in American money?"

2. *Day in court.* Prearrange a visit to the city or county courthouse. Often, a supervised class may observe a court session or tour the juvenile detention area. This excellent field trip experience can stimulate discussion on law, crime, and legal rights of youth.

3. *Colonial recipes.* Old colonial cooking recipes can be used to illustrate certain aspects of American history — the food available to colonists, techniques for food storage, other uses for food such as bartering or the use of flour to clean human hair. Have students actually prepare the old recipe, or have them find a current version of the recipe.

4. *Police awareness.* Many police departments have citizen information and public relations personnel who take small groups on shortened police work shifts. Such a field trip can be interesting, particularly if police personnel demonstrate police computer systems, traffic radar, and radio communications. This type of field trip also helps the students become aware of the police and their roles in society. As an alternative, many police stations will send officers to school classes to demonstrate safety ideas, self-defense techniques, or police procedures.

5. *Taste fair.* Conduct a weekly or monthly taste fair to widen students' interest. Each fair could have a specialty such as foreign, ethnic, health, or holiday items.

6. *Civil rights.* For a unit in ethnic history, one teacher had each student prepare a written report on a famous personality. Then each student made a picket sign with pictures and phrases representative of that personality. The student's written report was stapled to the back of the picket, which was then used as a basis for an oral report. The students also took their picket signs to another class, whose members tried to guess the name of each personality from the information presented on the front of the picket sign.

7. *Travel with the stars.* An individual student or the class selects a celebrity such as a sports figure, rock star, or TV entertainer and

records that star's activities for a specified time. Data can include performance dates, locations of performances, sizes of crowds, critic reviews, and other tangible efforts by the star. The format for record keeping can be decided by the student. Activities associated with the record keeping are encouraged, such as a map of the United States on which the travel route is traced.

Science

1. *Nature box.* Items from the natural environment can be placed in a container such as an oatmeal box or a three-pound coffee can. The container is covered with plain paper on which questions have been written like, "How does it smell . . . taste . . . touch?" "Where is it found?" "Did it grow?" The box should contain items that stimulate answers to the questions.

2. *Weather changes.* Take advantage of weather changes. On the day of the first snow, have the students turn their desks to watch the snow fall; the assignment could be to draw images of what they see. During a thunderstorm, the students could write about how storms make them feel.

3. *Science figures.* Every time a young student successfully completes a science lesson or unit, have him or her draw an animal, or cut an animal from construction paper, or find one in a coloring book to color and cut out or to use as a pattern. These animals are to be displayed within the room. Young children enjoy adding to the colorful animals which brighten the area.

4. *Atom splitting.* The principle of nuclear fission can be demonstrated with a balloon, dart, and candy. Each student in turn is blindfolded and asked to throw a dart at an inflated balloon containing several pieces of hard candy — demonstrating that the balloon is hit and the candy split by chance. In the demonstration, the student throwing the dart represents the cyclotron; the dart is the neutron; the balloon is the atom; and the split candy represents the particles and energy released from the split atom.

5. *Aerodynamic contest.* Paper airplanes and small plastic bags can be used to demonstrate how objects are able to fly. Paper airplanes can be folded in various ways to show how airplane surfaces enable flight. The hot air balloon principle can be demonstrated by inflating a plastic bag and carefully inserting a candle into the bag to heat the

air. (Caution: Do not let the flame come into direct contact with the plastic, which burns or melts upon contact.) When the air is heated, the bag will rise upon release because warm air expands and becomes lighter. A follow-up activity could be a contest between balloon and airplane flying, with the students' determining the highest flying balloon, the airplane that stays aloft the longest, the airplane that will travel the greatest distance, etc.

Reading

1. *Syllable rhythms.* The concept of syllables is difficult for some students to grasp unless it is put on a concrete level. Have the students beat out the rhythm of a word in some way such as clapping, tapping on the desk or floor. Once the students understand that each syllable corresponds to one beat, they frequently are able to count the syllables mentally.
2. *Word checkers.* Type a student's new words on paper, cut apart, and attach each to a checker until the set is complete. Play the game in the usual way, with the additional rule that a move or jump cannot be made until the word on the checker is read correctly.
3. *Word puzzle.* For young children, make a colorful design on one side of a square piece of posterboard. On the other side, draw lines to form squares; print four words in each square, one word on each side, as illustrated in Figure 4.7. Cut the puzzle along the lines and place the squares in an envelope. The students assemble the puzzle and then read all the words aloud. Geometric shapes other than a square also could be used.
4. *Teacher-made books.* Make high interest, low vocabulary books for the older student who is reading on a pre-primer or primer level. Write or type a narrative with basic beginning words to accompany illustrations from popular teen magazines like *Seventeen, Hot Rod, Car and Driver, Rolling Stones,* movie magazines, or recorded music magazines.
5. *Growing word stack.* Primary and intermediate aged students who are reading on a pre-primer or primer level often prefer having their own set of flash cards. Write each student's new reading word on a 3″ × 5″ card, and use these teacher-made flash cards when presenting new vocabulary. Establish a criterion level for the students' competency level, such as recognizing the word three times without error after

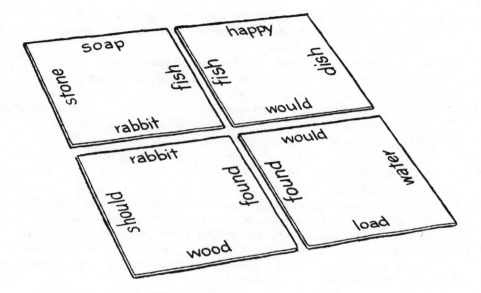

Fig. 4.7. Puzzle for reading improvement.

practice. When a student reaches the established criterion level, he or she keeps the card in a box or on a large notebook ring in the desk or a special location, and brings the cards out when needed for review and other uses during reading lessons. As new words are learned and kept, the stack of cards grows. Eventually, the cards can be taken home. Many index cards are needed, but this activity can give students a positive sense of accomplishment as a result of the visible evidence of their reading vocabulary growth.

Miscellaneous Activities for Young Students

1. *Paper bag search.* This activity focuses on auditory memory. Each student is given a small paper bag labeled with his or her name. The teacher then sequences a group of items that the students can find either outside or (on a bad-weather day) in the room. For example, a teacher of a young group might say, "Who can find a leaf, a rock,

a piece of paper, and a twig?" Following a signal to begin, the students try to find the items. This activity also may encourage group competition and interaction.

2. *Scent containers.* As an activity focusing on the olfactory sense, items having distinctive odors can be placed in separate baby food jars that have been opaqued by paint or other covering to conceal the contents. (Small plastic cartons could be used as an alternative.) Punch holes in the container's lid and cover with tape, which can be pulled back for smelling and guessing.

3. *Magnetic tower.* Attach to or embed a magnet in a piece of wood. Collect bolts and screws. The students can make pyramid designs using the magnetic base.

4. *Guessing game.* A guessing game at the beginning or end of the day is one way of calming a young group, as well as encouraging oral language. The teacher begins by asking a question about a classroom item, such as, "I see something that is big and red," and gives additional clues until the item is guessed. The first child with the correct answer begins the next round of the game.

5. *Listening games.* This activity provides experiences in listening to sounds and identifying them. The students have their eyes shut or blindfolded. Many classroom sounds can be used — a door opening, a pencil dropping, someone writing on the chalkboard, coins jingling, a window closing, coughing, clapping, etc. The teacher begins by making one of the sounds and calls the first student, who responds. If the student identifies the sound correctly, he or she becomes the leader.

   If the room has a piano, musical notes can be used for a sound discrimination activity. The leader plays two notes, one at a time. The children are asked to identify if the second note is higher, lower, or the same as the first note.

   Another listening game is to use rhythmic patterns to stimulate auditory recall. With a ruler or rhythm stick, the teacher beats a pattern; for example, tap . . . tap tap tap . . . tap . . . tap. A student is called upon to repeat the pattern. As the children become more proficient in their immediate auditory recall skills, the rhythmic pattern can be made more difficult by increasing the length of the rhythmic sequence and adding loud and soft beats.

6. *Tracing activities.* Simplified patterns of Peanuts, Raggedy Ann, Sesame Street characters, Spider Man, or other popular cartoon characters can be introduced into young students' tracing activities.

7. *Junk match.* Collect pairs of items and glue one member of each pair to a board or embed in plaster of paris. Place other items in a cardboard carton. Taking one item at a time, the young students search for its duplicate. Students can do this activity tactually or visually.

Social and Affect

1. *Who's who.* One teacher who worked with teenage girls used pipe cleaners as a way of introducing the students to their peers. Each girl was given a pipe cleaner with instructions to bend it according to some of the ups and downs of her life. The pipe cleaner was used by each girl as part of her self-introduction to the group. The teacher herself often began the session by sharing some personal experiences, using the pipe cleaner to illustrate.
2. *Buddy week.* As a good activity to promote affective involvement, each student is given or draws the name of a "secret buddy." Each day for a week the students leave their buddies notes, poems, and other surprises. The teacher can be included in the activity, if desired.
3. *Birthday photos.* A posed or candid snapshot of a student can be enlarged for a birthday gift (see the resource section in the appendix to this chapter). It becomes a unique gift if it is framed and has a special note attached.
4. *Solutions.* The teacher thinks of various situations that might occur in the classroom and presents some of the situations to the students during a group time. The students then consider and discuss solutions to each situation. Following that experience, the students possibly can determine solutions to some actual classroom conflicts as they begin to develop, before they get out of hand. If an incident already has occurred and the students offer a solution, the teacher should comment and indicate approval if the solution was appropriate; if the solution was inappropriate, the teacher should have a "counseling session" with the involved students, regarding appropriate solutions.
5. *Creative pamphlets.* For creative writing and affective development, a teacher can encourage students to create their own pamphlets, using blank papers with a colorful cover. The teacher could suggest titles such as, "The Fantastic Work of David" or "Everything You Wanted to Know About Lori." The students can design the covers, write stories and poems, and illustrate them. The teacher either can encourage total creativity or can present structured choices using

pictures, words, and phrases as stimuli; for example, "What kind of conversation could the two people in this picture be having?" or "Rain makes me feel _____ ."

Another potential use of pamphlets arises when a student is not quite ready to talk about feelings surrounding an incident. A pamphlet could be a good vehicle for venting some of these feelings. The blank pamphlets should be prepared in advance and accessible to the students. Pamphlets can consist of blank sheets stapled or laced inside a cover with titles such as, "How I Feel Today," "Happy Book," or "Mad Book." The students should feel free to either write sentences or draw pictures of their personal feelings.

This pamphlet technique allows students to express feelings in their own ways. At the appropriate times, the teacher can have individual, private discussions with the students about the contents and meanings of their pamphlets.

6. *Study carrel posters.* Self-concept materials can be part of a student's individual study carrel. The teacher- or student-made posters can be used to help students become aware of feelings. Poster titles can include "I am My Best Friend," "Hey, I'm Me," "I'm Glad to Be Me," "I am a Special Person," "This is Me — I am a Friend." Photographs of the student, thumbprints, body cutouts, special notes, and similar things can be attached to the posters.

7. *Affective discussions.* The end of the school day often is a good time to hold a group discussion about the happenings and feelings of that day. This gives the students a chance to think over the activities before daily reports are sent home. The students could sit in a circle on the floor or around a table. The teacher can ask the students, one by one, to express their accomplishments and plans for improvement. The group discussion period is a good time to praise both small steps and giant gains. The teacher and group can even use applause to reinforce special progress of younger children.

8. *Cooperative puzzles.* To involve a withdrawn child in cooperative play, mark the back of a puzzle: half of the puzzle pieces with the withdrawn child's name and the other half with another child's name. Assign the two children to work on the puzzle at the same time, with each being responsible for his or her own pieces.

9. *Story collage.* Identification with the feelings of characters in novels and short stories can spark interest in reading, as well as bring out a student's own emotions. An individual student or small group could read a story, make a collage of the story's theme, then explain

the parts of the collage and the collage as a whole to the rest of the class. This activity helps students express their own feelings and encourages interaction with other class members.

10. *Group design.* A free form or geometric design is drawn on a large sheet of paper on the floor. The entire class can color the design as one group or in smaller groups. Working on the design while it is on the floor encourages informality and conversation from shy students.

Art

1. *Pin art.* Provide or have students find simple printed designs, shapes, or symbols (stars, spirals, large musical notes, etc.). Each is attached with paper clips to colorful dark construction paper (blue, red, black, green) and then laid on a magazine or piece of cardboard. Using straight pins, the students poke holes at close regular intervals around the entire outline of the shape. The construction paper is removed and taped to the window, where the light filters through the pin holes to highlight the design.
2. *Pennants.* Students can make their own pennants by cutting felt material into pennant shapes. Designs can be added by gluing on other pieces of felt and by using felt tip pens. Each pennant is attached to a stick (dowel rod). The pennants make excellent room decorations.
3. *"Leather" bottles.* Cover glass jars or bottles with overlapping pieces of masking tape. Cover the masking tape with a shoe polish paste, and buff. The final leather-looking product can be an old-fashioned ink well or a flower container.
4. *Wire bending.* Obtain at least five colors of pliable cable and a pair of wire cutters. (Scrap wire from electric or phone companies is good.) Encourage students to select varying lengths and colors of wire to execute original ideas. Through bending, intertwining, and cutting, students can manipulate the wires into their desired creations.
5. *Personal placemats.* If students eat lunch in the classroom, personalized placemats can be functional as well as artistic. The students draw pictures on 12″ x 18″ paper, which is then laminated. Placemats also serve as physical boundaries if students (a) tend to use a larger area than desirable to eat; (b) argue about ownership of food; and (c) are responsible for cleaning their lunch table area.

Physical Education Activities

1. *Hot potato.* The students sit in a circle, with one student holding an object such as a ball, chalkboard eraser, or bean bag. When the teacher turns on the music, the children in turn pass the "hot potato" around the circle until the music stops. The student holding the "potato" when the music stops gets a tally point. The game continues for a predetermined time; the player(s) with the lowest number of points wins the game.

2. *Individual relays.* Individual relays can be played by students who cannot tolerate group relay competition. Team relays can be adapted to individual relays — that is, a student can compete with another student's record or a student can compete with his or her own record (for example, number of times the finish line is crossed in a predetermined time period). Have a stopwatch available for students who want to compete against their own time records.

    Relays can be played in the classroom, gym, or playground, depending upon the specific activity. Classroom relay activities include pushing a peanut across the floor with the nose; carrying a spoonful of navy beans without spilling; scooting across the floor with an orange tucked under the chin. Gymnasium relay activities include a hop, skip, and jump pattern, running backward, or doing the duck-walk across the gym. Another relay activity involves each student having a collection of three to five objects, like bean bags, erasers, clothespins, or balls, at the starting line. The student must carry the objects, one at a time, to the finish line. Another playground or gymnasium relay calls for the students to kick balls to the finish line (each student's ball must have an identification mark).

3. *Chair bounce.* Students can practice ball rolling and catching indoors with the following adaptation: Cut a two-inch strip from an inner-tube and stretch it between the two front legs of a straight chair, as shown in Figure 4.8. When a small ball is rolled toward the chair, it will bounce and return.

4. *Nerf ball activities.* Nerf balls, widely available, are made of soft, lightweight synthetic foam; they can be safely thrown, kicked, or batted around a room and do not hurt a student if hit. A Nerf football and two sizes of round balls (4″ and 7″) are available. A net and hoop (resembling a basketball ring) and brackets are available. Students can practice free throws or, if members of the class enjoy throwing the Nerf basketballs but vary widely in their skills, an adapted basketball

128

Fig. 4.8. Adaptation to practice ball rolling and catching.

game can be played as follows: Students decide in advance the number of free throws needed to complete the game. Each player takes a turn, and each time the ball goes into the basket, the player throws a die. The number appearing on the die is the amount the student scores for that successful throw. The students write their points on the chalkboard; when the game ends, they add up their scores. The winner is the player with the most points. Use of the die adds a gambling element that tends to equalize scores; for example, a less skillful player may score 6 points for a single throw while a skillful player may score only 5 points for two throws.

5. *Punching bag and kicking boxes.* A punching bag or empty cardboard cartons can be located in a special area where students can physically release aggressive feelings by kicking these inanimate objects rather than peers or adults. Also, rolled up newspapers can be given to children to hit against the wall or floor.

6. *Rainy day baseball.* Baseball can be adapted to indoor play. The ball can be made by stuffing one sock into the toe of another, tying the loose end, and cutting off extra material. Players use a hand for the bat. Regular baseball rules can be used, with the following additional rule: A player is out if hit by the ball while running to the bases.

Media

1. *"Sensational" slides.* A few inexpensive materials are needed to make unique, creative slides. Wipe bleach over old slides to remove the color. Add a small amount of petroleum jelly (e.g., Vaseline) to clean the slides. Cut a small section of transparent, self-adhesive paper approximately the same size as the slide. Place small feathers, colored cellophane, small dried, pressed flowers and weeds, etc. on the adhesive paper. Place the slide, Vaseline side down, onto the sticky side of the adhesive paper. Press the two materials together until the slide is as smooth as possible. These designs resemble kaleidoscope patterns when viewed through a projector. When music is added to a series of these slides, a "sensation" show can be presented.

2. *Overhead projector reading game.* Write instructions to the students on an overhead projector transparency. Have the students act out the instructions projected on the screen; for example, "Jeff, shake hands with the boy in blue pants." This activity provides practice in reading and in following written directions.

3. *Tape a story.* A student can audio-tape a story and present it to the class instead of merely reading it. Sound effects can be added to the tape, or additional sounds can be made as the tape is played — these effects add to the audio dramatization.

4. *Lucky five.* Teacher-made games can be used to help students learn and practice concepts. Lucky Five is a card game for practicing the identification of correct verb tenses; 25 tokens, a pair of dice, and a set of 50 to 70 verb cards are needed for two to five players. An example of a verb card is:

"Eddie _____ his packing for his trip."
    do, did, done

Usually, the correct answers are known by at least one player; if not, an answer key can be made. Directions are as follows: (a) Players throw dice to determine first player; player with the lowest total number on his or her dice begins the game; (b) Cards are placed face down to begin the draw deck; (c) Each player in turn draws the top card from the draw deck, reads aloud the sentence and verb tense selections, and responds with an answer; (d) If the player's first answer is correct, the player places the card in the discard stack and throws the dice; if a five appears on either or both of the dice or a combination of five appears on the dice, the player takes a token for each five; (e) If a player's first answer is incorrect, the other players give the correct answer and the player returns the card to the bottom of the deck; (f) The winner is the first player to get five tokens.

5. *Ping pong pumpkins.* One teacher used five orange ping pong balls for Halloween finger play activities. She drew pumpkin faces with a black felt pen, along with a circle of about ¾-inch diameter on the "bottom." She spread a line of liquid glue (Elmer's or Sobo) around the circle and, using an x-acto knife, cut a hole in each ball to allow room for inserting a finger. (Use of the glue prevents the ping pong balls from cracking when cut.)

6. *Family photos.* A teacher took snapshots of a young child's family. These were used in reading and language activities to help the child learn the meaning of words. Later, the teacher took action pictures of the child to further develop his vocabulary. Teachers also could ask the students to bring in family photos of their choice for the same purpose.

Making "Handy" Educational Materials

Teachers from time to time discover ideas and create gadgets that are both time and money savers and contribute to smoother classroom management. Some of these handy tips are:

1. Felt pens: Use water-base marking pens when preparing materials that are to be covered with transparent, self-adhesive paper. Markings from permanent ink pens "bleed," but water-base markings will

not. Spirit master work sheets also bleed after a period of time if covered with transparent, self-adhesive paper.

2. Scissors container: A scissors rack can be made by spray painting an inverted egg carton or decorating the outside of a coffee can (punch holes in plastic lid for scissors).

3. Chalkboard chalk: Permanent chalk is a useful material — The chalk remains on the board until it is removed with soap and water. (Available from school supply stores.)

4. Coded puzzle pieces: When a new puzzle is purchased, mark the back of each piece with numerals for some puzzles, alphabet letters for others, symbols for still others. When the pieces from several puzzles become intermingled, they are easier to locate if they have been coded in such a manner.

5. Name tags: If special stickers are unavailable or too expensive, masking tape can be substituted; it is easy to remove from clothing or desks.

6. Miniature chalkboard: Obtain a piece of 3-ply cardboard approximately 12″ x 12″ and paint one side with three to five coats of chalkboard paint (available in several colors at paint or school supply stores). Or, obtain masonite board; paint the smooth surface and use the other side as a flannelboard. A miniature board could be made for each student.

7. Flannelboard: Use the rougher side of a piece of masonite or cover a heavy weighted cardboard with flannel. Make flannelboard figures from foam-backed material or felt.

8. Game pieces: A cardboard carton can be used for games that include easily spilled or lost items — pick-up sticks, checkers, blocks, puzzles. Students can work with these items in the carton, but the sides of the carton need to be cut to facilitate arm movement.

9. Language art worksheets: Look in newspapers, commercial and educational magazines, discarded workbooks and textbooks for pictures that lend themselves to language art activities. Commercial adhesive stamp pictures also are available. Mount the pictures on cardboard or oaktag and cover with transparent self-adhesive material. Questions regarding the pictures can be written on a card attached below the picture or on worksheets accompanying the pictures. For example: "How many items in this picture begin with *ch*?" "Circle the fictional items on this picture."

10. Color coded materials: Colorful rolls of gummed-back tape are available from many school supply stores. These tapes can be used

to color code matching items, to make small badges and name tags, or to decorate bulletin boards.

11. Typewriter: A manual typewriter in the classroom can stimulate learning, as well as being fun. Many students who cannot write well may want to use the typewriter to compose stories. Typing sentences and paragraphs also can provide practice in capitalization, punctuation, and spelling. Titles on art work, science projects, or slides look more "professional" if they have been typed.

12. Bean bags: Find cloth material with large, appealing, simple print figures (animals, etc.). Cut around the figure outline, two layers thick, matching the figures. Sew sides, allowing an opening, fill with beans, then sew opening. The teacher can readily make a number and variety of bean bag shapes in this way.

13. Picture collection: Small pictures representing vowel and consonant combinations can be used for teacher-made worksheets. These pictures can be kept in small boxes or in a box with dividers. Separate them according to word lengths; for example, a box marked C-V-C (consonant, vowel, consonant) might include pictures of a cat, bed, and actions like hop and run. A different code can be designed for other academic subjects, but the C-V code is workable for locating pictures for teacher-made phonics and language worksheets.

14. Storing slides: Waxed paper and aluminum foil cartons can become storage containers for slides. The width is perfect to accommodate regular slides.

15. Sticky glue top: Elmer's or Sobo glue bottle tops sometimes are difficult to twist after first use. Before using the glue, remove the top and rub a small amount of petroleum jelly around the bottle's neck to prevent the lid from sticking.

16. Coat hanger chart: Cut an old window shade in half vertically. Cut the horizontal wire on the coat hanger and slip the shade onto the hanger, as shown in Figure 4.9. The shade can be pulled down to any length. Marking on the shade with a grease pencil allows it to be reusable.

17. Stapling: Staple papers at varied positions along the lefthand side, other than the upper lefthand corner only; this allows storage of more materials in a file. Staple a stack of duplicated pages with the printed side down if top sheets are to be removed sequentially for individual page work.

18. Durable materials: Cover frequently used materials with lamin, a transparent self-adhesive material, or plastic spray. The materials

Fig. 4.9.   Coat hanger/window shade chart.

will have a longer life, dirt and grime can be removed easily, and markings can be wiped off for repeated use.

CREATING LEARNING CENTERS

Learning centers can be designed in any number of arrangements and with a wide variety of materials. A center may be located in an area of the room designed with carpet squares, a table, and bean bag chairs;

134

or it could consist of displays on a bulletin board. Some suggested materials are games, audiovisual equipment, magazines, metric aids, and parts of broken machinery. Learning centers usually focus on a topic of interest such as science, library, communications, history, or problem solving. Directions for operation of the center should be clear, specific, and concise. The teacher and students can formulate verbal and/or written directions for operating the centers. Two learning centers are described below.

Learning Center: Me

The purpose of this learning center is to stimulate primary-aged children to think about and understand themselves better by increasing self-awareness. The learning center is divided into five sections.

Station 1

The child makes a book about himself or herself. Materials include construction paper, stapler, blank paper, file folders, scissors, crayons, magazine pictures, glue, and spirit master pages with sentences that offer possibilities for descriptions of oneself, such as: "This is my whole name written in my best handwriting.... Here is what I look like.... I am _____ years old. Students may want to use magazine pictures for decorating the book cover or illustrating pages. A poem about the child's individuality could be used as an introduction or page one of the book.

Station 2

The students view a filmstrip, *The Joy of Being You* (see Scholastic /Kimble, in the appendix to this chapter). Then they draw self-portraits of sad, happy, angry, and pensive times. Materials include the filmstrip and accompanying record, an individual filmstrip projector, a record player (if projector does not have one), blank pages, file folders, and colored pencils.

Station 3

The children open a closed cardboard box and remove the contents — a crystal ball and a cassette tape recorder. They use the crystal ball to predict what they will be or would like to be in the future. The teacher encourages them to give reasons for their predictions. Materials include a decorated cardboard box, cassette tape recorder, extra recorder batteries, two 30-minute cassette tapes, and crystal ball. The crystal ball can be a round fishbowl or a large light bulb. If a light bulb is used, a base is needed; this can be a small, sturdy cardboard box or plastic container, decorated appropriately. The base of the bulb is inserted through the container from the top and is secured with masking tape.

Station 4

The children listen to two different records that are color coded with purple and green markings. The selections on one recording suggest happy moods; those on the other record reflect sad moods. While the children listen to the record, they paint their feelings using water colors or felt pens. The drawing paper is color coded purple and green on the edges so the teacher is able to determine if the students have expressed two different feelings. Essential materials are the record player, two records as described, blank pages (color coded purple and green), water colors, felt pens, and file folders.

Station 5

The children guess what is inside four containers by using the sense of smell and four socks by using the sense of touch. After smelling or touching each of the items, they record what they think is inside each container and how they would use it. To assist the children, the work pages should have four color coded squares corresponding to the colors of the containers and socks; the children record their answers within the squares of the corresponding colors. Materials include the four different colored socks, color coded yogurt containers (with nail holes punched to let the scents escape), blank pages color coded to match the socks and containers, file folders, and a decorated box for the materials and completed work. Examples of items that can be placed in the yogurt containers are: peanut butter, ground coffee, cloves, mentholatum, peppermint, sachet (perfume). The socks can contain items such as: macaroni, jacks, coins, toothbrush, walnuts, yarn, straw, feathers.

Figure 4.10 illustrates the five stations of the above-described learning center.

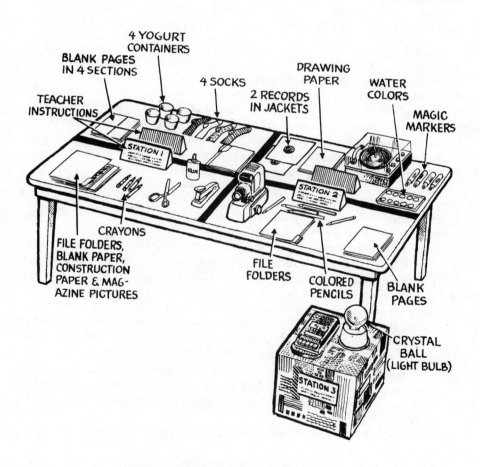

Fig. 4.10.   Learning center: ME.

Learning Center: Your State

The major purpose of this center is to acquaint intermediate and junior high students with specific information about their home state. The center contains a variety of materials designed to encompass different activities and to require more than one mode of response. Activities of this center could be initiated during the week of statehood celebration. The materials are displayed on a large conference table and are available to individual students as well as small groups. Possible activities and materials representing the state of Kansas are given below, as an example:

1. A game, "Across Kansas": The teacher-designed gameboard is an outline of the state's boundaries with the major and minor highway arteries identified. Historical landmarks on or near the highways are indicated. The players travel along the route following teacher-developed game rules, dice, markers, game cards, or other items (e.g., card representing 8 on dice states, "Camp overnight in Wichita.").
2. Reading books containing facts about the state are on display. Some topics include state products, lawmen and cowboys, Indian life, pioneer migration, and settlements. Comprehension questions accompany the books.
3. Patterns for Indian crafts, and materials such as beads, feathers, and thread, are available for student creations.
4. Sound filmstrips offer topics on Kansas animals and birds, historical events and landmarks, industries, and famous "Kansas Americans." The audio equipment includes several sets of earphones.
5. A decorated box contains objects from the outdoor environment. Students are encouraged to feel and identify these objects before seeing them. Paper is provided so each student can write as many facts as possible about any or all of the items. Descriptions could be submitted for a classroom contest.
6. The teacher designs several different seek-and-find word sheets — word puzzles containing hidden Kansas words. The puzzles are covered with transparent plastic so the students can use wipe-off markers to respond.
7. Phonograph records of folk songs and square dance music are used for large group experiences.

Figure 4.11 depicts this learning center.

Fig. 4.11. Learning center: Your state.

SUMMARY

Behavior disordered students can use some commercial materials with little or no modifications but, for the most part, the teacher should plan to revise and supplement these materials as necessary. The procedure of selecting and adapting materials is time consuming, but it is a stimulating activity because it summons initiative, creativity, and resourcefulness. Monotony is not part of a teacher's life when working with students who have behavioral disorders. Selection and adaptation of materials is contingent upon two other procedures — planning and academic diagnosis — and is coupled with three other procedures — programming, scheduling, and behavior modification. The total classroom milieu results from continuous change to meet the students' growth demands.

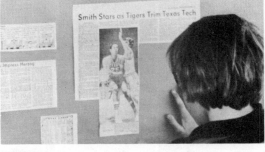

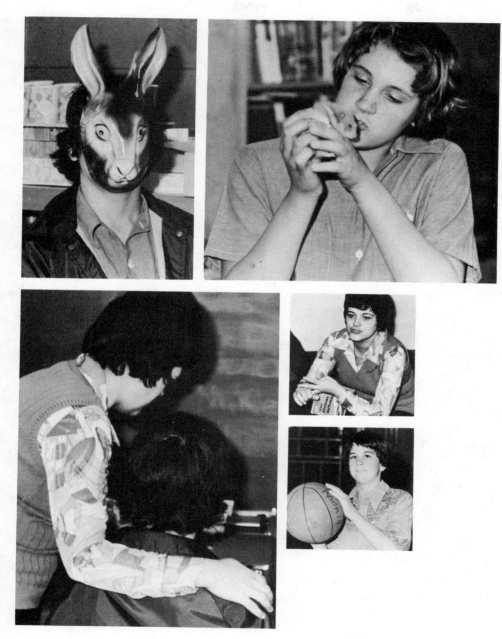

APPENDIX TO CHAPTER FOUR

RESOURCES FOR CLASSROOM MATERIALS

Abbey Press Offers posters, plaques, cards, gifts, and similar items, many of which are appropriate for the classroom. The "Write Your Own Books" are small, inexpensive booklets with beautiful designs and blank pages the students can use to create their own "best sellers." St. Meinard, IN 47577.

American Guidance Service Publishers' Bldg., Circle Pines, MN 55014

Coping With Series The series of 23 paperback books is written for adolescents and is appropriate for discussion groups and counseling sessions. The four major themes in the series are each represented by several books. Some of the titles: *Facts and Fantasies About Drugs, The Mind Binders, To Like and Be Liked,* and *Grades, What's So Important about Them Anyway?* A manual provides ideas and activities for use with all books in the series.

DUSO Kits The Developing Understanding of Self and Others kits are designed to stimulate social involvement, emotional growth, and language development (Kit D-1 is for kindergarten and lower primary; Kit D-2 is for upper primary and grade four). The manuals have a year's activities. The program emphasizes learning to talk more freely about feelings and behavior. Weekly activities contain problem situations, a story, a role play activity, a puppet activity, and supplementary readings and activities. Posters, records and cassettes, eight puppets, puppet props, group discussion cards, and role playing cards also are part of the kit (career awareness cards are part of Kit D-2).

Rub-on Rebuses 814 individual rub-on rebus symbols are available in a portfolio of nine sheets. The symbols represent common English words, numerals, and alphabet letters. The rebuses can be used on labels, in reading passages, and on worksheets.

Appleton-Century-Crofts Educational Division: *Slithery Snakes and Other Aids to Children's Writing* (Walter Petty & Mary E. Bowen, 1967) This book contains many specific ideas, invented circumstances, and nonsense titles for creative writing experiences. Meredith Corporation, New York, NY.

Bell Records: *Free to be You and Me* (Marlo Thomas and Friends) This record album describes freedom of choice for young boys and girls. The songs, stories, and poems can be used for group discussion and self-concept/awareness groups. One song, "It's All Right to Cry," is sung by Rosey Grier, former football player. 1776 Broadway, New York, NY 10019. (Book by the same title is published by McGraw Hill, New York)

Childcraft Educational Corp., 20 Kilmer Rd., Edison, NJ 08817

Classroom Camera This inexpensive camera is simple to operate, with two shutter settings, three distance ranges, and a lens cover. The student could use it for awareness activities and creative expression.

Feelings Books Childcraft has three books on expression of feelings and social relationships: *I Know What I Like* (Norma Simon), *Sometimes I Get Angry* (Watson, Schweitzer, & Hirschberg), and *No Kiss for Mother* (Tom Ungerer); these books encourage expression and discussion about feelings, reactions, emotions, and problems.

U Film It This kit contains a cardboard frame and 25 feet of film. Students can produce their own film using felt tip markers.

Children's Television Workshop: *Electric Company* and *Sesame Street* magazines. These monthly periodicals are based on the characters and concepts presented on the television shows. May be purchased at grocery stores or by subscription. One Lincoln Plaza, New York, NY 10023.

Collier Books/Macmillan Co.: *Secrets with Ciphers and Codes* (Joel Rothman & Ruth Ven Tremain, 1969) This book contains an assortment of codes for teachers to use as motivating features for basic skill activities. 866 Third Ave., New York, NY 10022.

Constructive Playthings Among other items, this firm has unbreakable toy cars and trucks, made from soft vinyl — bending, smashing, or stepping on them will not harm the vehicles. Each box contains two each of 18 different vehicles, three to four inches long. This firm also carries Nerf balls. 1040 E. 85th St., Kansas City, MO 64131.

Developmental Learning Materials (DLM) Co. — Clock stamp/coin stamp A three-inch rubber stamp produces a clock face with numbers; hands are omitted. The stamp is helpful in preparing time worksheets or for making daily scheduling charts depicting times for various subjects or activities. A kit of five U.S. coin stamps (penny, nickel, dime, quarter, and half dollar) is available with either head or tail side. The stamps are mounted on a clear plastic base with a handle, and the prints are of actual coin size. These stamps can be used for worksheets and games. Canadian coin stamps also are available. 7440 Natchez Ave., Niles, IL 60648.

Dramatic Publishing Co. Has a catalog of plays and musicals including class and school plays, full length, short royalty and non-royalty plays, musical comedies, Christmas plays, short entertainments, Shakespearian plays, and children's plays. Listings for each play include a short synopsis, casting requirements, and price. The catalog also contains information on ordering books on acting and producing, teaching aids, recorded interviews with actors and playwrights, sound effects, and publicity posters. 86 E. Randolph St., Chicago, IL 60601.

EDCOA Publications: *Each Day is a Special Day* This one-month calendar contains daily descriptions of special day designations and activities such as Secret Day *Shh*, Forgive Day, Touch Day, Prestige Day. Raspberry Reminders, P.O. Box 12212, Nashville, TN 37212.

Hubbard Scientific Viewing screen microscope, 50X and 100X power, from the *Biological Science Curriculum Study* (BSCS) materials, is inexpensive and can be operated easily by young children. Has a focus knob and on/off switch. Slides are viewed on the screen, similar to a single slide viewer. 2855 Sherman Rd., Northbrook, IL 60062.

Ideal Corp. Offers *Plastic Marks* — markers that resemble crayons and are used for writing on plastic surfaces; markings can be wiped off with a cloth. 11000 S. Lavergne Ave., Oaklawn, IL 60453.

Learning Handbooks: *Developing Individual Values in the Classroom* This handbook contains practical activities and strategies to help students clarify their own values. The projects help students examine feelings, participate in activities to build trust, and promote discussion. Department 1011, P.O. Box 818, Maple Plain, MN 55359.

Little Kenny Publications Offers game boards and game pieces for con-constructing handmade games — wipe-off spinners, wipe-off playing cards, wipe-off response cards, wipe-off crayons, dice, game markers or pawns. The open-ended game boards also are wipe-off. 1315 W. Belmont Ave., Chicago, IL 60657.

Love Publishing Co.: *Educational Games for Visually Handicapped Children* (Patricia A. Gallagher, 1977) This book contains descriptions of 100 board and card games designed for students' enjoyment as they practice learned concepts. Includes instructions for home-made construction of games for the blind, low vision and sighted student, which can be played with normally seeing children; ages 6-14. 6635 E. Villanova Pl., Denver, CO 80222.

Lyons Band Hap Palmer, a musician, has produced some record albums that provide effective musical activities. The songs are modern, clear tunes (many in rock style) with words that children learn quickly. The 21 titles include a variety of themes such as basic skills, creative expression, and self-concept. 530 Riverview Ave., Elkhart, IN 46514.

Macmillan Publishing Co.: *Coping* (Florence Freedman, John Korca-tante, Marjorie Smiler, & Jacqueline Tilles) The main approach of these reading materials is teaching the concept of "alternate" problem solving; the materials consist of dealing with confrontations with others who are selfish, bullying, authoritarian, prejudiced, or hypercritical. 866 Third Ave., New York, NY 10022.

McGraw-Hill: *Free to be You and Me* (Marlo Thomas and Friends) A book describing freedom of choice for young boys and girls. A record of the same title is available from Bell Records, 1776 Broadway, New York, NY.

Merrill (Charles E.) Publishing: *Teaching Children Self Control* (Stanley A. Fagen, Nicholas J. Long, & Donald J. Stevens, 1975) This book describes curriculum activities which are sequentially arranged and designed to teach children self control. Columbus, OH.

Novelty Features Each of three "Peanuts" cartoon grading stamp sets has five stamps featuring Snoopy, Linus, and Charlie Brown. Zodiac signs and holiday theme stamps also are available. 1902 Liberty St., Trenton, NJ 08629.

Open Door at the Redwood House: *Threads* This is a collection of 500 human relations activities for grades K through 12. It describes unique activities for affect and self-concept groups. 205 W. 16th St., Glencoe, MN 55336.

146

Public Broadcasting Service: *Electric Company Guide* and *Activity Books*
The guidebooks reinforce the skills presented on the **PBS** *Electric Company* programs. The two activity books have pages which can be duplicated for use with many children. Each section presents a different concept. Two newsletters are mailed to the purchaser each year. North Rd., Poughkeepsie, NY 12601.

Rand Co.: *Newspaper in the Classroom* (Hope Shackelford) This book contains a myriad of activities that elementary and secondary students can do with the newspaper. 510 S. Florence, Wichita, KS 67209.

Sanford Corp. - Ghostwriter and Developer Invisible ink pens; one pen is used to write invisible messages and a second pen is used to rub over the message area to reveal the writing. Bellwood, IL 60104.

Scholastic Magazines Publishes several periodicals, two of which are *Scholastic Scope* and *Let's Find Out* newspapers. *Scope* is a magazine for adolescents, published weekly during the school year. It is written in a high-interest, low vocabulary format; the material is contemporary, relevant, and focuses on modern adolescent interests. The "LFO" newspapers are for primary age children and are published monthly throughout the school year. A theme for the year is carried through each month. Three 4-page children's magazines are provided, plus a teacher's edition, a large fun calendar, posters, and special activities or booklets. The teacher's guide provides related activities that can be done in the classroom to expand the month's concept. 902 Sylvan Ave., Englewood cliffs, NJ 07632.

Scholastic/Kindle: *Joy of Being You* (from Unit 1) The Kindle sound filmstrip program includes units concentrating on feelings and emotions, for primary children. Each unit has five filmstrips, five records, and a teaching guide with the script presented in pictures and words. 900 Sylvan Ave., Englewood Cliffs, NJ 07632.

School Days 973 N. Main St., Los Angeles, CA 90012

> *Clever Characters Book I* This book is one of a series and contains 70 characters, each with a phrase or saying. The characters can be used directly on spirit master worksheets as motivational features or on construction paper for awards.

> *Library Card Pockets* Paper library pockets can be used as holders on charts and bulletin boards. A 3″ x 5″ index card will fit in the pocket.

> *Scratch 'n Sniff Library Kits* (3M Co.) Each kit contains 160 microfragance labels, 32 labels of five different fragrances, which release scent when scratched. Can be used repeatedly in con-

junction with stories, worksheets, science lessons, sense awareness activities, and creative writing units. Fragrances include chocolate, lilac, pizza, soap, smoke, etc.

Science Service Each month this firm sends to subscribers a small kit containing a science project that can be used for several suggested experiments. Project titles have included *Humidity, Biological Light,* and *Gravity.* 231 W. Center St., Marion, OH 43302.

Singer Educational Systems Has several different film projectors with small rear screens for individual or small group viewing; easily operated by students and can be used for interest centers or free time activities: *Study Mate Model II* (manual advance silent filmstrip projector, rear screen), *Sound Slide Projector Rear Screen* (carousel fits on top of small screen), *Auto-Vance Model II* (automatic advance sound filmstrip projector; rear screen, 3" x 4"), and *A-V Matic Sound Filmstrip Projector* (small screen for individual viewing; one model for cassettes and one model for records). Rochester, NY 14603.

U.S. Coast Guard Adopt a Ship Plan The Coast Guard will send the name of a ship and its captain for correspondence with a group of students. Propeller Club of the United States, 1730 M St., N.W., Suite 413, Washington, DC 20036.

Word Making Productions *Word Making Picture Stickers* is a collection of 600 different gummed picture stickers packaged in book format. *Language Making Action Stickers* is a collection of 480 different gummed picture stickers. These are good for teacher-made books, cards, and worksheets. Request *Discover the World of Words* catalog for descriptions of materials which emphasize language development. 70 W. Louise Ave., Salt Lake City, UT 84115.

Cross Reference by General Category

Adolescent Development   *See* American Guidance Service; Open Door at the Redwood House; Scholastic Magazines

Affective Development   *See* Abbey Press; American Guidance Service; Childcraft Educational Corp.; Learning Handbooks; Macmillan Publishing Co.; McGraw Hill; Merrill Publishing Co.; Open

	Door at the Redwood House; Scholastic/Kindle; U.S. Coast Guard Adopt-a-Ship Plan
Calendars	*See* EDCOA Publications
Cameras	*See* Childcraft Educational Corp.
Codes	*See* Collier Books/Macmillan Co.
Creative Writing	*See* Abbey Press; Appleton-Century-Crofts
Drama	*See* Dramatic Publishing Co.
Films/Projectors	*See* Childcraft Educational Corp.; Singer Educational Systems; Scholastic/Kindle
Games	*See* Little Kenny Publications; Love Publishing Co.
Language Development	*See* Public Broadcasting Service; Word Making Productions
Magazines	*See* Children's Television Workshop; Scholastic Magazines
Microscopes	*See* Hubbard Scientific
Motivational Aids	*See* Collier Books/Macmillan Co.; School Days
Music and Records	*See* Bell Records; Lyons Band
Newspapers	*See* Rand Co.; Scholastic Magazines
Organizational Aids	*See* School Days (library card pockets)
Rebuses	*See* American Guidance Service
Rubber Stamps	*See* See Developmental Learning Materials; Novelty Features
Science Activities	*See* Hubbard Scientific; School Days; Science Service
Toys	*See* Constructive Playthings
Sensory Awareness	*See* School Days
Writing and Marking Tools	*See* Ideal Corp.; Sanford Corp.

FIVE

PROGRAMMING

- Programming Guidelines
- Teacher-designed Programs
- Learning Principles and Programming
- Appendix to Chapter 5
  Sample Program
  Immediate Feedback Ideas
  for the Classroom
  Resources for Immediate
  Feedback
  Supplementary Readings

PROGRAMMING

Programming is a procedure in the structured approach that requires the teacher to arrange a behavior to be learned into a series of sequential, incremental steps. The goal of this procedure is to help the student acquire appropriate and productive behaviors and to maximize success. If the repertoire of inappropriate behaviors exhibited by students with behavioral problems is to be interfered with, the acquisition of new, successful behavior is paramount. Thus, programming is a critical procedure used by teachers to guide a student into a series of academic, social, and personal successes.

The programming process demands that the teacher be knowledgeable about the tasks to be learned by the students. Therefore, as the teacher develops a program and subsequently observes the students' responses to it, the teacher — being the program designer — can readily make evaluations of its effectiveness. If the student progresses successfully through all the program steps and achieves the established goal, the teacher's preparation efforts are verified. Should the student encounter difficulties, the teacher can analyze the program for deficiencies. Although the program is designed to enhance the student's growth, the teacher develops self-evaluation skills as well.

The teacher who programs the student's activities is an architect of learning and assumes primary accountability for preparation of an atmosphere that facilitates learning and social interactions. Special attention should be given to the following four general variables involved in learning: (a) the individual who does the learning; (b) the nature of the task to be learned; (c) the conditions in which the learning occurs; and (d) the person(s) associated with the learning. The wise teacher takes these variables into account when programming tasks for students.

153

PROGRAMMING GUIDELINES

The teacher must identify the *needs* of the individual student before a task is selected for programming. A program designed for one student seldom is given to another without modification. Furthermore, the uniqueness of each child prohibits the teacher's selection of a commercially prepared program designed to encompass a large number of students. Some commercial programs might be selected if they are modified to meet the needs of individual students.

Predetermined programs frequently focus on academic task behaviors; however, the teacher who implements the programming procedure can provide the student with a learning sequence having an academic or social goal. For example, a student may need to learn to button a coat, to use correct pronouns, to use a combination lock, to participate in biology lab work, or to follow game rules. Guidelines for programming each of those and other tasks incorporate many basic learning and program instruction principles.

For purpose of programming tasks for students with behavioral disorders, the following guidelines are suggested. These guidelines are accompanied by selected portions of two programs developed by two special class teachers. Program 1 was designed primarily to guide a student in acquiring an academic behavior, and Program 2 was designed primarily to guide a student in acquiring socially related skills. (Program 2 is given in its entirety in the appendix to this chapter.)

Program 1	*Program 2*
1. Establish a long-range goal.	
George will be able to tell time.	Lori will acquire leisure time skills.
2. Specify a target behavior. A target behavior frequently is referred to as *performance objective* or *task*.	
George will tell time to the hour when presented with a clock or worksheets with clock faces and clock hands set to specific hours.	Lori will make a terrarium when materials are provided in the classroom.

3. Determine the prerequisite skills necessary for the student to engage in the task.

George can count to 12.

George can read the numbers to 12.

George can write the numbers to 12.

George can read at the second grade level.

George can follow two-step verbal directions.

Lori has sufficient coordination to manipulate the necessary materials.

Lori is right-handed.

Lori knows left and right directions.

Lori is acquainted with the materials to be used.

Lori knows the arrangement of the classroom.

Lori can recognize the colors green and white.

Lori understands the following terms: *pick up, in front of, tilt, upside down, squirt, pour, rinse, full, empty, level, fill, approximate, middle, scoop out, surrounding, damp, sunken, press, teaspoon, base, wipe, small, large, inside, outside,* and *terrarium.*

4. List the major activities needed for development of this program; arrange the activities in a general sequence.

Read the sequence of concepts in a mathematics book regarding telling time.

Obtain a clock face rubber stamp, an old clock with movable hands, and a working clock with arabic numerals 1 through 12.

List steps on guide sheet.

Design worksheets.

Read terrarium building booklet.

Obtain a terrarium container and planting tools.

Purchase plants, dirt, and rock.

List steps on index cards.

5. Break down the sequence into incremental steps. This guideline is directed to maximizing success because each step presents an opportunity for success. If the student with learning and behavioral problems can proceed incrementally to acquire a skill in a 75-step

programmed task, the student has 75 opportunities for success. When steps are eliminated, the success element is still present, but reduced. Caution should be exercised when considering a reduction in program length. Success helps students perceive appropriate ways to behave. Failure can be tolerated only when an individual has a backlog of success.

. . . Put your finger on the short hand.	. . . Put the charcoal in the green glass until the glass is full.
What number is the hand pointing to?	Empty the green glass full of charcoal into the terrarium container.
Put your finger on the long hand.	With your hand, level the charcoal in the bottom of the container.
What number is the long hand pointing to? . . .	Put away the remaining charcoal, back of the counter . . .

6. Plan student responses. Attention to task is emphasized in this guideline; therefore, the student responses should be varied. Commercially prepared programs frequently require a student to respond in one manner; for example, the student presses a button, writes an answer, circles an answer, moistens a dot, or rubs a concealed image blank with a specially treated pen. Responses in teacher-made programs could include a combination of activities such as writing, manipulating, speaking, listening, pointing, selecting, matching, singing, digging, running, plucking, focusing, holding. The response activities also may include peer and teacher interactions. If the teacher is included in the program, the student has an opportunity to learn with an adult who is ready to give on-the-spot academic and emotional support, if problems occur.

7. Plan immediate feedback. After the student responds to a program item, the accuracy of the response should be determined immediately. If the response is correct, the student proceeds to the next step uninterrupted. If the response is inaccurate, feedback should redirect the student to a correct response. The teacher can be the important variable in this feedback system. If the teacher's interaction is programmed into the response section, the teacher can redirect the student to the correct answer when wrong answers are given, by doing on-the-spot adaptations, supplementing the program with additional steps, or temporarily terminating the program for subsequent refinement.

If a commercial program is under consideration for purchase, the feedback portion should be studied judiciously. Some programs have feedback systems that inadvertently teach the learner inappropriate responses. For example, one program requires a student to trace over symbols with a specially treated felt-tipped pen. If the student's tracing is accurate, the gray color of the traced symbol remains unchanged; if the student's tracing is inaccurate, the incorrect responses turn yellow. Many young children prefer seeing the yellow color so they make mistakes deliberately! On some machine programs, the learner responds to items appearing on the screen by depressing a button. If the response is correct, the frame automatically advances; if the response is incorrect, the same frame remains on the screen and the student has additional opportunities to respond. Students who enjoy mechanical gadgets have been observed to deliberately press incorrect buttons before depressing the correct ones! Other students who for some reason give many incorrect responses have learned to become good button pressers!

Immediate feedback is emphasized because it can prevent a student from going through a program in error. If an error has been made and feedback is delayed (given after the student has completed a number of steps) the student has been allowed to proceed incorrectly into the program — a debilitating experience. The immediate feedback technique has been used in activities other than programming. Some of these techniques are described in the appendix to this chapter.

8. Plan reinforcement of correct responses. Commercially prepared programs rely heavily on the premise that feedback in itself is reinforcing. This assumption is not always true. Can you remember a time when you worked diligently on a college paper, assuming you would receive a high score, but the paper was returned with a low one? You received feedback, but it probably was not reinforcing.

    Students whose academic experiences are replete with failures must experience feedback *and* reinforcement. The feedback may be accompanied by *extrinsic reinforcers* — for example, edible treats, pieces of model airplanes, or beads for a necklace; or feedback may be accompanied by *natural reinforcers* — for example, teacher's praise or grading symbols. Principles of behavior modification are useful in the implementation of reinforcers.

    The experience of teachers who have developed programs for disturbed students has shown that students who need some type of extrinsic reinforcement along with the feedback during the beginning program steps frequently have a shift in their needs before the program is completed — The success achieved at each incremental step appears to become intrinsically reinforcing and external reinforcers are dropped.

9. Allow the student to move at his or her own pace. The program is completed when the student can perform the target behavior; therefore, a time contingency does not need to be a critical factor in developing a programmed task. The student's behavior and the nature of the program indicate whether a task can be completed in one or more sessions. The academic task relevant to telling time to the hour, as described in guidelines 2, 3, and 4, was completed in a series of short sessions, whereas the terrarium making task was amenable to one session. The student's behavior is a good indication of the number of sessions needed.

10. Emphasize correct answers. Programs that include multiple choice responses should be designed so that the response selection is not misleading; trick response selections are not included. Why encourage students to give wrong answers? Provide answers which require discrimination and differentiation, but which are not misleading. Accent the positive.

11. Include evaluation components. Evaluation components are built into the program automatically if the previous guidelines have been followed. Since the incremental steps of the program are approximations of the target behaviors, the students can determine their progress toward completion of the target behaviors. Because the tasks have been specifically defined, the students' self evaluations can be objective. Furthermore, the student is not in doubt about the correctness of each response, as a result of the feedback system.

TEACHER DESIGNED PROGRAMS

When a teacher decides to develop a program, the guidelines given in the previous paragraphs should be followed, but the program presented to the student should be arranged in the following order: (a) target behavior, (b) prerequisite skills; (c) materials needed; (d) pretest; (e) feedback and reinforcers to accompany steps; (f) incremental steps; (g) posttest; and (h) observations and comments. (A program designed for a special student is included in the appendix to this chapter.)

Programs must include both a pretest and posttest. The simplest pretest is to ask the student to perform the task under consideration for a program. Sometimes, teachers select a task based on their observations alone and conclude that the student is unable to perform the activity; a more accurate assessment is made if a student is asked to actually do the task. The pretest will verify the teacher's observations. A posttest, additionally, can be developed when a student expresses desire to learn an activity, as in the case of Diana, a junior high girl in a special classroom who wanted to learn some advanced Origami. The teacher developed a program designed to teach Diana how "to fold an Origami flapping bird."

The incremental step format can be developed along various designs; for example, the steps may be written out for the student, but the teacher reads the steps to the student; the steps may be a series of diagrams accompanied by a sentence of information; or the steps may be a series of teacher-made worksheets, each containing one direction. The program design for Diana constituted a series of 72 5″ x 8″ cards, each containing a written direction and a piece of paper that had been folded as directed. Diana was given a sheet of Origami paper, which the girl folded according to the steps indicated on each card. Figure 5.1 provides an example of one programmed step. One commercially prepared Origami book had a set of 14 written directions and diagrams for folding the flapping bird, but Diana needed smaller steps to achieve that goal.

Development of a program requires a minimum of 40 to 50 hours. The most time consuming portion is to develop guideline 5 — breaking down the task into incremental steps. Prospective teachers enrolled in university methods courses have been required to program a task, as their major assignment. The primary rewards of that assignment have been the enthusiasm and success expressed and experienced by the special students for whom the programs were designed and the development of self-evaluation skills by the teachers. Any teacher desiring to use the above described programming procedure can follow all the guidelines as defined except guideline 5, which can be *approximated*.

Teachers are encouraged to do the following exercise to gain a "feel" for the development of incremental steps. First, take 15 minutes to write down the incremental steps necessary to "tie a shoe with laces through the last eyelet." Assume that the potential learner has the prerequisite skills for this program. Fifteen minutes is not sufficient time to write all the steps; however, writing the first ones gives the teacher a better idea of this component of programming. Ask someone to be the "learner" and

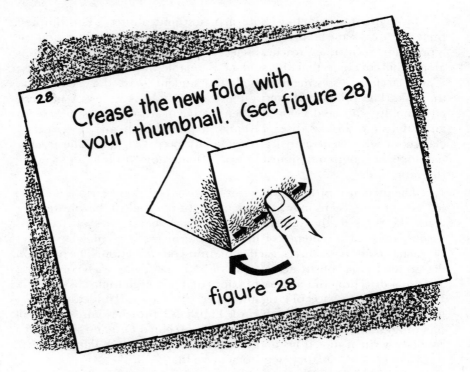

Fig. 5.1. One programmed step in Origami task.

follow the steps as given aloud. The learner probably will have difficulty because the steps are not as incremental as needed or essential information has been omitted. These unintentional omissions will give insight regarding the importance of attending to the number of incremental steps needed in learning.

The program guidelines also can be changed into questions to determine possible reasons for learning difficulties encountered by students. For example: Were the tasks specified? Were the directions on the written materials specific? Was feedback provided? Was this feedback given immediately? Was feedback accompanied by reinforcers? Did the process include sufficient incremental steps to meet the student's needs? If the answer to any of these questions is "no," the teacher can use some portion of the programming procedure to refine the activities originally planned. One student completed a paper as shown in Figure 5.2; if the teacher

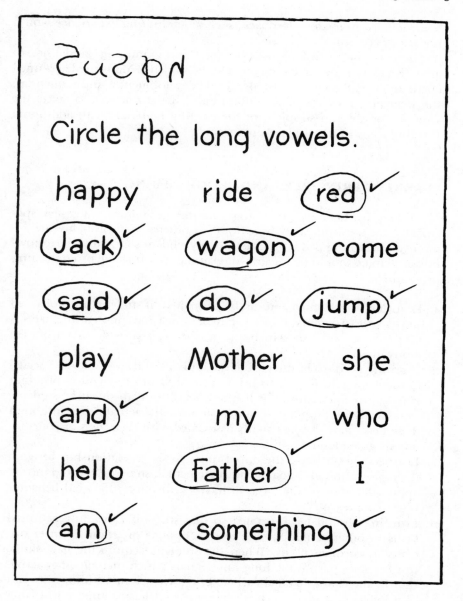

Circle the long vowels.

happy   ride   red ✓

Jack ✓   wagon ✓   come

said ✓   do ✓   jump ✓

play   Mother   she

and ✓   my   who

hello   Father ✓   I

am ✓   something ✓

Fig. 5.2. Student paper reflecting absence of immediate feedback.

had provided immediate feedback, such a debilitating experience would not have occurred.

The teacher also can use the above programming guidelines to analyze materials before giving them to the students. Many predetermined curriculum materials are designed to be developmental and sequential; the sequence, however, may contain gaps. If the teacher can detect the gaps, he or she can supplement the existing materials with additional learning steps in the student's program.

LEARNING PRINCIPLES AND PROGRAMMING

When teachers use the programming guidelines suggested specifically for students with behavioral disorders, they probably are reminded of learning principles basic to any student's growth. The following principles should be integrated meaningfully into the programming procedure:

1. Learning is facilitated and can be permanent if students are motivated sufficiently. Students' target behaviors must have motivating aspects or must be ones for which the teacher can provide or encourage motivation.
2. Learning needs to be directed to the individual learner's level. Specification of prerequisite skills prior to the student's entry into a program is useful in ascertaining the learner's level. Special education students are asked to perform tasks commensurate with their abilities, although these tasks may not be usually associated with their ages or concommitant grade levels.
3. Learners should have the opportunity to see a relationship between their work and the goal. The incremental steps of a program are approximations of the target behaviors; therefore, the goal behavior is always present.
4. Learning should be integrated so that students can apply acquired skills to other activities. The teacher designs programs to meet students' immediate needs. When the students acquire the new skills, this becomes part of the long-range goals which include other activities. In the example cited earlier, Lori's terrarium building was part of a long-range goal — the development of leisure time skills. After completing the terrarium, subsequent learning tasks might involve the care of plants, gardening, and similar activities.

164

SUMMARY

A definitive programming procedure should be used with emotionally disturbed children, especially during the students' initial months of enrollment in a special class. Its guidelines recognize techniques that can be used throughout the student's enrollment. An immediate feedback component benefits students who do not learn under conditions of delayed gratification. The response component prevents some students from withdrawing, because they must be active in the learning process. The evaluation component benefits students who view themselves as failures because, through evaluation, a student's progress is measured in relation to a specified task rather than to the achievements of other students or a standardized norm. Students' pretests are compared to their posttests; thus, students are their own control. Students who become overly anxious under time conditions are not threatened by that variable because they proceed through the program at their own pace.

An abundance of activities to facilitate learning and social interactions should be integral features of a classroom. Programming is the procedure that can maximize success in learning experiences. It incorporates techniques that can be used to interfere with and change a student's failure cycle. Programming a task is time consuming and sometimes difficult, but the benefits for both teacher and student are so rewarding that this effort cannot be overestimated.

APPENDIX TO CHAPTER FIVE

SAMPLE PROGRAM[1]

A. Target behavior:
Lori will make a terrarium when the materials are provided in the classroom.

B. Prerequisite skills:

1. Lori has sufficient coordination to manipulate the necessary materials.
2. Lori is right-handed.
3. Lori knows left and right directions.
4. Lori is acquainted with the materials to be used.
5. Lori is acquainted with the arrangement of the classroom.
6. Lori can recognize the colors green and white.
7. Lori understands the following terms: pick up, in front of, tilt, upside down, squirt, pour, rinse, full, empty, level, fill, approximate, middle, scoop out, surrounding, damp, sunken, press, tablespoon, base, wipe, small, large, inside, outside, and terrarium.

C. Materials needed:
One empty gallon jar; terrarium potting soil; dishcloth; dishtowel; dishwashing soap; terrarium plants (one large and two small); tablespoon; green glass, 8-ounce size; paper towels; tap water; small, orange aquarium rocks.

---

[1] This program was prepared by a teacher, Nan Hoffman, who read the steps to Lori because the girl did not have the sight vocabulary necessary to read the program herself.

D. Pretest:

Because of the expense of making a terrarium for a pretest, Lori was asked by her teacher *how* to make a terrarium. Her response was: "First you take some dirt and put it in a jar. Then you dig a hole and put the plants in it. Then you water it a lot, and if it needs more water, water it some more. The lid goes on real tight and you never take it off."

E. Feedback and reinforcers:

Teacher's comments and praise.

F. Incremental steps:

1. Place the container on a rubber pad in the classroom sink.
2. Pick up the white bottle containing the liquid dish soap.
3. Open the white bottle.
4. Tilt the bottle upside down into the terrarium container.
5. Put 2 squirts of liquid soap in the terrarium container.
6. Close the bottle.
7. Put the liquid soap away.
8. Turn the water on from the faucet until the container is almost full.
9. Wash the inside and outside of the container with the dishcloth.
10. Pour the soapy water into the sink.
11. Rinse the container with clear water until no soap bubbles are present.
12. Take the dishtowel from the counter and dry the container.
13. Place the dry container on its side on the counter in front of the soil.
14. Put charcoal in the green glass until the cup is full.
15. Empty the green glass full of charcoal into the terrarium container.
16. With your hand, level the charcoal in the bottom of the container.
17. Put the charcoal away, on the back of the counter.
18. Put the potting soil into the green glass until the glass is full.
19. Pour the soil into the terrarium container.
20. Repeat the last two steps four times.
21. Place the excess soil (that falls while pouring it into the glass) into the terrarium container.
22. Level the soil in the container.
23. Fill the green glass full of water.
24. Pour the water on top of the soil.
25. Level the soil again with your hand.

26. Pick up the tablespoon.
27. Put the tablespoon in the terrarium container.
28. Approximate the middle of the soil area in the container.
29. Place the tablespoon in the soil in the middle of the container.
30. Scoop out 3 tablespoons of soil from the middle of the container. (This will be done so that the 3 tablespoons worth of hole will make one big hole in the soil).
31. Place this soil in the green glass.
32. Feel the hole and the soil around it.
33. If the soil is damp, go on to the next step. If the soil around the hole is not damp, place 2 tablespoons of water into the sunken area in the container.
34. Pick up the large terrarium plant with your right hand.
35. Place this plant inside the container with the roots down.
36. Place this plant with your left hand into the sunken area in the container with the roots down.
37. Using your right hand, press the plant into the soil.
38. Take one tablespoon of soil from the green glass.
39. Using the spoon, place this soil around the roots of the large plant.
40. Repeat the previous two steps two times.
41. Using your right hand, press the soil firmly around the base of the plant.
42. Wash off the spoon at the sink.
43. Place the spoon in the container one inch to the right rear of the large plant.
44. Remove 2 tablespoons of soil from this spot.
45. Place this soil in the green glass.
46. Feel the area around this hole to see if it is damp.
47. If the area is damp, skip the next step.
48. If the area is dry, put 3 tablespoons of water on this spot.
49. Pick up the small plant.
50. Place this plant, with the roots down, into the sunken area in the container.
51. Press the plant into the soil.
52. Place the spoon in the green glass.
53. Get the soil out of the green glass with the spoon.
54. Put the soil around the base of the plant.
55. Press the soil around the base of the plant.
56. Fill the green glass half full of water.

57. Pour the water over the soil in the container.
58. Dampen a paper towel with water from the tap.
59. Wipe the excess soil from the sides of the inside of the terrarium container.
60. Take a dry paper towel from the counter.
61. Dry the sides of the inside of the terrarium container.
62. Fill the spoon with orange rock.
63. Put the spoonful of rock inside the container.
64. Place this rock in the container on the right-hand side in front of the plants.
65. Press the rock partly into the soil.
66. Twist the lid on the terrarium container.

G. Posttest:
Lori accomplished the task and was pleased to take the terrarium to her cottage.

H. Observations and comments:
"As Lori was working on the task, she was wary of her ability to complete it. As she went through each step, her smile got a little bigger. By the time the program was completed, she was about to burst with pride. She couldn't wait to get to the cottage to show her houseparents what she had accomplished. She told me that she was scared at first to do it, but now she wants to make another one. I feel she completely enjoyed being successful at this task."

IMMEDIATE FEEDBACK IDEAS FOR THE CLASSROOM

Idea 1

Several index cards, 3" x 5", can be cut down the center, each in a different pattern. The result is a collection of two-piece paper puzzles. Make a series of pairs, the left side of each paper puzzle containing a question, statement, or phrase, and the right side containing the answer. The left parts of the puzzle pairs are shuffled and placed face down to begin the draw deck. The answer parts of the pairs can be spread face down on a table or floor. Students take turns drawing a question card and giving answers; then the students find the matching piece and turn the matched pair to the printed side to determine if the given answer is correct.

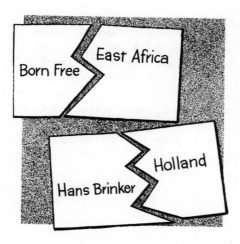

Idea 2

Many teachers have discovered a speedy way to give immediate positive feedback to a student. A special stamp resembling an eraser (see Resource Section of the appendix to this chapter) is attached to the end of a pencil. Stamps are available in star, checkmark, or happy face designs. Other choices also are available. Teachers checking students' work can immediately mark the correct responses with the special stamp. Using different colored ink pads can add to the uniqueness of this feedback technique.

Idea 3

Invisible pen sets provide the students with immediate feedback, and the teachers with an inexpensive teaching technique. The pens are available in packages of two — one pen writes invisibly (the teacher can use this pen to prepare response choices); the other pen makes the responses visible when the student rubs the pen point over the choice (See Resources section of this appendix). The example below contains a problem with a choice written under each box. Each box contains an invisible response. The student rubs the pen over the response choice and immediately finds if the answer is correct. If students enjoy this response format and use the "magic" pen to see *all* the feedback before attempting to figure out the right answer, encourage them to mark the correct answer only. After papers are returned, they can mark the other answers just for fun.

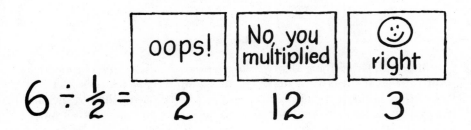

RESOURCES FOR IMMEDIATE FEEDBACK CLASSROOM MATERIALS

Daleen Publications Div., Allied Mfg. Co. — Invisible Pens Two felt-tip pens are in a package. Each has a different purpose; one pen writes invisibly, and the other develops the invisible writing. 815-25 E. Market, P.O. Box 1155, Louisville, KY 40201.

Effective Learning, Inc. — Concealed Process Self-correcting spirit duplicated materials can be prepared using the Concealed Process produced by this company. To make them: (a) prepare a spirit master in the usual way; (b) replace the carbon sheet with a Concealed Image Transfer Sheet and write or type information that should be invisible; (c) duplicate copies in the normal manner; and (d) have students use a Concealed Image Marker to make responses. Each transfer sheet can be used to prepare 10 spirit masters. Seven North MacQuestion Pkwy., Mount Vernon, NY 10050.

Field Educational Publishing — Cyclo-Teacher Cyclo-Teacher is a flat, small, lightweight case into which paper "cycles" of questions are placed, providing immediate feedback for learners. Cycles are available for social studies, science, reference skills, family activities, math, English, spelling, and primary skills. A "Do It Yourself Wheel" is available for making original cycles. The student pushes a lever to move the question into position, and writes the answer in the blank space provided. When the lever is moved again, the answer to the previous question appears. The student then scores the previous question before proceeding to the next one. Merchandise Mart Plaza, Chicago, IL 60654.

Jenn Publications — Know Now Workbooks *Know Now Workbooks* for primary aged students come with marking pens which, when used immediately, indicate whether a student's answer is right or wrong. 815-25 E. Market St., P.O. Box 1155, Louisville, KY 40201.

Laird, Stan — Individual Reading Job Cards Reading Job Cards, a packet of 156 individualized supplementary activities, can be used for students aged ten through eighteen. Each card has a unique activity on one side with answers on the back to provide immediate feedback. Individualized Game and Puzzle Cards (for reinforcing creativity and problem solving, Grades 4-12); Activity Cards (reading supplement for elementary grades); and Game and Puzzle Cards (elementary ages) also are available. 27948 Farm Hill Dr., Hayward, CA 94542.

Lee Publications — Invisible Ink Quiz & Game Books Invisible Ink booklets can be used as tree time activities or for reinforcing specific skills. Each booklet contains a "yes and know" pen which, when used to answer questions in the book, provides immediate feedback to the user. Available books include: *Yes and Know Quiz Books* (ages 5-15); *Yes and Know Quiz Books* (ages 8-18); *Yes and Know Game Books,* including *Baseball Fleet, Hangman Bingo, Twenty-One, Tic-Tac-Toe, Ultra Bowl* (football), *Basketball, Bowling, Dots, Bull's Eye,* and *Puzzlement; Guess and Show Educational Picture Books;* and *Cross and Know* (crossword puzzles). 815-25 E. Market St., P.O. Box 1155, Louisville, KY 40201.

School Days — Action/Mark Products With Action/Mark teaching materials, a student uses a pencil to write the answer to a problem on a pretreated sheet and then checks the answer by coloring in an adjacent box with an Action/Mark Crayon; the invisibly printed answer will emerge to provide immediate feedback. Math sets are available, each with 100 sheets. Answer sheets also are available; these are designed for use with any multiple choice or true/false questions and are available in 20, 30, 40, and 50 question format. 973 N. Main St., Los Angeles, CA 90012.

School Days — Know It All (Individualized Learning) Immediate self-checking is provided by the "Know It All," a small, flat plastic case into which discs are inserted. Each disc contains 20 to 40 questions and answers (the discs are available in grade sets containing math, language, spelling, and geography activities, or in single subject sets of math, time, geography, and money). The student checks each answer by lifting the answer tab. Individual sets include a plastic case, 12 interchangeable discs, and a teacher's guide. Classroom sets contain 10 plastic cases, five make-your-own blank discs, storage case, disc, and teacher's guide. Blank discs and plastic cases are available separately for student-designed or teacher-made lessons. 973 N. Main St., Los Angeles, CA 90012.

Summit Industries — Rubber Stamps Stamps resembling erasers can be slipped over the ends of pencils and used for feedback on student's papers. P.O. Box 415, Highland Park, IL 60035.

SUPPLEMENTARY READINGS

Learning on the Sneak[1]

Sherman G. Brett
Correctional Educational Supervisor, Baltimore, Maryland

I'm sure all of you are under the impression that Dr. Skinner is the father of modern-day programmed instruction. I would first like to correct this impression. With all due respect to Dr. Skinner, PI started in the Maryland Penitentiary. Allow me to explain. Years ago we had an inmate who during his free time would come into the recreation area of the prison and practice broad jumping. He started by setting up one folding chair and jumping over it. His explanation to all con-

---

[1]*NSPI Journal* 5 (1966).

cerned was that the chair gave him the height he needed to get more distance and that he only wanted to see how far he could eventually jump. Since this was a harmless pastime and excellent exercise, he was allowed to continue. After a week of jumping over one chair, he added a second.

Notice the features of PI here: He started in a way that was small enough to allow him success. He repeated the successful venture over and over or strengthened his basic knowledge and skills by reinforcing them. By setting up the second chair, he was being asked to respond to a new problem based on what he had learned in an earlier frame. This he immediately mastered.

His astonishing success led him over an increasing number of chairs. In just six short months he was jumping over a total of 14 chairs without a miss. By displaying his new skills, he attracted the attention of the entire inmate population and was cheered and given encouragement for each successful jump. The reward factor of PI is evident. He was also receiving the most important psychological boost a prison inmate can receive — recognition by his peers — and well he might have, for he was now jumping a distance of approximately 21 feet.

Now, as I mentioned earlier, this inmate jumped in his free time, a period from 4 to 6 p.m. Like every other inmate, he had a job at which he worked from eight in the morning until four in the afternoon. This particular inmate's job was running a sewing machine in one of the industrial shops. His shop was located on the top floor of a three-story building. As he approached the end of the building, he leaped with a tremendous motion, and just reached the top of the adjacent penitentiary wall. He quickly dropped over the wall. Before the startled guard could react, he was dashing down a nearby street in record time. During a subsequent investigation, the measured distance from the edge of the building to the edge of the institutional wall was found to be exactly 21 feet.

Poor Student or Poor School?
(author unknown)

No, I'm not very good in school. This is my second year in the seventh grade, and I'm bigger and taller than the other kids. They like me all right though, even if I don't say much in the classroom, because outside I can tell them how to do a lot of things. They tag me around and that sort of makes up for what goes on in school.

I don't know why the teachers don't like me. The never have very much. Seems like they don't think you know anything unless you can name the book it comes out of. I've got a lot of books in my room at home — books like *Popular Science, Mechanical Encyclopedia* and the *Sears' and Wards' Catalogs* — but I don't very often just sit down and read them through, like they make us do in school. I use my books when I want to find something out, like whenever Mom buys anything second-hand, I look it up in Sears' or Wards' first and tell her if she's getting stung or not. I can use the index in a hurry.

In school, though, we've got to learn whatever is in the book and I just can't memorize the stuff. Last year I stayed after school every night for two weeks trying to learn the names of the presidents. Of course, I know some of them like Washington and Jefferson and Lincoln, but there must have been 30 altogether and I never did get them straight.

I'm not sorry, though, because the kids who learned the presidents had to turn right around and learn all the vice presidents. I am taking the seventh grade over, but our teacher this year isn't so interested in the names of the presidents. She has us trying to learn the names of all the great American inventors.

I guess I just can't remember names in history. Anyway, this year I've been trying to learn about trucks because my uncle owns three and he says I can drive one when I'm sixteen. I already know the horsepower and the number of forward and backward speeds of 26 American trucks, some of them diesels, and I can spot each make a long way off. It's funny how that diesel works. I started to tell my teacher about it last Wednesday in science class when the pump we are using to make a vacuum in a bell jar got hot, but she said she didn't see what a diesel engine had to do with our experiment of air pressure, so I kept still. The kids seemed interested, though. I took four of them around to my uncle's garage after school and we saw the mechanic, Gus, tear a big truck diesel down. Boy, does he know his stuff!

I'm not very good in geography either. They call it economic geography this year. We've been studying the imports and exports of Chile all week, but I couldn't tell you what they are. Maybe the reason is I had to miss school yesterday because my uncle took me and his big trailer truck down state and we brought almost 10 tons of stock to the market.

He had told me where we were going, and I had to figure out the highways to take and also the mileage. He didn't do anything but drive and turn where I told him to. Was that fun! I sat with a map in my lap and told him to turn south, or southeast, or some other direction. We made seven stops, and drove over 300 miles round trip. I'm figuring out what his oil cost, and also the wear and tear on the truck — he calls it depreciation — so we'll know how much we made.

I even write out all the bills and send letters to the farmers about what their pigs and beef cattle brought at the stockyards. I only made three mistakes in 17 letters last time, my aunt said — all commas. She's been through high school and reads them over. I wish I could write school themes that way. The last one I had to write was on "What a Daffodil Thinks of Spring," and I just couldn't get going.

I don't do very well in school arithmetic, either. Seems I just can't keep my mind on the problems. We had one the other day like this: "If a 57-foot telephone pole falls across a cement highway so that 17-3/16 feet extend from one side and 14-9/17 feet from the other, how wide is the highway?" That seemed to me like an awfully silly way to get the width of a highway. I didn't even try to answer it because it didn't say whether the pole had fallen straight across or not.

Even in shop I don't get very good grades. All of us kids made a broom holder and a bookend this term, and mine were sloppy. I just couldn't get interested. Mom doesn't use a broom anymore with her new vacuum cleaner, and all our books are in a bookcase with glass doors. Anyway, I wanted to make an endgate for my uncle's trailer, but the shop teacher said that meant using metal and wood both, and I'd have to learn how to work with wood first. I didn't see why, but I kept still and made a tie rack at school and the tailgate after school at my uncle's garage. He said I saved him ten dollars.

Civics is hard for me, too. I've been staying after school trying to learn the "Articles of Confederation" for almost a week because the teacher said we couldn't be good citizens unless we did. I really tried, because I want to be a good citizen. I did hate to stay after school, though, because a bunch of us boys from the south end of town have been cleaning up the old lot across from Taylor's Machine Shop to make a playground out of it for the little kids from the Methodist Home. I made the jungle gym from old pipe, and the guys made me Grand Mogul to keep the playground going. We raised enough money collecting scrap this month to build a wire fence clear around the lot.

Dad says I can quit school when I am fifteen, and I am sort of anxious to because there are a lot of things I want to learn how to do and, as my uncle says, I'm not getting any younger!

BEHAVIOR
MODIFICATION

- Intervention: A Basic
  Modification Plan
- Behavior Modification
  Techniques
- Reinforcement, or Reinforcers
- Behavior Modification as a
  Diagnostic Technique
- Cautions in Behavior
  Modification
- Appendix to Chapter 6
    Reinforcer Ideas for the
      Classroom
    Resources for Reinforcers

BEHAVIOR MODIFICATION

Behavior modification, another procedure in the structured approach, is aimed at analyzing the variables affecting behavior, and managing behavior. It frequently is integrated with the procedures, pre-academic year planning, educational diagnosing, selecting and adapting educational materials, programming, and scheduling. Behavior modification differs from the other procedures because it focuses primarily on the consequences of behavior, whereas pre-academic year planning, selecting and adapting educational materials, and programming center on the antecedents of behavior, and educational diagnosis focuses primarily on response. Behavior modification does have similarities to the other procedures in that its implementation is highly individualized as a result of the great differences among students with emotional problems.

Behavior modification can be defined further as the application of behavioral principles based on operant conditioning. The behavioral principles have been used in a variety of settings such as regular and special classrooms, homes, industries, rehabilitation and psychological treatment centers, and in fact any setting where the modification of behavior has been sought. *The basic premise is that all behavior, normal or abnormal, is learned, and that behavior is a function of its consequences.* That is, the probability of behavior occurring depends upon the consequences that follow it. Behavior can be strengthened or weakened by consequences. Behavioral principles are applied to *overt* behaviors and their relationships with the environment. Many individuals using these principles to change behavior do not deny that abnormal behavior may have antecedents in the individual's past but contend that their reconstruction isn't necessary for behavioral change.

If teachers approach a student's behaviors as learned behaviors, they must conclude that inappropriate behaviors are learned behaviors. Thus, the responsibility of teaching becomes more than a modification of students' academic knowledge. The teacher is challenged to become involved with identifying student behaviors that (a) need encouragement, enrichment, and maintenance; (b) need weakening or decreasing; (c) need to be acquired; and with providing environmental variables that can bring about desirable changes.

Behavior can be measured objectively if it is observed directly and recorded in its environmental setting. Direct observations should be made and recorded over time rather than during a single session. These observation efforts also are made to describe the environmental variables that influence the behavior. Observations and recording activities can increase a teacher's sensitivity to student needs; can increase precision in teaching techniques; and can reaffirm the need to be consistent in working with emotionally behaviorally disturbed youth. Finally, recorded observations provide the students and teachers with feedback relevant to behavioral occurrences and changes.

Functionally analyzing a student's behavior can be accomplished by identifying the four components of a behavioral act — stimulus, response, contingency, and consequence. A *stimulus* is an antecedent event that causes a response. For example, if paper scraps are on the classroom floor and the teacher picks them up, the paper is a stimulus because it caused the teacher's response — picking it up. If the teacher did not pick up the paper, the paper was not a stimulus because it did not cause a response. A *response* is an individual's action, frequently referred to as "behavior."

A *consequence* is a subsequent event that follows an individual's response and determines the probability of its future occurrence. The type of consequence is determined by its effect upon the response. If the consequence increases the response, it is called an accelerating consequence. An oversimplified example illustrates this: A student was dawdling on his math worksheet. He was told that if he completed the assignment by 10:30, he could be the line leader for recess and lunch. The student did complete the math within the specified time. Being line leader was the accelerating consequence because it increased the student's responses — working on the math sheet.

If the consequence decreases a response, it is referred to as a decelerating consequence. As an example: A student pounded his desk and the teacher wanted to decrease the pounding. The teacher told the student that for each series of pounding, he would spend two minutes in the classroom after class was dismissed. The amount of pounding decreased. Staying after school for two minutes was a decelerating consequence because the response — pounding on the desk — decreased.

If, in the two cited examples, the students' responses had not changed the behavior in the desired direction, being line leader and staying after school would not have been consequences. One cannot say that being a line leader for recess and lunch is an accelerating consequence for all students, nor can one say that staying after school for two minutes is a decelerating consequence for all students. Selection of a consequence is highly individualized for each student.

Contingency refers to the arrangement between the response and the consequence. The teacher in the previously cited example had said to the student, "Complete your math worksheet by 10:30 and you will be line leader for recess and lunch." Doing the math is the response; being line leader is the consequence; and "by 10:30" is the arrangement, or contingency. The several types of contingencies are discussed later in this chapter.

INTERVENTION: A BASIC MODIFICATION PLAN

Individual consequences can be used effectively by the regular classroom teacher who has three or four children in need of special help, as well as by the special class teacher who has a group of students with academic and behavioral problems. In either situation, a certain amount of teacher time and thought is involved in the selection and consistent application of consequences, but the hours spent will pay great dividends in terms of student progress.

For consequences to be effective in changing behavior, the basic modification plan follows these steps: (a) Select a "target" behavior; (b) Find a consequence that *works;* (c) Determine the arrangement between the "target" behavior and its consequences; (d) Discuss the planned program, clarifying all details; (e) Implement the program; (f) Record the behaviors throughout the program; (g) Evaluate the plan; (h) Fade the program.

If a teacher wanted to apply the above modification plan to specific situations, individual intervention programs would be planned, each requiring the following steps:

Make Preliminary Observations

1. Observe the student's behaviors.
2. List the behaviors to be modified. An example of a list for one student was:
   a. Assignments (doesn't finish them).
   b. Focus the microscope.
   c. Use the interest center.
   d. Read library books.
   e. Fighting on the playground must be reduced.
   f. Same for blow-ups and outbursts.
   g. Papers are too messy.
   h. Eliminate cursing and swearing.
3. List the behaviors in ranking order, with those of highest priority appearing first on the list. The example list was:
   a. Blow-ups.
   b. Incomplete assignments.
   c. Interest center.
   d. Focus microscope.
   e. Cursing and swearing.
   f. Fighting.
   g. Messy papers.
   h. Read library books.
4. List potential accelerating consequences. An example of a list for one student was:
   a. Assisting the custodian in his duties.
   b. Using a piece of A-V equipment.
   c. Watching the tropical fish in the acquarium.
   d. Free time.
   e. Playing Nerf basketball with a friend.
5. Rank the consequences in order of their potential interest to the student. The example rankings were:
   a. Nerf basketball.
   b. Assisting custodian.
   c. Free time.
   d. Watching fish in acquarium.
   e. Using A-V equipment.
6. List potential decelerating consequences; for example:
   a. Staying in during the 7th hour.
   b. Eating lunch in the room instead of the cafeteria.

c. Cleaning the classroom.
d. Staying after school.
e. Working in an isolated area of the room.
7. Rank the decelerating consequences in order of the student's dislikes. The example list was:
a. Staying in for 7th hour.
b. Staying after school.
c. Cleaning the classroom.
d. Eating lunch in the room, not cafeteria.
e. Working in isolated area of room.

The teacher can observe behavior and consequences during the school day and jot down observations. During some free minutes the observations can be studied in more detail, followed by the priority ranking. Since the teacher has specific purposes in mind, the student's strengths and weaknesses, likes and dislikes, and other traits and interests may manifest themselves.

Select a Target Behavior

From the list of behaviors to be changed, choose a specific target behavior. If the program is designed to decelerate a behavior, selection of only one target behavior is recommended. If several inappropriate behaviors are selected, the program could be overwhelming to the student. If a teacher is using behavior principles for the first time, the selected behavior should be one that occurs fairly frequently or is relatively lengthy in duration. In the example above, the first behavior appearing on the list is "blow-ups," but since blow-ups occurred only once a week or so, the teacher unfamiliar with behavior modification would not be able to gain much experience with such episodic behavior. "Cursing and swearing" and "incomplete assignments" occurred frequently; therefore, selecting one of these behaviors for the teacher's first modification program would be a better choice. The teacher gains experience in using behavioral techniques more readily if high frequency behaviors are selected.

Define the Behavior

The behavior should be defined specifically. The behavior selected in the example was "incomplete assignments" — specified to mean: "To finish a teacher-directed written assignment within the prescribed class time." This definition was individualized for the student and would not necessarily apply to other situations. To expedite communication after the specific definition has been established, the teacher may refer to the target behavior in a general way, such as "incomplete assignments."

Select the Consequence

The teacher can approach the use of consequences in two ways. One approach is to select a decelerating consequence from the list, such as "staying in for 7th hour," and arrange for it to follow the target behavior "incomplete assignments." The teacher may consider the following arrangement: "The student will stay in for 7th hour to finish each incomplete assignment." If on subsequent days, the number of incomplete assignments diminishes, staying in for 7th hour was a successful decelerating consequence. Research and data support the effective use of decelerating consequences.

The teacher, however, can approach modification of inappropriate behaviors in a positive way. Inappropriate behaviors can be redefined by using a "flip side of the coin" definition. For example, the opposite of "incomplete assignment" is "completed assignment." The teacher could select one of the accelerating consequences, such as "playing Nerf basketball with a friend" and arrange for it to follow "completed assignment." The teacher may consider the following arrangement: "The student can play Nerf basketball five minutes for each completed assignment." This second way of changing inappropriate behavior may be termed *accent the positive*. It should be a prevailing theme to accompany all the procedures of the structured approach — especially behavior modification, which often is concerned with inappropriate behaviors. Emotionally disturbed students frequently have a repertoire of maladaptive behaviors that tend to disguise the presence of appropriate behaviors. If accelerating consequences are used to increase the positive counterparts of inappropriate behaviors, the repertoire of appropriate behaviors widens.

186

The structured approach emphasizes that students have behaviors which need accenting. Accenting the positive through use of accelerating consequences also helps students learn alternate behaviors. "Completed assignment" is an alternate way to perform. If, in contrast, a student receives decelerating consequences for inappropriate behaviors that subsequently are weakened or eliminated, the student only has learned what *not* to do.

The rate of behavior change is dependent upon the strength of the consequence. Ranking potential consequences can assist the teacher in determining the strength of the consequence. "Playing Nerf ball with a friend" was judged as the favorite consequence so it probably has the most strength. Ranking consequences also can assist in determining whether a consequence is possible to implement in the classroom. If "playing Nerf basketball with a friend" is ranked as the highest consequence but the friend isn't available when the student is ready for the consequence, what happens? The effect of arranging a consequence that can't be delivered is deleterious. The teacher could determine the priority rank of playing Nerf basketball without the buddy. If it still ranks "1," fine; if lower, the potential consequence "2" should be considered.

Select a Contingency

How long, how often, how much, and when should the student receive the consequence? Selecting the right arrangement is an important decision. Ideally, each time the target behavior occurs, it is followed immediately by the selected consequence. (For each completed assignment, the student immediately plays Nerf basketball for five minutes.) This arrangement is referred to as a *continuous schedule,* the most effective and expedient arrangement to facilitate behavioral change; but it is the least practical arrangement for teachers to implement because attending to one behavior of one student on a continuous basis within the classroom is almost impossible. An intermittent schedule then is selected.

An *intermittent schedule* is one in which some but not all responses are followed by a consequence. Intermittent schedules are subdivided into two major categories: ratio and interval. A *ratio schedule* refers to consequences contingent upon a number of responses. An interval schedule refers to consequences contingent upon a time lapse. Ratio schedules are subdivided into two types: fixed ratio and variable ratio.

187

Interval schedules are subdivided into two types: fixed intervals and variable intervals. These schedules are defined as follows: (a) Fixed ratio: Requires the same number of responses for each consequence, such as five math problems for each Snoopy sticker (5:1); (b) Variable ratio: Requires that the number of responses for each consequence be irregular, such as five math problems for one Snoopy sticker (5:1); eight problems for one sticker (8:1, 7:1, 4:1, 9:1, etc); (c) Fixed intervals: Requires that the same amount of time elapse before each response is consequated, such as remaining in seat for 20 minutes for a Happy Face Circle (20 min.:1); (d) Variable interval: Requires that the amount of time elapsing before each consequence be irregular, such as remaining in seat 20 minutes for a Happy Face Circle (20 min.:1); in seat 15 minutes for a Circle (15 min.:1, 35 min.:1, 10 min.:1, 25 min.:1, 15 min.:1, etc.).

What schedule should the teacher select? The schedule selection is dependent upon the behavior to be modified. In one classroom situation a student's frequency for being out of seat was minimal, but the amount of time he was out of seat was lengthy. The teacher selected an interval schedule because the amount of time when the student was out of seat was the concern. Furthermore, the teacher selected a fixed interval schedule, which was stated as follows: "For every 10 minutes you remain in seat, you will receive a Snoopy sticker." Students can make easier discriminations and form quicker associations of the expectations if arrangements are in fixed intervals. The arrangement was a positive approach, as discussed earlier.

For another student, whose English assignment required the selection of correct verb tenses, a fixed ratio schedule was selected. The concern was for the number of accurately selected verbs and not for the length of time needed to complete the assignment.

Many emotionally disturbed students panic when they are uncertain about controlling their own behavior, and about the outcomes of their behavior. They need to be able to predict their behavior and its outcome — the consequences. Fixed schedules "spell out" the arrangement. Thus, the student can predict, "If I follow the arrangement, the following will happen: . . ." The response decision is the student's. During a student's initial months in a special classroom, some selections are limited to two choices; but the decision making process is expanded gradually so that multi-choices are available. This expansion usually occurs as a student is acquiring new behaviors.

Continuous schedules should be used for *acquisition* of behavior, and intermittent schedules should be used for maintainance of behavior.

Because the impracticality of continuous reinforcement in the classroom precludes its use by most teachers, intermittent schedules are selected for the acquisition of behavior. The selection of a fixed ratio or a fixed interval schedule for the acquisition of behavior is a less precise but necessary choice. Moreover, the teacher needs to be aware that a behavioral change may not occur as quickly with an intermittent schedule as it would with a continuous one.

When a student's behavior reaches a pre-established goal, the schedule can be "thinned" by extending the frequency or duration of responses for one consequence. A classroom example clarifies this technique: A student was on a fixed schedule, 5:1 — five multiplication facts for one sticker. When the math work reached the pre-established goal, increases in the ratio were set at 7:1, 10:1, 15:1, and finally 20:1, to maintain the goal. Such shifts in schedule are usually explained to the student.

More than one schedule can be used to modify behavior. A beginning typing student was required to type two accurate lines on a fixed ratio of 2:1. When the student maintained the goal on a consistent basis, the teacher added a fixed interval schedule; that is, the student was required to type two accurate lines within a specified time for the one consequence.

After the contingency has been determined, the teacher should discuss the intervention plan with the student before it is implemented. Again, students can be guided to change gradually, building upon a series of successful steps. The teacher in the previous example initially could have required that the student type two accurate lines in a specified time for one consequence. This plan, using a fixed ratio and fixed interval, may have asked too much from the student. A wise teacher avoids planning potential failure for students.

Record Behaviors

Why is it necessary to record? If behavior is recorded, changes and degree of changes can be determined. A classroom example illustrates the need to record: Raymond, a six-year-old emotionally disturbed boy, was enrolled in a special classroom. School personnel knew Raymond because his screams were heard frequently in the building. For unexplainable reasons, Raymond screamed high-pitched "e's" which often interrupted the day's activities. The teacher implemented a behavior modification program designed to decrease the screams. Raymond's "e's" were counted during a 20-minute period per day at random times for one week. Each "e" received a count; for example, "e-e-e" equaled 3 counts. The mean rate of "e's" was 175 per 20-minute period before intervention. Obviously, Raymond's screaming behavior needed modification. During modification, the teacher continued to record so it could be established readily if Raymond's screamed "e's" were diminishing. On one occasion, shortly after implementation of the intervention program, while sharing conversation with another teacher, Raymond's teacher mentioned that Raymond was screaming *only* 125 times. The other teacher was aghast, repeating "125?" Raymond's teacher then related that the boy formerly had screamed 175 "e's" per 20 minutes. The second teacher encouraged Raymond's teacher to continue the progress!

Recording also can add precision to the initial target behavior definition because the observer attends more acutely to events surrounding behavior. A classroom teacher discovered this while planning an intervention program for a visually handicapped student who was dependent upon others. Dependency was described as, "The girl will not walk alone during change of classes; she depends upon others for mobility." Observation and recordings revealed that in four days the student had 17 between-class changes. During these class changes, the girl had walked alone two times and began walking alone 15 times until her closest friend told her to wait so they could walk together. The recording revealed that the teacher's target behavior description was partially erroneous because the girl did initiate independence in walking to classes. Her independent mobility was interrupted by a friend who wanted to walk and visit on the way to other classes. The teacher learned from direct observations and recording that the girl actually demonstrated independent rather than dependent mobility.

What is recorded? Any or all of six major variables could be recorded: (a) frequency (the number of times a behavior occurs; for example, 12 times a day); (b) duration of behavior (the length of time the behavior continues; for example, 20 minutes); (c) quality of behavior (for example, 95 percent accuracy); (d) intensity (as shown, for example, by sound level in a room); (e) a product (the tangible evidence of an endeavor with aesthetic expression, such as watercolor drawing or a creative poem); (f) skill (for example, how high did the athlete jump? Or, how many yards can the student swim?). Some recordings include more than one variable, such as frequency and duration which result in a rate measurement.

When is behavior recorded? Several options are available: (a) continuous (each time a behavior occurs, it is recorded); (b) time sample (refers

190

to a specific time period selected for recording, such as the first 15 minutes of each hour); (c) random spot check (recording is aperiodic; the student is observed at irregular times. Note: Two recordings must be made — the number of observations and the number of target behaviors observed); (d) specific spot check (predetermined brief intervals, such as the first seconds of every hour and half-hour.

How does a teacher know what and when to record? The target behavior is the first determinant. For example, if the target behavior is, "late to class," the teacher may be more concerned with how late the student is than with how many times. Hence, a duration measurement rather than a frequency count is selected. The second determinant is the amount of time available to the teacher. Continuous recording is the ideal choice because it reveals every target behavioral occurrence, but it also is the least practical form of classroom recording. The teacher engaged in classroom activities cannot direct undivided attention to one student. Thus, the teacher will have to select another recording time option.

How is behavior recorded? If the frequency of behavior is recorded, a teacher could make hash marks on a sheet of paper or use a mechanical counting device. A stopwatch can be used to record duration of a behavior. Some other recording devices used by teachers for frequency counts are shown in Figure 6.1.

Who does the recording? Teachers using behavior modification techniques for the first time should do it themselves. As they become familiar with the techniques, recording can be shared by training aides, parents, observers, and students. Students can be taught to do self-recording; but self-recording also has been used in itself as a consequence to bring about changes in behavior.

How long is behavior recorded? Behavior is recorded during the intervention program, which consists of two major time periods: (a) baseline (the pre-intervention period), and (b) modification (the intervention period).

Baseline period

Baseline recording is done before the intervention is introduced. This recording is valuable because it represents a standard against which behavioral changes and the extent of change can be determined. The recording should be unobtrusive because if students are aware that their behavior is being recorded, they may deliberately modify their actions and cause a false picture.

191

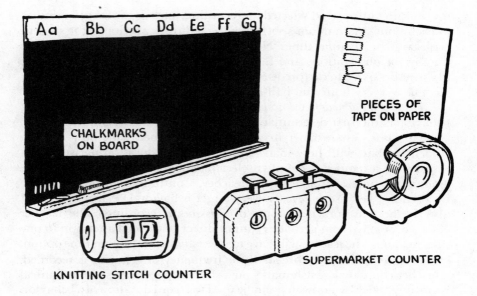

Fig. 6.1. Behavior recording devices.

Baseline recording adds precision to the teacher's evaluation of a student's behavior; terms like *always, constantly,* and *never* lose credence. For example, the teacher introduced earlier who was concerned with the out-of-seat behavior of one student had made comments like, "He is always out of his seat." But when this behavior was recorded, the student was found to be out of his seat 80 percent of the time and in seat 20 percent. Thus, "always" was not an accurate description. The recording did confirm the selection of a target behavior, and it also eliminated an inaccurate description, replacing it with an accurate one.

Baseline recording is continued until the observer notes stability in the behavioral occurrences or a pattern of occurrences. An example of a stable duration recording is as follows: A teacher used a stopwatch to time Jeff, a sixth grade boy, who sucked his right index finger. The boy was right-handed, so the finger sucking prevented him from using his pencil for work activities — hence, the selection of finger sucking for the target behavior. The teacher recorded the behavior in the morning from 9:00 to 11:00 a.m. The amount of time Jeff sucked his finger for eight consecutive school days was: 50 min., 56 min., 68 min., 62 min., 54 min.,

64 min., 66 min., and 69 min. The finger sucking ranged from 50 to 69 minutes. Jeff's teacher determined that the eight-day record, as seen in Figure 6.2, revealed a stability in duration of finger sucking.

To demonstrate how a pattern, rather than stability, in behavior determines length of baseline: A fourteen-year-old student in a residential setting had a number of mini-assignments to complete each day. The

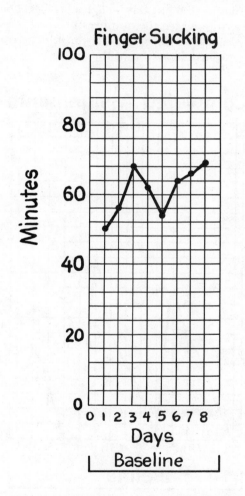

Fig. 6.2. Baseline recording reflecting stability of undesirable behavior.

number of assignments ranged from 10 to 15 a day and the student was not turning in many of these assignments. The frequency recording of assignments turned in beginning with Monday revealed the following: Monday — 0, Tuesday — 2, Wednesday — 5, Thursday — 7, Friday — 10; the following week, Monday — 1, Tuesday — 3, Wednesday — 5, Thursday — 7, Friday — 12; the third week's pattern, Monday — 0, Tuesday — 0, Wednesday — 4, Thursday — 6, Friday —8. The frequency count indicated a pattern in which the number of turned in assignments was low the first days of the week, increasing during the course of the week. Figure 6-3 is a graphed depiction of these data.

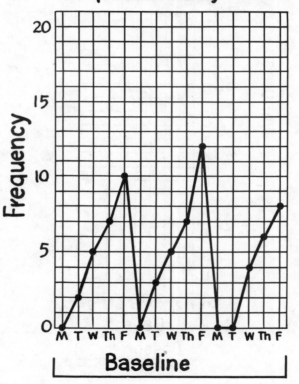

Fig. 6.3. Baseline recording showing pattern of behavior.

The teacher also recorded the number of assignments the student was expected to do, and computed a daily percentage of assignments turned in. This added more precision to the baseline recording. A comparison of the first week's frequency recording of assignments turned in with the percentage of turned in assignments, as shown in Figure 6.4, illustrates this point.

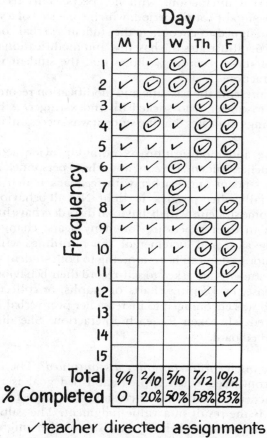

✓ teacher directed assignments

⊘ student completed assignments

Fig. 6.4. Percentage comparison of teacher directed and student completed assignments.

Modification period

Modification recording is the continuation of baseline recording, but it is done during the intervention period when the contingency and consequences are in effect.

In one special classroom, a teacher did a baseline frequency recording of a student's verbal interactions with her peers. This recording was continued into the modification period, which consisted of a social interaction program designed to encourage the student's verbal contacts with her peers. Figure 6.5 illustrates the baseline and modification recordings. A comparison of these recordings shows that the student was able to increase her interactions.

Figure 6.6 represents the baseline and modification recordings of the student referred to earlier who sucked his index finger. A comparison of the two recordings indicates that the student was successful in changing his behavior.

The baseline and modification recordings provide accountability records for the teacher, student, parents, and school personnel. The records also provide the student and teacher with feedback which is critically important, especially when progress is slight. Not all behavioral changes are giant steps. Some students with behavioral disorders have had inappropriate behaviors in their repertoire for many years; changes in those behaviors may be slow and incremental, but recordings will reveal the changes. This information can be reinforcing to both student and teacher.

Frequently, students are asked to self-record their behavior during the modification phase, by keeping charts or graphs, or collecting tokens. The student who was encouraged to increase her peer verbal interactions received a colored felt token for each interaction. She displayed the tokens on a flannelboard.

When is an intervention program discontinued? The intervention program is discontinued when a pre-established goal is reached and maintained. Teachers and other modifiers should remember that establishment of a goal is the result of a value judgment. The value judgment could be based on peer comparison; that is, a teacher might set a goal for an individual student's target behavior, based on what is expected of students in that class. The teacher may set a goal based on expectations of children of the same age, such as all ten-year-olds. The value judgment may be based on a comparison of the individual to himself or herself; how does he or she perform now as compared to an earlier performance?

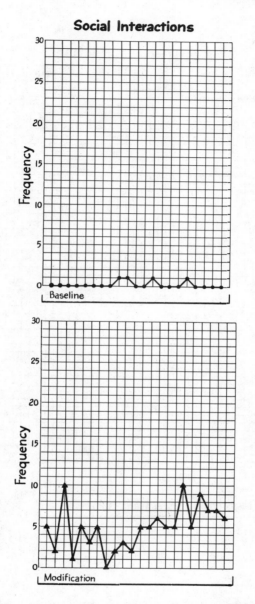

Fig. 6.5. Baseline and modification recordings showing improvement in social interactions.

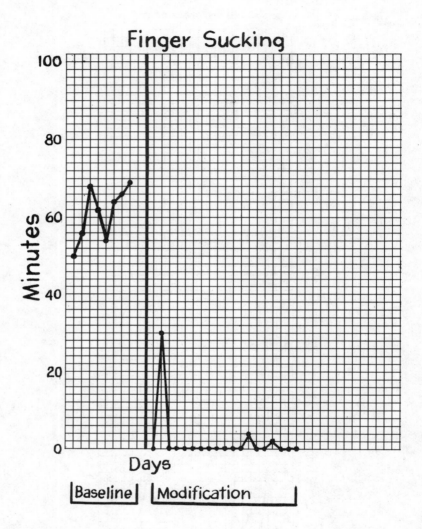

Fig. 6.6. Baseline and modification recordings showing improvement in behavior.

BEHAVIOR MODIFICATION TECHNIQUES

Two behavioral techniques teachers can use to develop learning activities are discussed below. These techniques — shaping and fading — were selected from others usually associated with management programs.

Shaping

In this process, portions and/or approximations of a goal behavior are reinforced. This technique is important in helping students acquire new behaviors and in reaching levels of expectations. Dramatic changes in behavior seldom are acquired immediately; therefore, teachers can subdivide goal behavior into successive steps and provide reinforcement.

A vignette illustrates the technique of shaping: Larry, a fifteen-year-old boy in a special class located in a regular school, was physically disoriented when he was out of the classroom. He became lost if he were six feet or more away from his classroom. Larry was targeted to learn routes within the building for his own safety, independence, and future integration into regular classes. The teacher listed the locations and routes Larry would need to learn, requiring that he learn one at a time. The first four locations were: (a) restroom; (b) the adjacent special classroom; (c) fifth grade room; and (d) playground exit. A drawing of the school's floor plan, as seen in Figure 6.7, shows the locations and routes Larry was to learn.

Initially, the teacher had to physically demonstrate and teach Larry how to stay near the hall walls so he would not become lost in the hall space. The teacher had to determine legitimate reasons for Larry's "practice" trips. The restroom trip was a particular challenge to the teacher's ingenuity; she resolved the situation by introducing several classroom projects that required water (obtained from the restroom), giving legitimacy to Larry's trips to the restroom. The teacher knew Larry's trips were successful if he returned with water in a container. Reinforcement was in the form of social praise and Larry's own knowledge that he was able to leave and return to the room unaided.

After six consecutive successful trips, Larry was taught to find the next location — another special classroom adjacent to Larry's room. The teacher prearranged for the forthcoming trips with the next door teacher. Larry was sent to borrow items such as paper clips, construction paper, chalk, or to remain in that room to participate in an activity with

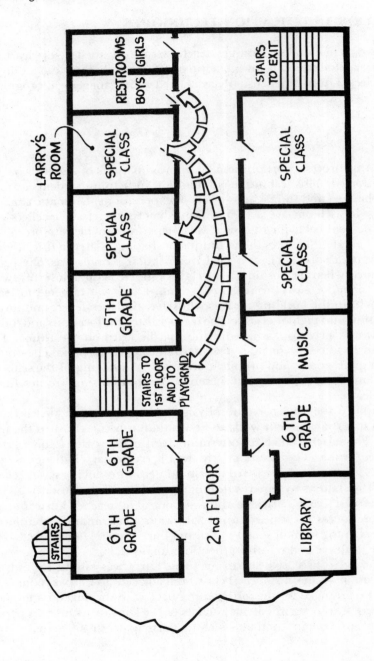

Fig. 6.7. Layout and routes for student behavior goal, using shaping techniques.

younger children for whom he had fondness. After his visit, he would take the borrowed items or one of the young children's papers to his own classroom. Larry needed something tangible to remind himself of the purpose of the trip. The tangible item also served as feedback to Larry's teacher; if he returned with an item, he had made a successful trip. As seen in Figure 6.7, learning each location was built upon Larry's existing knowledge of the previous location; thus, as he passed a known location(s), his knowledge of it was reaffirmed.

To review Larry's "travel" knowledge, the teacher intermittently asked him to make round trips to the known locations. Gradually, Larry learned his way to the principal's office and all necessary locations such as outdoor exits, custodian's room, library, music room, and the regular classroom he would enter someday.

Shaping — the reinforcement of successive approximations — is a teaching technique of paramount importance to teachers, and a learning procedure of paramount importance to all students, especially those with emotional and academic problems. The programming procedure described in Chapter 5 is based on successive approximations.

Fading

Fading is a technique that gradually reduces the number of cues needed to learn a response. An example: Doug, a seven-year-old student in a special class, had failed kindergarten but was socially promoted to first grade, which he also failed. His parents, who had unrealistic goals for Doug's performances, were angered by his failures. Doug's poor self-image was reflected in his low tolerance for performance, hesitancy to engage in activities, slumped shoulders, drooping head, and other indications. The teacher observed that coloring was one of his frustrating experiences, so all coloring except free style activities was terminated — except for a series of tasks that would employ the fading technique. Each day, Doug was expected to complete one coloring task, using simple, large, geometric shapes drawn on sheets of paper with wide black lines. The dark outlines gradually were faded until they were similar to the ones provided in curriculum materials. Figure 6.8 provides an illustration of this technique. Doug completed a series of squares, rectangles, triangles, and circles plus a series of large simple picture shapes. The basic shapes then were reintroduced in reduced sizes. After Doug completed the teacher-made learning sequence, he was able to successfully complete the coloring tasks presented in the curriculum materials.

A serendipitous event occurred which enhanced the coloring sequence. When Doug began the learning sequence, he tried to keep his

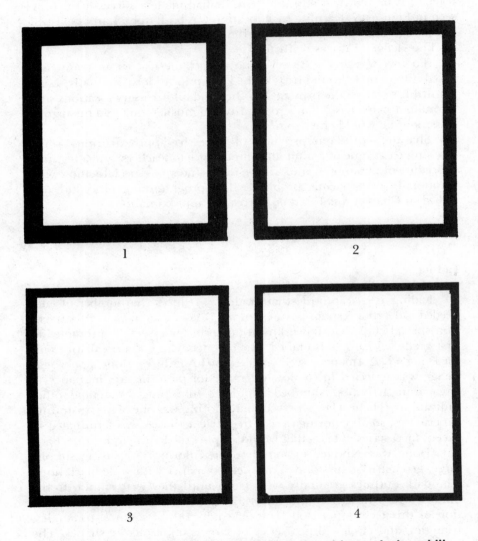

Fig. 6.8. Example of fading technique in teaching coloring skills.

coloring within the inner edge of the wide outline, and while many strokes went past the inner edge, only a few strokes went beyond the outline's outer edge. The wide, dark outline negated some of Doug's errors. Figure 6.9 illustrates this concept.

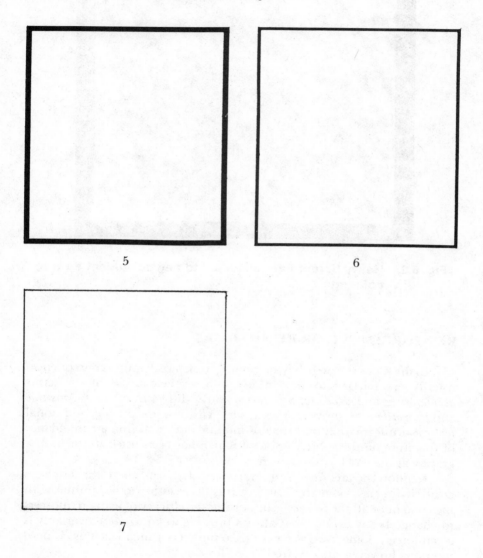

5

6

7

Fig. 6.9. Heavy border lines as an aid to negate student error in coloring.

REINFORCEMENT, OR REINFORCERS

In the literature on behavior modification, accelerating consequences usually are referred to as reinforcers. Nevertheless, use of the terms *accelerating* and *decelerating consequences* differs from use of *positive* and *negative reinforcers*. The reader wishing to pursue additional technical information on behavior modification will find an abundance of literature on the subject, some of which has been listed in the bibliography at the end of this chapter.

Reinforcers are interesting variables that can elicit the teacher's creativity in classroom applications. It isn't necessary to be familiar with the content of all the research supporting the efficacy of using reinforcers to change behavior, nor is it always possible to know *why* a variable is a reinforcer. Some aspects regarding reinforcers which teachers *do* need to know, however, are described as follows.

Hierarchy of Reinforcers

Reinforcers exist in the lives of all persons. These reinforcers can be ranked in order of each person's preference. This priority is referred to as the hierarchy of reinforcers. The hierarchy of reinforcers is not a constant; shifts occur because of a number of variables including the person's age, needs, level of maturity, deprivation, and so on. Teachers should keep the hierarchy in mind as reinforcers are selected and provided in the classroom. The list of reinforcers which a teacher ranks for each student can change; reinforcers often shift priority positions. Some or all reinforcers will or can be replaced with new ones. No one reinforcer heads the priority list for all persons. Normally, reinforcers associated with physical comfort, such as food and shelter, precede qualitative levels of reinforcers such as cognitive learning, social approval, and aesthetic qualities. Food, however, will not head the list of an anorexic nervosa student. The individuality of reinforcers cannot be overemphasized.

Materialistic and Natural Reinforcers

To ask an emotionally disturbed student to competently complete academic work and to "act your age" because it is the right thing to do is absurd! If emotionally disturbed youth responded appropriately to reinforcers naturally occurring in the environment (such as social approval, grades, success, and praise), they would not be in a special classroom. Analogous to this situation is to ask whether adults would fulfill their work obligations because it is the right thing to do. Some reponses in human life are made because of their "payoff" value. Some of these "payoffs" are materialistic, such as paychecks, acknowledgments, and recognition; other payoffs are intrinsic, such as a feeling of accomplishment, appreciation of beauty, and the satisfaction of reaching a goal. A goal in the special education program for students with behavioral disorders is to help the student learn to achieve and accept a balance of materialistic and intrinsic reinforcers.

If more materialistic reinforcers are utilized in the special classroom during the student's initial months in a program, they can be replaced gradually with intrinsic reinforcers. A shift from materialistic to intrinsic

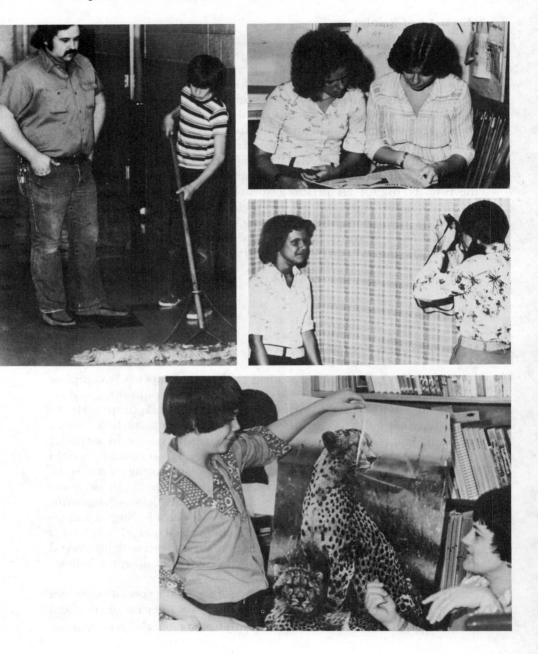

reinforcers is illustrated by the following classroom experience: Six young emotionally disturbed children received frequent materialistic reinforcers for a series of small tasks during the first hour of scheduled work activity. If all their tasks were completed during the first hour, the children participated in a 15-minute orange juice and vanilla wafer break period. Initially, the children ate vigorously and talked simultaneously. As the school months elapsed, their social graces improved. The children ate smaller portions of the snacks and monitored their own conversations. Meanwhile, they had requested and were learning how to serve the cookies and pour the juice. Several months later, all the students were participating appropriately in conversation and refusing most of the food. The materialistic payoff — food — gradually shifted into an instrinsic payoff — the enjoyment of conversation with friends after a work period.

Short-Term and Long-Range Reinforcers

Another goal in the special program is to teach students to wait for reinforcers. A gradual change in the schedules of reinforcement, as described earlier, is one technique that can help students learn to wait. This goal has become increasingly difficult to achieve, however, because our society has become accustomed to immediate reinforcement. Food, entertainment, and mobility can be attained instantly after some simple responses. An individual can twist a dial and immediately view a TV movie; can place coins in a machine and receive food and beverages; flip a switch and receive light; twist a key in a car ignition and have power to move at varying speeds; or dial a telephone number and be in contact with an individual thousands of miles away.

Tokens

Tokens are a medium of exchange used in lieu of reinforcers for the desired responses and subsequently exchanged for reinforcers. Teachers have used points, theater tickets, plastic discs, happy faces, coins, pieces of felt, paper clips, and poker chips for tokens. Sometimes, tokens are parts of total reinforcers, as in pieces of a model car, pieces of a puzzle, or beads for a necklace. If time is associated with a reinforcer, it is frequently difficult to have a time period follow a response, especially if the student is doing a number of short tasks or if the student needs a certain amount of time for enjoyment of the reinforcers. Examples of time-related reinforcing activities could include time with an object (working on a model plane); time with a person (conversation with a friend or counselor; or time for self-development (trying a new facial makeup or workouts in a gym). A student working on a series of short tasks could receive tokens representing time, such as one token per one minute of time. When the student accumulates a requisite number of tokens, these can be exchanged for the earned amount of time.

Tokens also can be used to help students learn to delay gratification. Dispensing tokens on a frequent basis (using a low frequency ratio 2:1 or a low frequency interval 2 min.:1) can sustain some students' interest for a long-range reinforcer exchange. In many cases, the reinforcer has been decided upon in advance by the student and teacher. Students have asked to eat dinner at a teacher's house, to bowl with a child care worker, to have a mod T-shirt, and to have their hair styled. The agreed-upon reinforcer is something of value to a student and is within reason of a teacher's budget. Teachers who have diagnosed a student as described in Chapter 3, and have functionally analyzed the student's behavior as described in this chapter, will have reached an understanding of the timing needed for token exchange. Students' needs for token exchange periods range from a few minutes to daily, weekly, or monthly exchanges. Students who need frequent exchanges can be guided gradually into waiting longer between each time of token exchange.

Tokens can be used as an intermediate stage to guide students from materialistic reinforcers to social ones. A brief description of a teacher's program for a sixteen-year-old adolescent girl in a residential setting illustrates this point. Ruth had a negative self-image and poor personal body habits. All of the students in Ruth's class were receiving tokens for their individual behaviors, exchanging the tokens at the end of each week for a variety of items available in the canteen, including potato chips, coke, teen magazines, or events such as movies, parties, or shortened school days. Gradually, items like lipstick, makeup, eye shadow, soap, deodorant, brushes, and combs were added to the canteen's inventory. Ruth was encouraged to try the cosmetic items. Lowered prices and attractive packaging were instigated to encourage selection of these items. A beauty corner with mirror, renovated dressing table, cosmetic lighting, and attractive posters were arranged in a corner of the classroom, which also included magazines with articles on body care, hair styles, and cosmetic application. The teacher was available to give "beauty hints," if requested.

Cautiously, Ruth began to buy and use some of the beauty items. The improvement in physical appearance became apparent to her classmates and personnel in the residential setting, who complimented her on these changes. The compliments served as social reinforcers which encouraged Ruth's continued use of the beauty items. Gradually, the canteen introduced employment opportunities within the residence, such as "Help the cook clean out storeroom, 2 hours — $2.50." Ruth was then encouraged to work for wages, which she subsequently did. When she went on "off grounds passes," she spent some of her money for notions and cosmetic items in community stores.

Some teachers use tokens because they are easier to dispense than a variety of tangible reinforcers. If many individual modification programs are occurring concurrently in the classrooms, teachers simply cannot dispense different reinforcers for the many different behaviors without sacrificing teaching and personal contact time with the students. Tokens can make classroom reinforcement of many behaviors manageable.

When teachers consider establishing a token system for a student or class, they need to plan carefully how each student is to earn tokens and lose tokens. A plan to make up for loss of tokens should be included. A student must not be cornered. In anticipating that need, many programs include provisions for earning bonus tokens. Figure 6.10 lists some of the school behaviors in an adolescent girls' treatment center which earn points or cause loss of points. The non-school staff used an additional point system specifying behavior in residence and recreation areas. The point program was integrated with the entire treatment program and was coordinated by each girl's counselor. A committee including child care workers, teachers, counselors, therapists, recreation personnel, and students made decisions relevant to the selected behaviors and their corresponding points. The committee also continuously reviewed and updated its decisions.

Token giving should be accompanied by praise, encouragement, a pat on the back, or other forms of social approval. A teacher in a residential setting had just initiated a sticker token system in his primary class when an unexpected influx of new students overcrowded his room. In his efforts to individualize the students' academic programs, he became hurried in dispensing tokens — leaving them on the students' desks without comment. As a result, student behaviors did not change, nor were tokens accrued as anticipated. When the teacher added enthusiastic

Points

Ways to Earn Points in School

1-2	Appearance (1 extra point for extra sharp appearance)
1	On time at 8:30
1	On time at 10:15
1-2	Being prepared
4-10	Academic points (1 point for each assignment completed and corrected to 85%; 2 points for each assignment that is 100% on first try).
1	Returning progress report signed by counselor
1-2	Behavior (1 extra point for exemplary behavior)

Ways to Earn Bonus Points in School

1	½ hour of work — tutoring, librarian, helping the corrector
1-5	Creative writing or drawing
5	Book report or artist of week
3	Current events summary
5	Getting more times tables correct than previous one-minute trial test
1-2	Doing classroom chores — filing, cleaning bulletin boards
1+	Anything a student does that is above and beyond what is expected; for example, "supporting another resident" or making a good decision such as pulling oneself out of a bad spot.

Unacceptable School Behaviors that do not Allow Earning of Behavior Points

Cursing, especially when meant to be verbally abusive.
Eating or drinking in class
Cheating
Yelling out windows to strangers
Leaving class without permission

Figure 6.10. Behaviors resulting in points.

social approval to the token giving, student behaviors changed and tokens accrued in greater amounts.

Record-keeping is essential to a token system. Some teachers record each student's earned and lost tokens in a standard record book. Others devise their own recording forms and keep the sheets in a notebook. Some teachers transfer information from recording sheets to graphs. Many teachers use points for tokens. Points are marked on each student's academic worksheet schedule or on a point sheet. If points are exchanged during the day, a record of "spent" points is included. If any or all points are saved, teachers could provide students with a savings record form. Figure 6.11 gives some recording format ideas for token systems used in the classroom.

Programs that should be avoided are ones which provide students with a fixed number of tokens at the beginning of a day (for example, 100 points) and deduct points for inappropriate behaviors. This approach provides the initial amount of points noncontingently, accents the negative, and does not offer the students alternate ways to behave. On rare occasions, a single inappropriate behavior can be modified using this technique — if a positive atmosphere prevails in the room. In one special class, a teacher introduced a program for a student who persisted in asking unnecessary questions. Under the program, this student began the day with a fixed number of "tickets." Each ticket represented one question. If any tickets remained at the end of the day, the student was free to redeem them. This program was added judiciously to the existing token reinforcement program and was terminated as soon as the student replaced unnecessary questions with legitimate ones.

The previous pages of this chapter contain descriptions of techniques which can be used to modify behavior through the systematic arrangement of consequences. In classrooms a multitude of responses are evoked from educational materials. When the teacher presents a curriculum material, after careful selection and adaptation, and/or programmed tasks, and/or arranges the classroom environment, concentration is directed to the antecedent events to stimulate and change the students' responses. The activities described in chapters 2, 4, and 5 primarily focused on techniques designed to change behavior by arranging stimuli. Teachers should be fully cognizant that the availability of the most powerful reinforcer could be to no avail when a student cannot make the desirable responses. If a teacher can include all four components — stimulus, response, contingency, consequence — in the planning, then a more inclusive approach to behavior modification is used.

Fig. 6.11. Format examples for recording token exchanges, and recording forms.

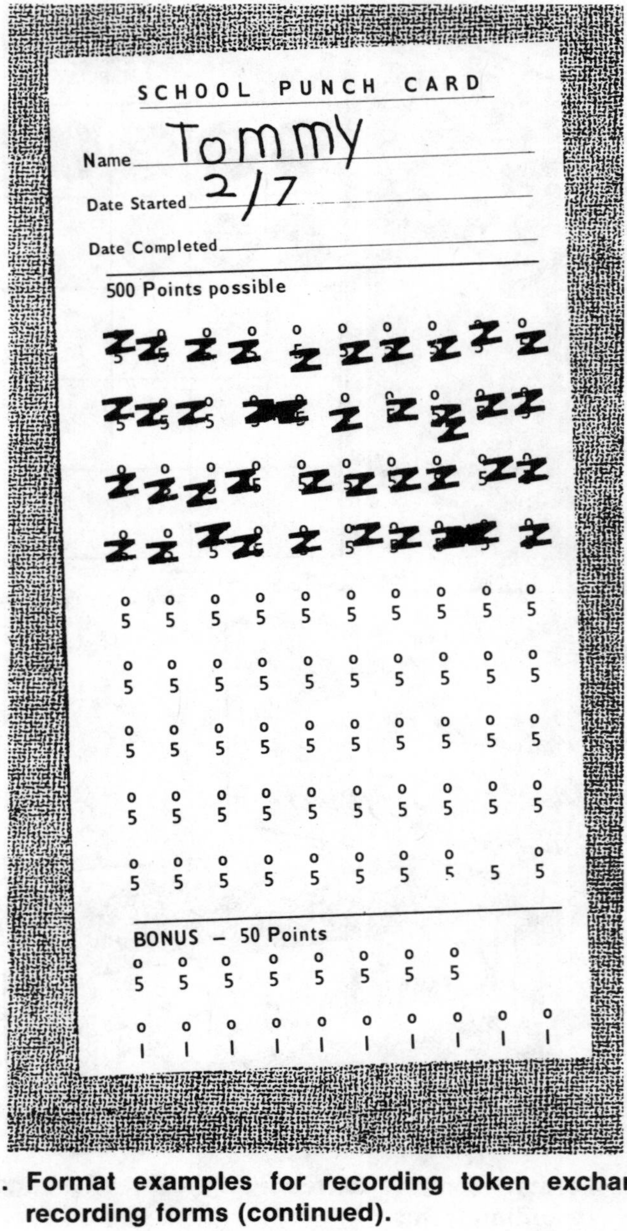

Fig. 6.11. Format examples for recording token exchanges, and recording forms (continued).

Free Time Area

Many special classrooms have a free time area, a special location in the room where students can engage in favorite activities. Tokens often are used to gain admission to the area. Teachers have discovered that designation of a free time area is a useful and meaningful technique in providing various reinforcers that interest the students. Teachers usually realize, however, that a few ground rules should be established for the free time area. The area, first, should have specific physical boundaries. It should be a physically attractive area, offering a variety of activities to meet students' current interests and to entice new interests. The area should include activities and materials that can be completed in a single free time period, as well as longer term activities. Some students may need to be guided and encouraged in their selections of activities. Aides, volunteers, and students from regular classrooms have been used effectively as support personnel in this effort. Some reinforcers used in free time areas and throughout the special classrooms are listed in the appendix to this chapter.

BEHAVIOR MODIFICATION AS A DIAGNOSTIC TECHNIQUE

Teachers involved in identifying the stimulus, response, contingency, and consequence of student behaviors are in fact using behavior modification as a diagnostic procedure — one of its most valuable features. This application extends the diagnostic procedure described in Chapter 3 and reiterates the importance of ongoing diagnosis. A classroom example illustrates the value of behavior modification as a diagnostic procedure: All the students in a regular classroom were taught a new concept that involved subtracting a three-digit number in the subtrahend from a three-digit number in the minuend with borrowing from the 100s column. After group instruction, the students were asked to complete a worksheet in 30 minutes. Figure 6.12 is a copy of a student's worksheet.

The teacher studied results of Ray's efforts and listed possible reasons for his incomplete, inaccurate worksheet, then categorized the speculations under *stimulus, response, contingency,* and *consequence* as follows:

1. Stimulus: The sheet contained too many problems. Ray's handwriting through the first row of problems was legible, but legibility steadily worsened. The workbook page was aversive to Ray.

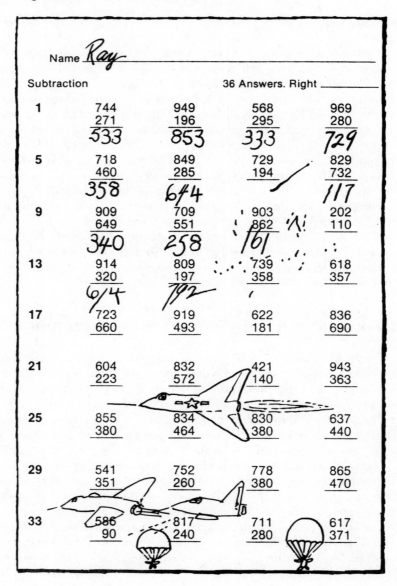

Name *Ray*

Subtraction   36 Answers. Right _____

1   744   949   568   969
     271   196   295   280
     533   *853*   *333*   *729*

5   718   849   729   829
     460   285   194   732
     358   *644*   *117*

9   909   709   903   202
     649   551   862   110
     340   *258*   *161*

13   914   809   739   618
     320   197   358   357
     644   *792*

17   723   919   622   836
     660   493   181   690

21   604   832   421   943
     223   572   140   363

25   855   834   830   637
     380   464   380   440

29   541   752   778   865
     351   260   380   470

33   586   817   711   617
     90   240   280   371

Figure 6.12   Example worksheet used in behavior modification diagnostic technique.

2. Response: Ray didn't understand the concept of borrowing from the 100s column because he subtracted the smaller number from the larger number regardless of its appearance in the subtrahend or minuend. Ray was not as interested in doing the math worksheet as he was in drawing jets and parachutes.
3. Contingency: Thirty minutes was not sufficient time to complete the worksheet.
4. Consequence: The teacher's instructions did not include a reinforcer for completing the paper.

This single observation analysis of Ray's work provided cues for modifying his next math assignment. The teacher had many options from which to choose; for example:

1. Stimulus: The teacher could make a worksheet with fewer problems, or circle only some of the problems on a full page which Ray is to complete.
2. Response: The teacher could tutor Ray in the new concept, giving him opportunities to use manipulative aids for understanding the units, 10s, and 100s concept.
3. Contingency: The teacher could provide more task completion time.
4. Consequence: The teacher could provide a reinforcer such as a sheet of drawing paper and colored pencils for Ray to complete his jet drawings.

Ray's next math assignment can be the result of the teacher's conscientious selection of a specific variable(s). The teacher could: (a) reteach the concept, providing experiences in using manipulative aids for understanding the concept of units, 10s and 100s; (b) provide a handmade worksheet with a fewer number of problems; and (c) provide a sheet of drawing paper and pencils for Ray's drawings. Should the teacher proceed as described, one cannot know if only one variable would have changed Ray's responses; but during a student's initial months in a special education class, emphasis is on providing successful experiences — so the teacher may not be wise in always testing out only one variable at a time to determine its appropriateness. In some situations, the teacher should present a "package" of changed variables to ensure success.

CAUTIONS IN BEHAVIOR MODIFICATION

Students — particularly emotionally disturbed students who have academic and/or social problems — need to be understood before implementing techniques to bring about desired changes. If students are "listened to," teachers can be more astute in selecting intervention procedures. If behavior modification is used without (a) analyzing environmental conditions, (b) assessing the student's developmental growth stages, and (c) planning in advance, behavior modification practices can have deleterious efects on the student. Behavior modification accompanied by sensitivity, however, can bring about successful experiences to enhance a student's growth.

SUMMARY

Behavior modification is another procedure used to implement the concept of *structure*. It often is of greatest value during the student's initial months in a special program, when external controls are needed as new behaviors are acquired. The procedure is not an entity unique to educating disturbed youth — it sets forth techniques that can be used to individualize any student's program. Its strength is in its integration with other procedures. The use of behavior modification also causes changes in the teacher's behavior which in turn causes changes in the students — an ongoing procedure.

BIBLIOGRAPHY

Addison, Roger, and Homme. Lloyd, "The Reinforcing Event (RE) Menu," *National Society for Programmed Instructional Journal* 5 (1966): 8-9.

Axelrod, Saul. *Behavior Modification for the Classroom Teachers*. New York: McGraw-Hill, 1977.

Gallagher, Patricia. *Recording Classroom Performances: Techniques for Recording Behavior*. Sioux Falls, SD: Adapt Press, 1975.

Gallagher, Patricia. "Behavior Modification? Caution!," *Academic Therapy* 11 (1976): 357-363.

Homme, Lloyd. *How to Use Contingency Contracting in the Classroom*. Champaign, IL: Research Press, 1970.

Krumboltz, John D., and Krumboltz, Helen. *Changing Children's Behavior*. Englewood Cliffs, NJ: Prentice-Hall, 1972.

Lindsley, Odgen. "Direct Measurement and Prothesis of Retarded Behavior," *Journal of Education* 147 (1964): 62-81.

MacMillan, Donald. *Behavior Modification in Education*. New York: Macmillan Co., 1973.

Meacham, Merle, and Wiesen, Allen. *Changing Classroom Behavior: A Manual for Precision Teaching*. Scranton, PA: International Textbook Company, 1969.

Ross, Alan. "The Application of Behavior Principles in Therapeutic Education," *Journal of Special Education* 1 (1967): 275-286.

Whelan, Richard, and Haring, Norris. "Modification and Maintenance of Behavior through Systematic Application of Consequences," *Exceptional Children* 32 (1966): 281-289.

Zigler, Edward. "Research on Personality Structure in the Retardate." In *International Review of Research in Mental Retardation* (Vol. 1), edited by Norman R. Ellis. New York: Academic Press, 1966, pp. 77-107.

APPENDIX TO CHAPTER SIX

REINFORCER IDEAS FOR THE CLASSROOM

Verbal or Written Words, Symbols, Phrases, and Sentences

Teachers should emphasize the student's role by using statements beginning with *you* — "You really did it" rather than *we* statements ("We really did it"). First, the latter is erroneous when a student, not the student *and* teacher, did an activity; and, further, the *you* emphasis is one small technique to enhance students' self identification.

Teachers who offer social approval as a reinforcer should use a vocabulary that is meaningful to the student. In written comments, some teachers highlight key words, etc. with colored pens or pencils or special note paper. The following words and terms in themselves are reinforcing, or accompany other reinforcers. Although these words and phrases may be overused or objectionable in some adult circles, one cannot dispute their value as social reinforcers for children.

Fantastic!
Wonderful!
Super!
Out of sight!
All *right!*
That's very clever!

Imaginative!
Dynamite!
We're so proud of you!
This is a biggie!
Beautiful!
Great!

Social Interaction

—Helping the custodian in his duties.
—Telephone praise — the teacher makes a telephone "brag call" to the parent about a positive achievement of the day, with the student listening to the conversation.
—Popcorn film festival — students invite a class or special friend to the festival, fix popcorn, and share it with their guest(s).
—Helping other students in the class or in other rooms.
—Assisting teacher, coach, secretary, cook.
—Presenting a talent show.
—Showing work to a special adult (child care worker, counselor, building principal).
—Break time with a friend.

Body Proximity and Contact

After making sure that the student can accept proximity and/or contact as a positive act, the following are possible reinforcers:

—Patting a shoulder
—Hugging
—Walking along side of
—Placing arm around waist
—Sitting side-by-side
—Special handshakes
—Kneeling by a young student

Short-Term Activities

Short-term activities refer generally to those which can be enjoyed during a 15-minute period or discontinued at any point without loss of enjoyment. A small sampling includes:

—Using a View-Master™
—Reading horoscope books
—Binocular watching from windows, possibly recording observations such as climatic activity, animals, etc.
—Listening to records and tapes (provide headphones)

—Running errands
—Sharpening pencils for the class
—Playing card games
—Doing Spirograph drawings
—Thumbprint art, using ink pad and watercolors to create thumbprint
    animals such as rabbits, frogs, mice.
—Making junk sculptures
—Using a manual adding machine or typewriter

Long-Term Activities

Long-term activities usually require several hours for completion; they could be accomplished in an extended session or continued from session to session. Some of these are:

—Constructing crossword puzzles for someone else to complete
—Learning magic tricks to perform for the group
—Making macrame items
—Making recipe card files after collecting and selecting recipes
—Making psychedelic posters with irridescent paint
—Building a transistor radio
—Tinkering with an old radio, TV set, machine motor, bike
—Training a pet hamster or gerbil
—Sewing patches, emblems, or studs on jeans or jackets
—Staging a puppet show, using a hollowed out, discarded TV set

Materials

Reinforcers can be almost anything. Some time-proven examples are:

—Postcards with special messages
—Drinking mugs with student drawings on side of container
—Wild colored paper for assignments
—Pencils imprinted with student names
—Plants
—Paper clips
—Paper (construction, drawing, graph, art, wrapping, etc.)

—Miniature soldiers, cars, furniture, appliances
—Jumping beans
—Cosmetics
—T-shirts

Awards and Privileges

Some of the more effective reinforcers include:

—Having one's name on the "Brag" list
—Student teacher for a day (involves correcting papers and answering others' questions)
—Super Citizen award. (Take Polaroid pictures of student; display or give to student. Present a trophy.)
—Wearing a teacher's watch for the day after learning how to tell time.
—Early dismissal
—Longer lunch period
—Washable tattoos
—Lunch, snack, or dinner with teacher
—Skipping study hall

Food Items

If food is a necessary reinforcer, nutritional food is preferred over "junk" food. Provide food that is consumed readily. Avoid foods like hard candy, gum, and caramels if work activity immediately follows. A caution: Students could be enjoying the food and acting inappropriately at the same time; hence, the student in this situation is receiving reinforcement for inappropriate behavior. Also, be sure a student is not diabetic, allergic, or has other health-related factors that prohibit using certain foods. Some suggestions:

Cereal	Marshmallows
Raisins	Flavored, colored ice-cubes
Peanuts	Celery filled with peanut butter or cheese spread
Animal Crackers	Crackers
Ice Cream	Fruit Juice

224

RESOURCES FOR REINFORCERS

Tangible reinforcers, again, could be almost anything. Teachers who wish to invest a little more effort, time, and dollars, could consider some of the following:

Costume jewelry	Postcards
Badges	View-Master™ Sets
Games	Small puzzles
Posters	Washable tattoos
Drinking mugs	

Some of these items are available in any dimestore; others can be ordered from the sources given below.

Brilliant Enterprises "Pot-Shot" postcards are colorful, meaningful contemporary cards; 931 different sayings, include themes of love, life, reality, health, travel, friendship, religion, you and me, family, marriage, and politics. Examples: "Life is a very special occasion"; "Don't be afraid to give some of yourself away. It will all grow back"; "When last seen, I was heading in a circular direction." For a small fee, the company will mail a catalog of titles plus 10 cards in a starter set. 117 W. Valerio St., Santa Barbara, CA 93101.

Constructive Playthings A free 96-page *Carnival Catalog* provides information about ordering small items to be used as classroom rewards (rings, badges, games, carnival-style items). 1040 E. 85th St., Kansas City, MO 64131.

Creative Teaching Press, Inc. Has scratch 'n sniff labels containing fragrances such as orange, rootbeer, candycane, strawberry. Labels are circular, worded "well done" or "good work" and available in two fragrances per package. 5305 Production Lane, Huntington Beach, CA 92649.

Doodle Art Distributors Doodle Art posters come in various sizes and subjects; fine-tipped Doodle Art pens can be purchased separately. 208 W. Third St., Mansfield, OH 44902.

Grant Photos, Inc. Has a wide variety of posters from which to choose: art reproductions, travel posters, NFL posters, personalities in American History, animals, "concern" posters, months of the year, and world neighbors. Request brochure, which contains miniature illustrations of the posters. Box 406, Rockford, IL 61105.

Kiddie Kreations Mugs — A special kit provides enough die-cut drawing paper to make up to 50 drawings. Designs can utilize many materials — crayons, oil, watercolors, felt tip pens, etc. When completed, the drawings are mailed to this company, which uses the designs to make thermal insulated mugs. (Mug charges and postage constitute additional fee.) 4301 Lasher Rd., Bloomfield Hills, MI 48013.

Lectro-Stik Corp. Stikki-Wikkis are self-clinging building sticks that can be bent into any shape. The ends of the stick are covered with a wax that never hardens. 3721 Broadway, Chicago, IL 60613.

School Service Co. Happy Stamps — Small stamps that fit over the end of a pencil and do not require ink are available in a variety of designs including Happy Face, Panda, Sylvester, Road Runner, etc. 647 S. LaBrea, Los Angeles, CA 90036.

Teech-Um Co. Has Winner Circles — colorful pre-stick badges for achievement, illustrated to accompany their wording. Available: Happy Face, Good Worker, I Know My _____ , Busy Bee, Bookworm, Super Star, Math Whiz, Good Citizen, Reading Whiz, Good Helper, Happy Birthday, and blank badges. P.O. Box 4232, Overland Park, KS 66204.

Walter Drake Company Photo Puzzle — A jigsaw puzzle can be made from a color or black-and-white photo. The firm returns the photo along with the die-cut puzzle. 94 Drake Bldg., Colorado Springs, CO 80901.

SEVEN

SCHEDULING

- Schedule Guidelines
- Daily Scheduling Techniques
- Appendix to Chapter 7
  Vignettes

SCHEDULING

Scheduling is a procedure in the structured approach that provides the framework for progression of classroom activities. The procedure is comprised of guidelines, each establishing a hierarchy of phases through which the student advances. The guidelines presented here are designed to expedite the teacher's interference with debilitating effects of the student's previous classroom failures and ineffectual, interpersonal experiences and to maximize the student's opportunities for appropriate behaviors and personal successes.

Behaviorally disordered youth must be recipients of systematic planning so that their work is accomplished in an organized manner toward a final goal which, for many students, is their return to the mainstream of peer group activities, after acquiring the skills necessary to participate responsibly and with inner satisfaction in society. Some of the guidelines help students achieve autonomy in group interaction skills. Other guidelines prepare students to participate in regular classroom environments. Still other guidelines help establish a success pattern that can be maintained by natural reinforcers and, in some cases, intrinsic motivation. In each guideline, students are encouraged and expected to be responsible for their actions and their consequences. The teacher's knowledge of the five previous procedures — pre-academic year planning, educational diagnosis, selecting and adapting educational materials, programming, and behavior modification — is a requisite to implementation of the scheduling procedure.

Of course, students progress at varied rates and frequently are in phases different from their peers on the guidelines' continua. For example, in one special classroom of eight primary aged, emotionally disturbed children, the students varied in their abilities to function in

229

group situations. One guideline states: *Instruction Directed To Individual Student Is Prepared For a Group Of Students.* For this young group, the guideline was implemented as follows: Doug, Peggy, Mac, and Jody did all basic reading activities individually with the teacher, followed by independent activities. Mac joined Mark for oral reading; Steve and Kim were paired for all reading activities; Randy read with a regular class. This same guideline for another subject area did not have the same groupings for these students. Figure 7.1 is an example of the students' placement on a continuum.

Even if an entire special class was in the same phase on a guideline continuum, the students likely would not be engaged in the same activities. For example, one technique in Guideline 3 suggests that short work periods be extended to longer work periods. All of the students may require short work periods, and for three students this may mean that each can work independently for five minutes. One of these students may work on a paper and pencil activity; another may work on a coloring paper, and another may read orally to the teacher. Each student has five minutes of work (which is the same phase of the guideline — short work period); however, the work itself is different. No restriction exists to the creativeness by which the teacher implements the guidelines. Ingenuity, knowledge of curriculum materials, and a sensitivity to students' needs are highly desirable skills. How can a task as small as a student's five-minute coloring activity entail creativity? A cursory glance at the variables considered in this five-minute activity reveals the teacher's ingenuity. Since a teacher knew that a student has extreme difficulty

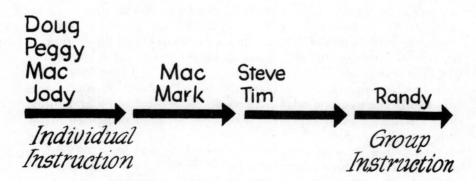

Fig. 7.1. Student placement on a guideline continua.

coloring within outlines, liked airplanes and other flying objects, and that cartoons were a favorite pastime, she provided a simple picture of a Mickey Mouse balloon, heavily outlined with a black pen, and replaced the regular sized crayons with primary ones. A visitor walking into the classroom scarcely would take note of the task, but the teacher knew that the work had been individualized and scheduled for a five-minute period, and the student knew he could successfully complete it during that time. Many of these short work periods were planned before the time span was extended.

The twelve scheduling guidelines that follow are based on a student's progression from the initial days of special classroom placement to the final days. This progression could occur in one academic year, but the time varies. Some students may require more years of special help and others may advance at a faster rate. Further, not all students begin in the same phases of the guideline continua. The student's level of academic instruction and personal development are the main determinants for placement on each continuum.

SCHEDULE GUIDELINES

The following guideline statements suggest techniques that can be used from the beginning to the final days of a student's program. Ideas for guiding the student's progression through each continuum also are presented.

Guideline 1 — Extend Day-By-Day Planning to Advance Planning

Initially, the teacher does not schedule for a week or a month in advance but, rather, plans day-by-day for each student, basing each succeeding day's activities on the student's current day's performance. Perhaps a student will encounter unexpected difficulties when presented with a new concept; for example, reversing integers in the multiplication process. The followup activity would be postponed until the student would gain understanding of the mathematical process. The teacher's instruction could be rescheduled for the following day. Perhaps a student may be so withdrawn one morning that he or she is unable to function adequately on the assigned tasks. If the teacher had scheduled a week's activities in advance, repeated adjustments would be necessary. Many

231

emotionally disturbed students' behaviors are unpredictable during their initial weeks and months in a program; thus, the teacher is more efficient in planning lessons on a day-by-day basis. At a later time, weekly plans are possible.

Once the teacher has projected a day's work for each student, another important aspect of scheduling — time distribution — becomes apparent. A plan book can be divided into areas for each student's work activities, indicating where teacher instruction and contact time with aides, volunteers, or student tutors are needed. For example, one student may be scheduled to receive instruction before proceeding to completion of a task; some students are working on their individually planned tasks; and still others are working with the aide. Students and adults alike must know with whom and when designated activities occur. No two days are exactly alike regarding distribution of time.

During the initial weeks of a new program, events that can interrupt the class schedule (like visitors) should be avoided until the students are familiar with the routine. Sometimes a day's routine, carefully planned, is interrupted suddenly by unforeseen incidents such as a student's temper tantrum, followed by another student's crying, while the teacher is occupied with yet another student. When these unanticipated incidents occur, they are resolved and the schedule is resumed, but the original schedule may need readjustment before it is resumed.

Guideline 2 — Prepare Instruction Directed to Individual Students for a Group of Students

Because every student presents a myriad of responses which frequently are dissimilar from the peers', the student's materials and instruction have to be individualized. The student's responses may vary within and between academic subjects. A brief sketch illustrates this point: Fifteen-year-old students usually perform at the junior high level; however, one fifteen-year-old emotionally disturbed girl had the following skills: (a) oral reading and comprehension at grade level; (b) arithmetic, a threatening subject even though it was planned for her instruction level, fourth grade; (c) grammar skills at the sixth grade level; and (d) creative writing and poetry at the adult level.

Or, consider the possibility that two students would be at the same reading level and use the same curriculum materials; one may read at an average rate but cannot manage an interruption while reading, and the other student may read slowly and methodically. To present the same lesson simultaneously and expect the same behaviors is anathema, especially if either student is intolerant of the other's individuality.

Grouping begins whenever the teacher observes an opportunity for two students to engage in an activity. Perhaps two students can work at opposite ends of a large work table when they have an art project to complete; or three students can respond to a chalkboard lesson and then proceed individually on seatwork assignments. As different combinations of grouping present themselves, the network enlarges and the technique is expanded to involve more students. Group instruction for students performing at the same grade level then becomes possible.

Some special classes have a daily group period in which grade level is not the critical variable. The group period may consist of a discussion on current events or feelings; work on art or science projects; listening to the teacher read a storybook, novel, biography, poetry, or play; participating in music activities; or playing board and card games. Many teachers begin group activities with the students remaining at their desks. If the desks are located in study carrels, students turn their desks to face the center of the room. Gradually, the physical distance is narrowed and physical properties are omitted until students eventually learn to sit on the floor in groups, sit at large tables for a group project, or stand in a circle with joined hands. During the final phase of this guideline, the activities closely resemble those in a regular classroom.

Guideline 3 — Extend Short Work Periods and Small Task Steps to Longer Work Periods and Larger Task Steps

Tasks often must be scheduled into mini-assignments. A student having the ability to succeed on a 40-minute social studies assignment that includes reading factual information, answering comprehension questions, using map skills, and writing a short, creative passage may not be able to stay with that task for a 40-minute period. Thus, the teacher can break the task into short sessions which the student can tolerate. Subsequent lessons in social studies should be continued in this manner, with time increased by increments until the student can work longer periods. Other students may need short work periods because they are not developmentally mature or because they lack the skills necessary to proceed on lengthy or complicated assignments.

Task complexity rather than time may be a student's academic hurdle. The procedure of programming, breaking a task into incremental steps, can be used to enable a student to proceed in a series of mini-tasks that lead to completion of the final goal. Time and task complexity are stretched gradually to assure that the student has the tolerance to function commensurate with ability.

Some students become overwhelmed by the physical presence of materials, especially hardbacked textbooks and workbooks. Many classroom ideas have been conceived to distribute the workload so the student perceives the work as being possible to do. One idea is to remove all materials from the student's desk and locate these things in another part of the room; the student can pick up the materials for one assignment at a time. Or, using "in" and "out" file trays, work to be completed is placed in one tray and completed work in the other.

Worksheets can be torn from consumable workbooks so the physical appearance of a workbook is not defeating; or worksheets can be subdivided into sections and presented one at a time to the student. One teacher cut each arithmetic worksheet into individual problems until the student was capable of completing a single row of problems, then half pages, and ultimately the entire page. When worksheets are cut into smaller portions, the completed sections can be glued to a piece of cardboard in increments until the entire worksheet is completed. The student can then keep the cardboard as evidence of his or her efforts. Some teachers omit hardbacked texts from the curriculum by presenting all materials in softbacked books or folders. Seeing small amounts of work accumulated into larger amounts often pleases students, in realizing how much work actually has been accomplished.

Guideline 4 — Arrange Individual Work Areas into Group Work Areas

A feature of the individual's program is the individual work area. One specific arrangement consists of each student's desk and chair placed in a designated area, which may or may not be partitioned from the other individual work areas. These work stations frequently are referred to as "offices." Various methods can be used to enclose work areas, including portable wooden or cardboard partitions placed between desks, study carrels, or cardboard partitions temporarily attached to the desk. Thus, the student is physically oriented to individual work activities and individual

instruction. The arrangement is designed to enhance a one-to-one pupil-teacher relationship. The reduction of visual stimuli resulting from the physical arrangement is beneficial to some students. Headphones or earplugs can be used to reduce audio stimuli, if necessary. Care should be taken, however, to assure that individual study arrangements are not abused. In some situations, students have been assigned inappropriately to carrels as a means of punishment. Special classes should give top priority to individuality and helping the students view their physical arrangment as an aid to overcoming academic hurdles. Individual work areas are physical reminders that individuality reigns.

If a student does all the academic work in an individual work area, he or she must have legitimate reasons for leaving it and moving around the room. One reason could be a requirement to place completed tasks on the teacher's desk. Another successfully employed technique has been to place "in" and "out" baskets (such as two-tiered file trays) in a certain location, such as on a work counter, table, or bookshelf, but far enough away from individual work areas so that the students must walk to and from them. The students need their own work spaces, but they also need legitimate reasons for moving about. Execution of this principle relies upon the teacher's resourcefulness.

The teacher also should watch for opportunities to place students in close proximity. Perhaps two students could have their desks located adjacent to each other for a spelling test, or four students could convene at a large table if a student is located at either end of the table and the other two are seated across from each other. Although the students are seated together at one table, they each have a separate work area.

Gradually, the individual work area arrangement is abandoned and the grouping of physical property is established. Some classes retain several individual work areas for students who prefer to work privately on certain activities.

Guideline 5 — Reduce Curriculum Adaptations and Include Regular Class Material

During the initial months of placement in special self contained classrooms, curriculum materials are adapted to a greater extent to meet needs of individual students. When the adaptations include selection or construction of materials different from those used in the regular classroom where the student will be mainstreamed, the student should be guided into using these materials (such as hardback textbooks and workbooks) and participating in activities associated with the materials (such as taking lecture notes and learning new concepts from large group instruction). Many special education teachers obtain copies of the materials that will be used in the receiving classroom and introduce them into the student's educational program as the last link in the chain of curriculum adaptations before the student is transferred to the regular classroom.

Guideline 6 — Change Definite Class Periods to Flexible Periods

Initially, every minute of the student's class time is scheduled, with few deviations. Each student should have an established routine upon entry into the room. For example, when the students walk into the class, they should know where to place wraps, homework, notes, forms, and other items. The student then follows the established schedule. If reading is the first activity, then English — that order is maintained. If the student uses a thin, soft lead pencil, that remains the writing tool. The student is not left in a quandry about behavioral expectations and should not be in doubt as to when a daily activity will occur. After the student becomes familiar and comfortable with the schedule, independence can be assumed because the routine is known and the student is not left guessing about what to do and not to do.

The definite work periods, however, eventually should be replaced with flexible class periods. The teacher must be alert to initiating a shift in the student's routine, which could be a simple substitution of a different stimuli for the same lesson format. For example, the teacher's handmade handwriting lesson might be replaced with a workbook page; an English period could be replaced with an extended reading lesson; a special event such as a school assembly or a birthday party could be substituted for some of the routine activities. Thus, the student is guided in the direction of flexibility.

Guideline 7 — Expand Teacher Planned Activities to Include Student Planned Activities

The teacher plans the daily assignments, selects and adapts the materials, and instructs the students. During the initial days of a program, some students may require a miniscule plan for some activities, as exemplified by a nine-year-old girl's actions: Susan had completed a series of short work periods which totaled an hour of work, and had earned 15 minutes of free time. She went to the play area, where she selected a large sheet of drawing paper and a box of crayons. During the entire free time, Susan repeatedly fondled each crayon. As soon as she brought one crayon close to the paper, she replaced it with another. Susan was upset when her 15 minutes were over, protesting, "I didn't have my free time. I didn't color my picture!" After an on-the-spot counseling session, the teacher required Susan to return to her schedule; but that evening the teacher developed another free time plan. If Susan were to earn 15 minutes of free time the next day and again decided to color, the teacher would direct her to draw, with a red crayon, Susan's favorite color. Susan did earn the free time, went to the play area, and selected a large sheet of drawing paper. The teacher suggested that she use a red crayon. Susan executed the entire picture in red and proudly displayed the finished product. Subsequently, the teacher suggested two colors, red and blue, whenever Susan selected coloring as her free time activity. The progressive suggestion of additional colors continued until Susan's repertoire consisted of eight colors. Eventually, her ability to choose from a small assortment of colors grew until she was able to make her own selection from a box of 24 crayons. Susan had learned how to make choices. In this example, the teacher initially provided definitive directions, which steadily diminished.

The student can be introduced incrementally to planning activities. The student's initial planning can be as simple as selecting records to be played for the noon hour activity, selecting a physical activity for the morning exercise, or selecting the order in which daily assignments are completed. Then the student can begin planning work in one academic subject. Experience tells us that junior high and senior high students plan too much work for themselves when they first begin scheduling their work. Hence, consultation with the teacher after students plan for their academic subject(s) is advisable. Eventually, some students plan their entire schedule. After students have engaged in planning an operable schedule, they have their own framework for an efficient and rewarding work routine.

Guideline 8 — Replace Teacher Supervision of All Activities at Times With Students' Self Supervision

The teacher must act as the cohesive element in a diverse, often fragmented atmosphere that can exist with a group of behaviorally disordered children. In addition to teaching, the teacher spends time making observations for intervention cues and scheduling changes; umpiring incidents, intervening when negative contagion or crises develop; and supporting egos when anxiety arises. Some behaviors, if not interfered with, can be catastrophic for a student. Thus, the teacher must be available at all times. This, of course, places heavy demands on teachers' time.

Fortunately, the aforementioned situations do not prevail throughout the year. Their frequency diminishes when the students learn self-control skills and alternate solutions to problems; students also learn to proceed with the day's schedule when an adult figure is not present. Early in the program, a student's needs may require the teacher's presence in the form of physical contact. This contact can be changed gradually to close proximity, and later extended to greater distances. The student begins to realize that a teacher is not needed at all times. Occasionally, the teacher can step out of the classroom for brief periods, and these intervals can be lengthened as the student gains independence and self-direction. At some point, students learn to monitor their own behavior without the teacher's presence.

Guideline 9 — Phase Students Into the Special Class and Out to Regular Classes

If a new group of students is scheduled to enter a special classroom, the students should be enrolled in successive order, with an interim period between each student's entrance. When disturbed youth enter a special class, they usually need much attention. Each student should receive individual orientation to the classroom structure and guidance in the routine, support for feelings of anxiety, bewilderment or fear, and understanding for feelings of hostility. The teacher, having specially designed the student's activities based on the individual educational program goals and objectives, needs time to establish the program to determine its effectiveness. After each student has made some adjustments, another student is introduced to the classroom. Again, the same planning and support is required. Phasing in also gives the teacher the time necessary to prepare in a maximum way for each new student.

Phasing out is the technique by which a student is introduced into the mainstream of regular class activities. Frequently, the decision to begin the process is based on the student's demonstration of a skill(s) that

240

will enable successful participation with some of the nonhandicapped students. Science may be the ideal subject for one student's integration; with another student, science may never be an area of interest, let alone a skill. No hard and fast rule applies to the day or month when all students with behavioral disorders are phased out of special classes. Usually, the phasing out process begins as soon as a student reaches grade level on any one skill and reaches a point at which some failure can be accepted. Some students, however, are phased out initially for specific activities within a content area because of their interests and good verbal skills only. Others are phased out to special activities such as art, music, and physical education, in which academic skills are not required. The special student's behavior and opportunities for interaction with peers are the most significant clues in a decision to begin phasing into a regular class. The guideline as discussed here, of course, can be implemented only if it is in accordance with the individualized education program (IEP).

Guideline 10 — Transform Materialistic Reinforcers into Natural Reinforcers

Emotionally disturbed students are removed from typical classroom settings and placed in special environments for many reasons, including their inability to understand, cope with, or receive the benefits of natural reinforcers such as teacher and peer approval, report card grades, positive social comments, visible evidence of progress, sense of mastery, and satisfaction of learning. These types of reinforcers either lost or never had influence in bringing about desirable behaviors in the student. Therefore, extrinsic reinforcers are used to motivate the student toward desirable academic and social behaviors. Sometimes, even money or holidays from school are used as reinforcers. But materialistic reinforcers are only a means to achieve the use of natural reinforcers. Materialistic reinforcers can set into motion desirable behaviors so often missing from the student's repertoire. After the student acquires the desired behaviors, the teacher should begin the shift to natural reinforcers.

Use of extrinsic reinforcers varies among students. One student may need materialistic reinforcers for 80 percent of his or her efforts, and another student may need extrinsic reinforcers for only 20 percent of the work.

Using extrinsic reinforcers for all of a student's behavior is a cardinal error when a student is capable of handling higher levels of reinforcers.

If a student is enjoying success or seeking appropriate peer approval for accomplishments in an academic area, for example, and the teacher provides tangible reinforcers, the student is regressed to a primary level of reinforcement. The teacher has a responsibility to be constantly alert to the student's needs along the reinforcement continuum. Selection, amount, and provision of extrinsic and natural reinforcers should be reviewed continually.

Guideline 11 — Present Reinforcers on a Fixed Schedule Followed by a Variable Schedule of Reinforcement

During the early stages of the academic program when students are acquiring many new behaviors, they should receive reinforcement on a fixed schedule; that is, once the duration or frequency of a response is determined, it is followed by a reinforcer for each correct math problem or for one minute of attention. The technique is designed to give students a backlog of success by accenting many responses. The student probably has been a failure either in school, with society, or self, and may not be able to perform adequately or appropriately without receiving something "extra" for the work.

Perhaps many failure experiences have been associated with errors on a completed worksheet; if reinforcement had been presented for each item, the margin of error could have been reduced. A fixed ratio is suggested until the student achieves a level at which change is indicated; that is, the student works a pre-selected number of responses before the reinforcer becomes available. For example, a student receives reinforcement for each row of completed math problems rather than for every problem; or for each paragraph, not each reading page. When a success pattern is established, the student is reinforced for varying amounts of completed work. The variable schedule then is used to maintain the behavior.

Guideline 12 — Shift from Immediate Presentation of Reinforcers to their Long-range Presentation

During the beginning days of a student's enrollment in a special class, immediate presentation of reinforcers is recommended strongly. The importance of immediate reinforcement cannot be overemphasized. A classroom situation illustrates the necessity of avoiding a time lapse in presentation of reinforcers: A student working on a reading task shot paper wads while the teacher instructed another student. Following completion of the task, the student received reinforcement for the reading task. If this student could not perceive the relationship between behaviors and their consequences, the other behavior, shooting paper wads, also was reinforced. To avoid reinforcing wrong behavior, immediate reinforcement is imperative, but immediate presentation of reinforcers is often an impossible task for a teacher. Since the teacher is in contact with myriads of behavior, immediate reinforcement is aproximated (given as soon as possible). Many teachers have their aides assist in presenting reinforcers. Knowing that the reinforcement is delayed, the teacher or aide should accompany presentation of reinforcers with acknowledgment of the recipient behavior.

Assume that a student is scheduled to receive a reinforcer for each one-half hour of work but the teacher or aide is delayed in presenting the reinforcer. When the reinforcer is given, the behavior is acknowledged; for example: "Great, Lee, you completed your punctuation page in the scheduled half hour of time." Had Lee acted inappropriately in the interim of waiting for the reinforcer, he would be less likely to confuse the wrong behavior with the recipient one if it is clarified.

Immediate presentation of reinforcers is necessary whenever possible until the student progresses through a systematic delay of reinforcers and is able to wait for reinforcers presented after longer intervals. The student needs to learn to accept delayed reinforcement because long-range and intermittent reinforcers prevail in our society. In most regular classrooms, approving comments are intermittent; graded papers are returned at the end of the day, the following day, or end of the week; report cards are distributed every six to nine weeks. Consequently, the adjustment to delayed reinforcers should be considered before the student is fully integrated into the regular classroom.

DAILY SCHEDULING TECHNIQUES

The following techniques are suggested as aids in effectively carrying out daily activities scheduled for the group and each student. These techniques are most meaningful for students during their initial months of a program.

243

1—*Provide each student with a daily schedule.* The format depends upon the student's level of understanding. Many teachers design a schedule using a subject or time block format. Duplicated copies of the schedules are made in advance, completing sections as they pertain to each student. Teachers also save the individual schedule sheets because they provide an excellent record of each student's progress. The forms for two daily schedules are given in Figure 7.2.

Intermediate, junior, and senior high students can have their daily schedules placed on their desks, or on a clipboard hanging from a hook attached to the side of the desk, or taped to a side of the study carrel. For primary children, the work can be placed in a series of folders representing time blocks. Non-readers can have their worksheets numbered within the folders, according to the order in which they are to be completed. Numbered slips of paper can be attached to materials which cannot be easily placed inside the folders, such as books, manipulative aids, or filmstrips. Regardless of the format, each student receives a daily schedule of activities and, thus, expectations and order of activities are known in advance. Students may not always like the work to be completed, but they know what is planned and what the options are. There is little room for argument since the schedule is a "black and white" arrangement. The teacher can make adjustments if circumstances indicate the need for on-the-spot rescheduling. Inherent in the schedule is careful teacher planning for work geared to each student's current level of ability and the amount of teacher instruction necessary for guidance in the daily work.

2—*Alternate high probability tasks with low probability tasks.* The Premack principle can be used with regularity — that is, of any two responses, the one that is more likely to occur is the preferred response (high probability behavior). It can reinforce the lesser frequent response (low probability behavior). If, of two academic subjects, reading is preferred to mathematics, reading is the high probability behavior and is scheduled after math. The student's preferred and less preferred activities are scheduled alternately. If a student has no preferred academic activities, favorite non-academic activities can be scheduled as high probability behaviors.

3—*Schedule work that can be finished by the end of the school day.* Students need the opportunity to begin each day with a "fresh slate." This technique appears to reduce anxiety in some students because they do not have a long period in which to worry about any of their previous day's unfinished work. They know where they stand before

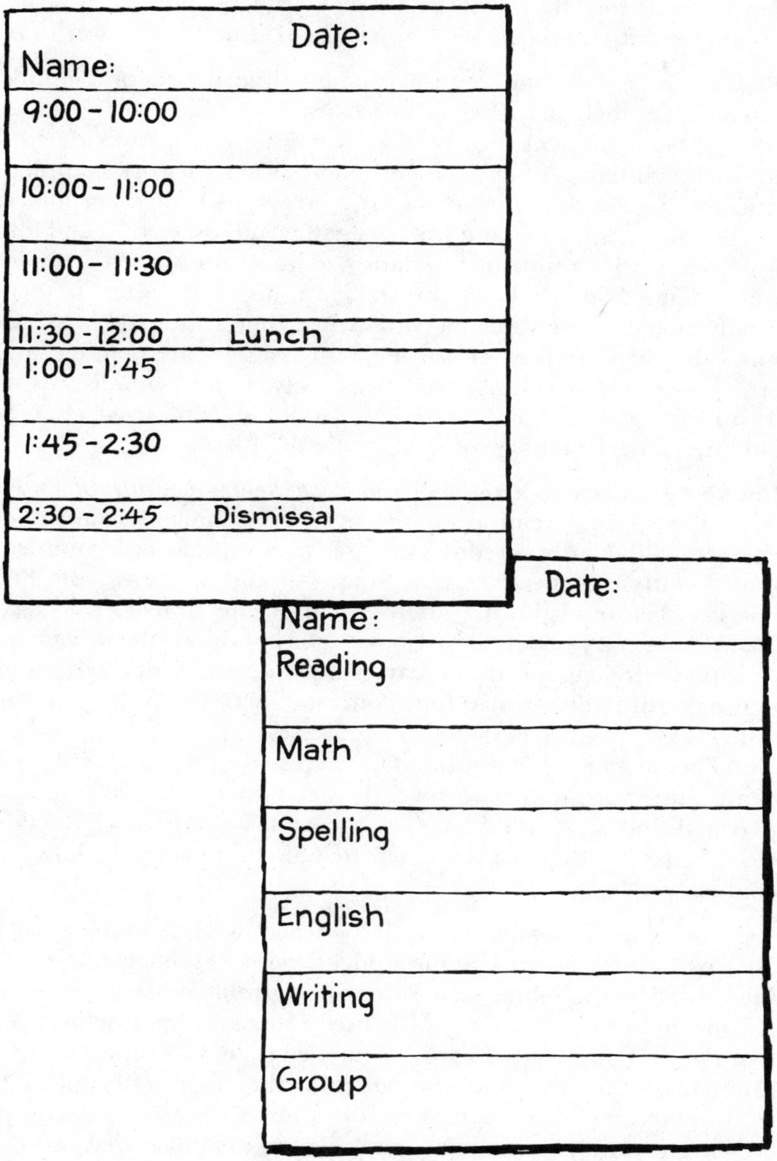

Date:	
Name:	
9:00 – 10:00	
10:00 – 11:00	
11:00 – 11:30	
11:30 – 12:00	Lunch
1:00 – 1:45	
1:45 – 2:30	
2:30 – 2:45	Dismissal

Date:
Name:
Reading
Math
Spelling
English
Writing
Group

Fig. 7.2.   Two forms for daily schedules.

they leave at the end of the school day. Students have been heard to say after a difficult day, "Well, tomorrow I can start all over again."

4—*Plan for leeway time.* After estimating the time needed for the students to complete their activities, allow extra time for feedback and new concept development. Also allow time to cover unexpected but inevitable situations such as legitimate delays in work completion, students having difficulty in putting on wraps, collecting materials to take home, students and teachers gathering loose ends, and for the teacher's overly optimistic estimation of time commitments. Students' time planned to the last minute before dismissal often is to their disadvantage. Some students panic when they anticipate missing the bus; others rush in their efforts to finish assignments, making careless errors — and thus ending a day negatively. In allowing leeway time, a student's work occasionally will not be completed, but such situations can be managed on an individual basis.

5—*Require students to complete one task before beginning another.* Reinforcers, time reminders, physical environment arrangements, and individual daily schedules are used to encourage task completion. Additionally, a general rule of thumb should be conveyed: "Finish one task before beginning another." Jumping from task to task or completing only preferred tasks may compound a student's inability to cope with demands of the environment. Furthermore, the student may have difficulty or encounter confusion in resuming an incomplete task.

This technique is not intended to restrict work habits; after students integrate productive work habits into their lives and accrue personal and academic successes, they can become more flexible in work behavior. By that time, they are able to discern flexibility from confusion.

6—*Provide time reminders.* The daily schedule designates the times allotted for assignments. Some students need reminders as a result of inadequate work habits, time orientation problems, or other reasons. A concrete time reminder can be used in lieu of the teacher's verbal reminders. Thus, students are encouraged to monitor their time commitments. A kitchen timer can be set for the amount of time allotted to the assignment or the number of minutes remaining to complete an assignment. The audible sound of the timer also may serve as a stimulus that reminds students to continue working. Timers could be placed on students' desks or other location in the students' view.

Some students have carried set timers to the playground or free area as a physical reminder of the time allotted for their activities.

Individual cardboard clocks or clock faces stamped on paper can be used as time reminders for assignments or special periods when the student is to be out of the room. A colored felt pen could be used to outline, highlight, or underline special times on a student's daily schedule. Figure 7.3 gives samples of time reminders teachers have used in their classes.

7—*Don't assign additional work if tasks are completed ahead of schedule.* Should students complete work in advance of the assigned time, provide something pleasant or encourage them to seek out pleasurable activities. Do not have the student complete another assignment. If teachers give additional work, they are conveying the message: "When you have finished all your work, you'll just be given more." Students may begin to gauge the planned work accordingly and move at a slower pace, or may become so discouraged that work completion no

247

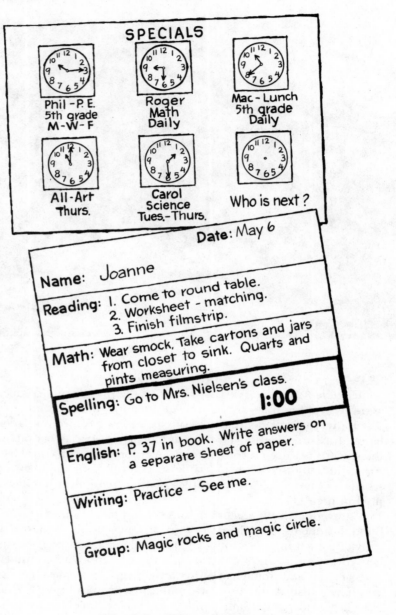

Fig. 7.3.   Time reminders.

longer will be maintained. Sometimes a student (usually one who has advanced along the guideline continua) will ask to go ahead on work, ask for homework, or pursue an academic related task. Encourage this type of endeavor, recognizing that such examples represent a concept different from the preceding statements.

8—*Plan ahead and anticipate student needs.* Many preventive and anticipatory measures can be considered to ease anxieties or facilitate activities. For example, if the room has no wash sink and the students enjoy creating with paints, paste, clay, chalk, etc., bring a bucket of water in the room; also, a bucket of water and old rags are handy for minor spills. If a student has planned to work with special materials, be sure that these materials are accessible.

9—*Establish expectations in advance and do not introduce unexpected activities.* If the daily routine is to be interrupted, do not let the students know too far in advance, but do tell them in time to avoid total surprises. Fire drills, birthday parties, and school assemblies are some activities that can over-excite students, but undue excitement can be reduced if announcement of the activity is well timed.

   The teacher also should discuss expected behaviors with the students. Students with emotional problems engage in unacceptable behaviors, sometimes unexpectedly and, when consequences are not established in advance, an endless match of wits can ensue if the teacher attempts to decelerate every new, inappropriate response. For example, if a student responds unexpectedly, by shouting a series of obscene words or smearing paint over walls and on another student, offer a plan. Briefly explain the inappropriateness of the behavior. Explain the future consequences of the behavior should it be repeated, and restate the existence of pleasant reinforcers that are always available when the student is engaged in appropriate behavior. Present the alternate choice and consequences of repeating or refraining from the behavior. If the inappropriate behavior occurs a second time, the teacher must be prepared to follow through with the consequence. Be sure the consequence is one that can be implemented. "Cleaning the room" is an empty consequence if it is not administered.

10—*Include feedback and evaluative marks with a student's daily schedule.* Some daily schedules are designed with space for comments. Other schedules are accompanied by an evaluation sheet. Students should receive written as well as verbal feedback throughout the day, along with evaluative information on separate forms at the end of the day or week. If parents or child care workers need more than

249

the planned feedback, teachers should provide it. The written feedback is in addition to individual conferences, phone calls, and group meetings. If tokens or points are used in the class and are representative of evaluative information (such as six tokens for an "A" grade), this information likewise should be shared.

11—*Provide positive feedback.* Many students have been subjected repeatedly to papers graded by checkmarks to indicate incorrect responses. Because the errors receive attention, the negative aspect of the work has been emphasized. A large number of errors on the page could result in an excruciating and debilitating experience. This negative grading technique can be reversed by marking all correct responses with *C* or *OK*. With some emotionally disturbed students, the correct responses may need to be highlighted further. A heavily outlined *C* or a large *OK* can be entered by the accurate responses, and a small checkmark or light underline can be used to indicate the wrong responses. And the teacher could stand beside the student and say, "Great," and "Good," or "OK" as a paper is graded. This additional feedback encourages students who are described as "defeated children." Smiling faces (☺) can be substituted for *C* marks on the papers of young children.

Only the number of correct responses should be indicated at the top of a worksheet, or the number correct could be written above the number wrong. Encouraging statements should be substituted for warning ones. Feedback, howevep, cannot be equated with reinforcement. Feedback is knowledge of results which may or may not be reinforcing. Some positive feedback ideas are shown in Figure 7.4.

SUMMARY

Scheduling guidelines provide the framework for progression of classroom activities and.techniques for implementing daily schedules. Students can be expected to "test" the schedules, but the teacher must maintain them until the students learn how to budget time and are able to positively direct their own structured and unstructured time. The scheduling procedure cannot be implemented until the teacher has a working knowledge of the other procedures in the structured approach. Since students progress through the continua of the scheduling guidelines, their final days in the special class differ markedly from their initial days. Thus, scheduling is another ongoing procedure accompanied by changes in the students and teacher.

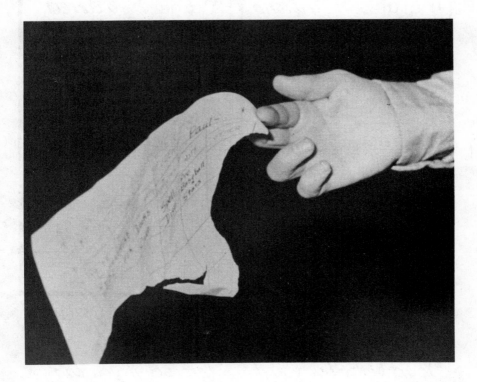

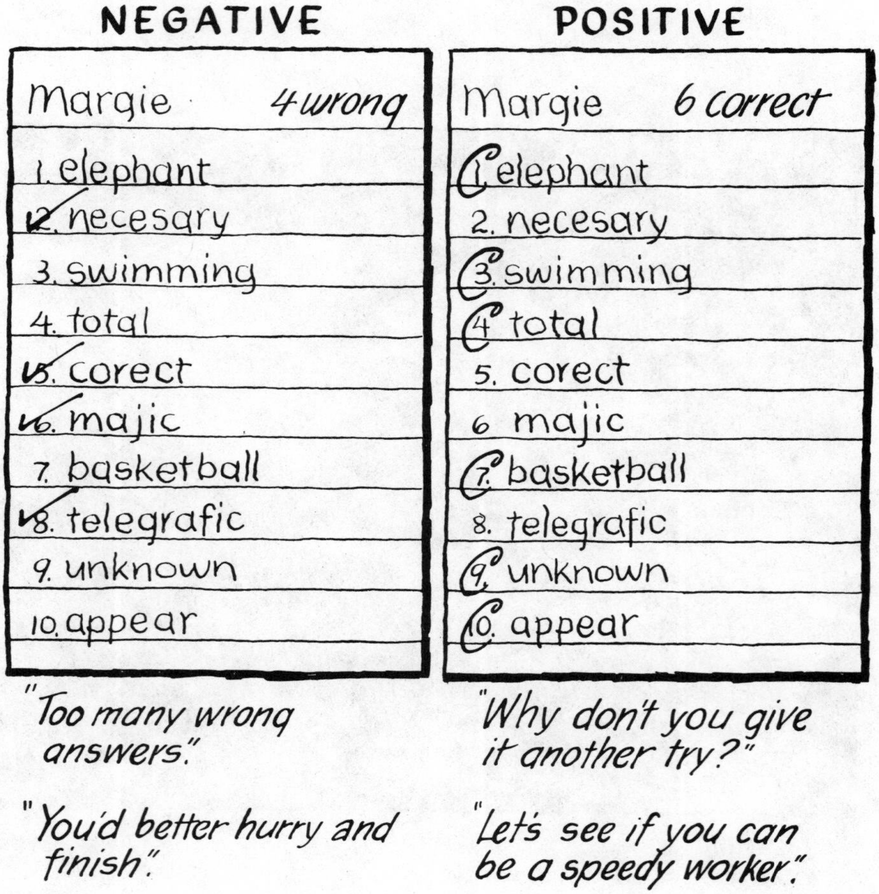

NEGATIVE	POSITIVE
Margie 4 wrong	**Margie** 6 correct
1. elephant	1. elephant
2. necesary	2. necesary
3. swimming	3. swimming
4. total	4. total
5. corect	5. corect
6. majic	6. majic
7. basketball	7. basketball
8. telegrafic	8. telegrafic
9. unknown	9. unknown
10. appear	10. appear

"Too many wrong answers."

"You'd better hurry and finish."

"Why don't you give it another try?"

"Let's see if you can be a speedy worker."

Fig. 7.4.   Positive vs. negative feedback.

252

APPENDIX TO CHAPTER SEVEN

VIGNETTES

The following three vignettes present actual class situations using techniques and guidelines described in the chapter. Illustrated material is italicized in the text.

Vignette 1 — Integration of Scheduling, Evaluation, and Feedback in a Special Self-Contained Primary Classroom

A primary class used different colored folders representing specific time periods for three daily work blocks. Sets of folders for each student were located in desk file trays stacked on a counter. The teacher numbered papers or task descriptions within the folders in their plan for completion. Usually, the aide assisted the students in their individual assignments while the teacher worked with students in groups. When the children successfully completed the tasks for each work block, they were free to use materials in the room or to participate in free time activities.

The children earned chips representing points for academic and social behaviors throughout the day. Bonus chips also could be earned. The students placed their chips in individual special containers on the teacher's desk whenever they wished; the teacher could remove chips from the container for inappropriate behaviors after a warning had been given. The teacher and aide kept an ongoing account of earned chips on a *recording form*. Near the end of the day, the students counted their chips, and each visited with the teacher to review the day's events. The *daily reports* were marked and given to the students to take home.

Date:	Dick	Beth	Don	Rollie	Floyd	Al	Mary
Beginning the day	2						
Block I	1 2 1 ④						
Recess	2						
Group Time	2 2 ④						
Block II	4						
Lunch Rest	2						
Block III	4						
Recess	2						
Group Time	4						
Ending the Day	2						
Total							

Daily Report

Name: Date:

                        Points Earned

Beginning the day	_____
Block I	_____
Group Time	_____
Recess	_____
Block II	_____
Lunch - Rest	_____
Block III	_____
Recess	_____
Group Time	_____
Ending the day	_____
Total	_____

Comments:

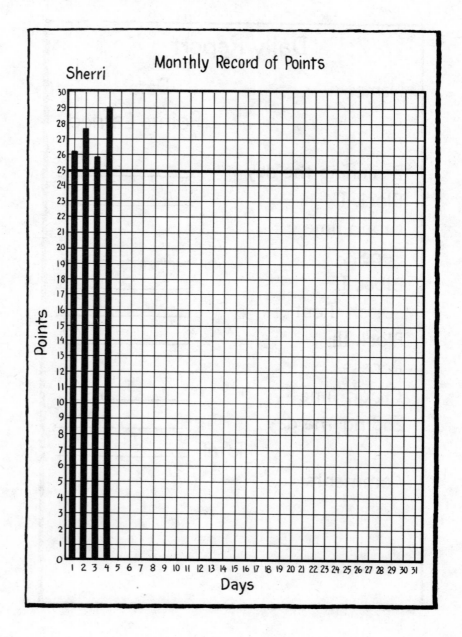

Students who earned 25 or more points received a paper happy face, a happy face on the daily report, and a small snack. They also colored the amount of earned points on a *bar graph* that was part of a permanent bulletin board display. The graphs changed once a month. The chips then were turned in to the teacher — they were not saved for long-range reinforcers.

The parents had been involved in conferences and were thoroughly acquainted with the evaluation system. They could discern how and where points were earned or not earned on the daily report.

These techniques were integrated in a classroom with prevailing empathic relationships, individual and group teaching, firmness in expectations, and consistent support. The teacher and aide were partners in this special primary classroom.

Vignette 2 — Integration of Scheduling, Evaluation, and Feedback in a Special Self-Contained Intermediate Classroom

An intermediate class used a week's *assignment schedule;* however, only one day's activities at a time were written on the schedule. The school day was subdivided into five major work periods, and the times associated with the work periods were written on the chalkboard. Students kept their schedules in their desks, along with a token *recording sheet* taped to the top of their desks.

Grades were given for academic behavior, and points were given for academic and social behaviors. The points could be used to buy free time or be saved for a previously agreed upon reward. A record of the unspent points was kept in a simulated savings *passbook*. Each student took home a *daily report*. That report and the savings book were marked at the end of the day, when the teacher and each student spent a few minutes reviewing the day's happenings. The passbooks were kept in a metal *"strong box."*

The teacher used a lesson plan book to plan daily activities, which then were marked on students' schedules. A *recording sheet* was kept for the students' earned points and grades.

These techniques were used in a classroom of seven highly aggressive boys who had individual programs consisting of remedial activities. Many curriculum motivation aspects embellished their assignments. The aide was largely responsible for the motivation features while the teacher interacted with the students in the academic and interpersonal domain.

ASSIGNMENT SCHEDULE

Date: _____

Student: _____

	READING	PHONICS	LANG. ARTS	SPELLING	MATH	OTHER
MON.	Read P. 37-45 W.B P.4	Homonyms crossword puzzle	Make a secret box for yourself & write 5 secrets.	Make Spelling list to take home.	Alphabet Math	
TUES.	Discuss 37-45 & design a book jacket	N P W U P.94	Write a story about the lonely snowman	Alphabetize spelling words	Boardwork with Mrs. McGuire (Multiplication)	
WED.						
THUR.						
FRI.						

Student's Daily Point Sheet

Name:
Date:

Academic	Reading	Phonics	Lang. Arts	Spelling	Math	Group	Bonus + Social Behaviors
Starting							
Finishing							
Following Directions							
Neatness						X	
Listening							
Working Quietly							
In Seat							
Raising hand							
On Task							
Out of Class							
Earned							
Spent							
Saved							
Comments:							

DAILY FEEDBACK REPORT_____	
READING	
PHONICS	
LANGUAGE ARTS	
SPELLING	
MATH	
OTHER	
POSSIBLE CREDITS	
TOTAL CREDITS	
BEHAVIOR REPORT	
NAME:	

Date	Amount Deposited	Amount Withdrawn	Balance	Initial

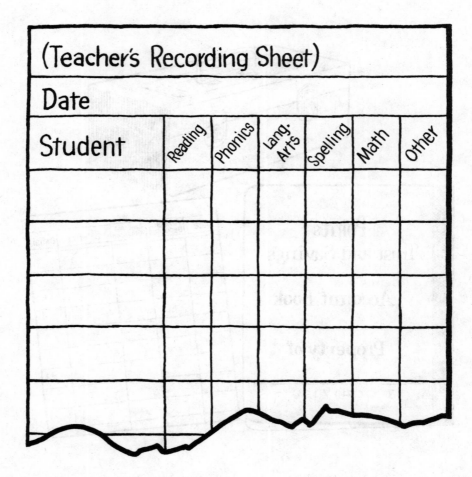

(Teacher's Recording Sheet)

Date

Student	Reading	Phonics	Lang. Arts	Spelling	Math	Other

Vignette 3 — Integration of Schedules, Evaluation, and Feedback in a Special High School Classroom

Adolescent girls in a residential setting used a weekly *contract sheet* for their schedules. The week was scheduled from Thursday to Wednesday so school performance could be tied into the availability of weekend passes. Girls were assigned to one of four homerooms, where they spent a major portion of their school time. They went to other rooms for science and electives, which included drama, basic sewing, furniture refinishing, typing, and sensory awareness. The teacher responsible for teaching a subject wrote the assignment on the contract form. Assignment percentages and points earned also were marked on the contract. At the end of the day, the teacher totaled the points earned and wrote a comment on the weekly *behavior chart* while the student wrote her evaluation comments on the contract.

In addition to earning points for academic behaviors, the students earned points for social behaviors in school, in residence with child care staff, and in recreation. A point committee with representatives from each discipline (child care, counseling, teaching, and the student group) determined how points were earned and spent. The point committee continually updated the point system. Each homeroom teacher kept a running account of points earned on a *daily record sheet*. Earned points always were recorded over points possible (e.g., 27/30).

At the end of the week (Wednesday) each student averaged the percentage grades from her contract and recorded them on a *weekly average percentage sheet*. The teacher rechecked the math and signed the form, which was kept in a specially marked folder until the end of the six-week grading period. At the end of six weeks, each student averaged all of her subjects for the marking period and completed a *six-week report* that was accompanied by *instructions on averaging* grades.

The weekly school progress report was used as feedback from teachers of girls attending neighboring high schools. The report was returned by the girl to her former homeroom teacher at the residential setting prior to the weekly meeting. In the weekly team meeting, the teacher shared this information, along with the homeroom reports, to other staff members.

The homeroom teacher completed a *weekly progress report* which each student shared with her counselor. The counselor signed the report and returned it to the teacher, who placed it in the special file folder with the schedule contracts and weekly average percentage sheets.

Teachers, child care workers, and recreation personnel made daily recordings on a weekly *behavior chart*. The charts could be seen by the students at any time and were kept on a clipboard (one clipboard per counselor) in the child care station except during the school day; during the school day the charts were kept in the homeroom, where teachers recorded earned points and wrote comments. The charts were color coded to facilitate daily sorting of homeroom charts. The counselors discussed the behavior charts with each of their girls and recorded significant behaviors in the girls' medical records.

At the end of the week (Thursday morning) a teacher or teacher's aide gathered the recordings of points earned and spent in all areas — recreation, school, and child care. This information was summarized and marked on each teacher's *total points sheet* at a weekly meeting attended by the entire staff. This meeting included discussions regarding the girls' eligibility for passes and the levels of residence privileges open to the girls. Girls also could spend points in a variety of other ways. The point system supplemented the girls' treatment program, so even if a girl had earned enough points for a pass, her therapist may consider the inadvisability of the girl's going on leave at that time; another girl may not have earned enough points for a pass, but the therapist may suggest one, whereupon the student could borrow points from the point bank for the pass.

At the staff meetings, members reached a decision to phase out the point system. This was an important step in the program for the girls who moved to a group home or who attended public school while living within the residential setting.

Integration of a schedule, evaluation, and feedback system in this residential setting was a vital link in the communication network among staff members. Consistency in behavioral expectations and adult support was enhanced by the described services.

Student's Weekly Schedule
CONTRACT

I, _____ , contract to do the work listed below for the days of the week of _____ . I will work ahead in my free time and study hall to complete all the work I have contracted to finish by the end of the school morning (12:00 noon).

Subject	Thursday	Friday	Monday	Tuesday	Wednesday
Elective Points & Comments					
Literature	__% __pts	__% __pts	__% __pts	__% __pts	__% __pts
Math	__% __pts	__% __pts	__% __pts	__% __pts	__% __pts
Social Studies	__% __pts	__% __pts	__% __pts	__% __pts	__% __pts
Science	__% __pts	__% __pts	__% __pts	__% __pts	__% __pts
Other	__% __pts	__% __pts	__% __pts	__% __pts	__% __pts
Total					
Points earned over Points lost					
Student Comments:					

Teacher's Daily Record Sheet

Date Student		APPEARANCE	ON TIME	BEHAVIOR	PREPARED	STUDY BEHAVIOR	ACADEMIC POINTS	CORRECTOR LIBRARIAN OR TUTORING	ELECTIVE	SCIENCE BEHAVIOR — LAB	BONUS POINTS	TOTAL POINTS	ACADEMIC %

Needs Help:
1.
2.
3.
4.
5.
6.
7.
8.
9.
10.

Ready to Check Out:
1.
2.
3.
4.
5.
6.
7.
8.
9.
10.

Weekly Average Percent Sheet

Name of Student: _____ :

WEEK OF:	WEEK OF:	WEEK OF:
ENGLISH/ LITERATURE	ENGLISH/ LITERATURE	ENGLISH/ LITERATURE
MATH	MATH	MATH
SOCIAL STUDIES	SOCIAL STUDIES	SOCIAL STUDIES
SCIENCE	SCIENCE	SCIENCE
OTHER	OTHER	OTHER
Checked by:	Checked by:	Checked by:

Averaging Instructions

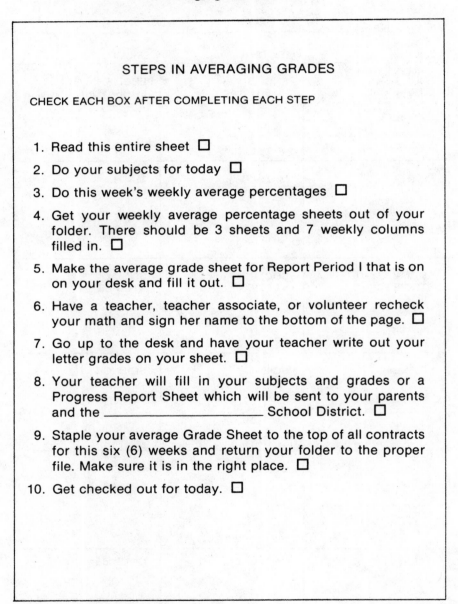

STEPS IN AVERAGING GRADES

CHECK EACH BOX AFTER COMPLETING EACH STEP

1. Read this entire sheet ☐

2. Do your subjects for today ☐

3. Do this week's weekly average percentages ☐

4. Get your weekly average percentage sheets out of your folder. There should be 3 sheets and 7 weekly columns filled in. ☐

5. Make the average grade sheet for Report Period I that is on on your desk and fill it out. ☐

6. Have a teacher, teacher associate, or volunteer recheck your math and sign her name to the bottom of the page. ☐

7. Go up to the desk and have your teacher write out your letter grades on your sheet. ☐

8. Your teacher will fill in your subjects and grades or a Progress Report Sheet which will be sent to your parents and the _____ School District. ☐

9. Staple your average Grade Sheet to the top of all contracts for this six (6) weeks and return your folder to the proper file. Make sure it is in the right place. ☐

10. Get checked out for today. ☐

Report Form for Students Attending Regular Classes

Weekly School Progress Report				
Student:			Week of:	
Courses	Perfect Attendance, if not please list dates absent	All Assignments Turned In	Acceptable Behavior In Class	Teacher's Signature and Comments

Homeroom Teacher's Weekly Point Form

Progress Report						
Student:				Week of:		
	Thursday	Friday	Monday	Tuesday	Wednesday	Thursday
Points Earned						
Points Possible						
Average Daily Percentage						Avg. % for week
Teacher's Comments:						Circle in red if attained honor roll

Counselor's Signature

269

Weekly Behavior Chart

NAME _____ BEHAVIOR CHART WEEK OF: _____ COUNSELOR

	SCHOOL			CHILD CARE			RECREATION						
	PTS.	BNS.	SPT.	PTS.	BNS.	SPT.	PTS.	BNS.	SPT.	PTS	BNS	SPT	TOT
THURS.													
FRI.													
SAT.													
SUN.													
MON.													
TUES.													
WED.													

Point Record Sheet for School, Residence, Recreation

Teacher _____ Week of: _____

TOTAL POINTS SHEET

Name	Combined Pts. So/Rec/Sch	Pts. Spent	Grand Total	Pass	Class

½ DAY PASS COSTS: 42 points (8 hrs. or less)
1 DAY PASS COSTS: 85 points (over 8 hrs. — not overnight)
2 DAY PASS COSTS: 170 points (overnight)
3 DAY PASS COSTS: 200 points (Fri. night to Sun. night)
(for passes over 3 days: add 30 points for each additional day)

EIGHT

MAINTENANCE AND PHASING OUT

- Substitute Teachers
- Parent Communications
- Phasing Out
- Appendix to Chapter 8
    Books about the Lives of
    Emotionally Disturbed
    Children

MAINTENANCE AND PHASING OUT

Maintenance and phasing out — the two remaining procedures of the structured approach — were touched upon in the previous chapters, and are expanded upon here. Maintenance refers to continuance and enrichment of the special class environment after it has been established. Although an inordinate amount of time is spent in developing a special educational environment for disturbed youth, its maintenance cannot be assumed. Planned techniques designed to carry on the program must be implemented. One consideration is in planning for the substitute teacher, to continue the structured approach during a teacher's absence. Another consideration, communicating with parents, is designed to establish cooperative home-school relationships for the purpose of expanding the special environment.

The special program also assumes some of the responsibility for directing habilitated students to other educational opportunities. Phasing out is the procedure for establishing a link between special education and regular education so the student can make a successful transition into the mainstream of activities.

SUBSTITUTE TEACHERS

The need for a substitute teacher arises for many reasons including illness, maternity leave, emergencies, death of a family member, unavoidable commitments, attendance at professional meetings, and personal business. The amount of time a substitute spends in a class varies from several hours to weeks or months.

Schools have various procedures for obtaining substitute teachers. For some, a central office is contacted; for others, the building principal is contacted; for still others the absentee teacher contacts a teacher from a list of available substitutes. The experience level of substitute teachers ranges from those who have had no contact with exceptional children to those who have had successful teaching experiences with emotionally disturbed youth. Regardless of the extent of time substitute teachers are needed, their levels of experience, or procurement procedures, advance planning should be done to prepare for a substitute in the special class. The substitute should be the recipient of a plan for a well organized day and should have to make few decisions regarding the daily functioning of the class, so that the students can enjoy a productive day.

The advance planning can be subdivided into two major categories: routine entries (information that remains relatively unchanged, such as the school's procedure for fire drills), and room entries (activities such as lesson plans for the students). Information in routine entries requires frequent updating. If all the information were placed on 5″ x 8″ index cards and kept in a file box, or on single sheets of paper kept in a notebook, replacements could be accomplished more readily.

Information items the teacher may want to include in instructions to the substitute are outlined below.

1. Routine entries. (Most of these are associated with the school building and remain relatively stable.)

    a. School routine.

        (1) Names of building principal, assistant principal, and teachers in adjacent rooms.
        (2) Room number.
        (3) Bell schedule.
        (4) Schedule if other teachers come to the special class to instruct.
        (5) Schedule of students who go to activities away from the special classroom.
        (6) Routes to and from special rooms such as art, music, physical education, and lunchroom. Add a note if the student is to be accompanied by teacher or aide to any of the rooms.
        (7) Lunch, attendance, and tardy counts, and routing of that information.
        (8) Seating arangements for school assembly.
        (9) Lunch period times.

(10) Lunch procedure, such as assigned tables for students or cleanup responsibilities.

(11) Lunch arrangements for the teacher, such as requirements to eat at an assigned table and staying in the building during the lunch time; or places for eating lunch such as the faculty lounge, designated areas, or restaurant facilities.

(12) Routes to building exits.

(13) School rules for students, such as no talking in the hall, having passes when walking in the halls during class time, or no smoking on the school premises.

(14) Playground rules.

(15) Free period (if any). Indicate where faculty members congregate, location of coke, coffee, and vending machines, restrooms.

(16) Dismissal routine.

(17) Duty assignments such as hall, playground, bus, or telephone.

(18) Room routine, such as closing windows, locking doors, pulling window shades to a certain level.

b. Teacher's desk and materials.

(1) Location of keys if needed for desk, closet, file cabinets, or audio-visual equipment.

(2) Location of books, materials, and A-V equipment.

(3) Procedure for library, hall, nurse, and counselor passes.

(4) Description of what constitutes a "tardy" or a pass to the nurse and counselor.

(5) Procedure for checking out materials from the classroom.

c. Disaster instructions.

(1) Description of procedures if they are not posted in the room.

(2) Order in which students leave and return to the rooms.

(3) Route taken to the safe area.

(4) Description of warning and/or all-clear signals.

(5) Map of the school showing north and south streets. (Identify major areas of building.)

(6) Closing or opening of windows and doors.

(7) Indication if advanced warning of disaster drills is given to teachers.

d. School discipline hierarchy.

(1) Usual techniques for inappropriate behavior, such as subtle kinds of disapproval, removal of tokens or points, private warning, or on-the-spot mini-conference.

      (2) Additional channels for misbehavior, such as time-out, conference, or assignment of a time and place for confinement (e.g., 8th hour in study hall).

      (3) Explain "misbehavior" referrals to the principal's, counselor's, or crisis teacher's offices.

  e. Resources.

      (1) Names of one or two students who are trustworthy.

      (2) Names of teachers to call upon for assistance.

      (3) Emergency telephone numbers.

2. Room entries, (Most are associated with the special classroom and need frequent updating.)

  a. Room organization.

      (1) Names of students; include photographs (e.g., school pictures or snapshots).

      (2) Seating chart or study carrel assignments.

      (3) Self-adhesive nametags for students and/or their desks.

      (4) Morning routine such as flag salute, lunch count, group or individual counseling sessions.

      (5) Line leaders or buddy arrangements.

      (6) Student duty roster, such as sharpening pencils, watering plants, or collecting feedback sheets.

      (7) Class time schedule (e.g., 9:15-10:30 for Work Block 1).

      (8) Dismissal routine including materials that go home, transportation used by each student, any special seating arrangements on bus, etc.

  b. Special situations.

      (1) Names of children on medication, the medications, and any possible side effects.

      (2) Information about any unusual health conditions and their management, such as a student who has seizures, or one who has a bladder problem.

      (3) Information about students who have hearing, visual, or physical impairments that necessitate special locations in the room, require curriculum adaptations, or limit the student's activities.

      (4) Names of person(s) student can turn to if extremely emotionally upset.

(5) Students' reactions to certain techniques used in the room.

c. Lesson plans.
   (1) Teacher plan book and/or student assignment sheets. Leave specific instructions and directions with these plans. Some teachers do board work, make daily plans, organize materials, etc., after school. This habit can benefit the substitute if the special education teacher is absent unexpectedly.
   (2) Teacher's recording sheets for grades.
   (3) Students' evaluation sheets.
   (4) Location of answer keys.
   (5) Location of teacher's manual(s).
   (6) Description of how incomplete assignments are managed.
   (7) Description of grading system; include requirements for correcting errors in assignments.
   (8) Description of which assignments are returned to the students and which are kept by the teacher.
   (9) Description of any reinforcement or token systems. Describe the reinforcers, contingencies, and behaviors that can earn or lose reinforcers.
   (10) Description of free time rules or how to structure free time.
   (11) Teacher's recording sheets for token accumulation.
   (12) Include a reinforcing note to the substitute somewhere within the plan; for example, "Hang in there! The kids need you."
   (13) Make all instructions concise and understandable.
   (14) Allow time in the morning schedule for the substitute to have a "breathing spell" in which to review plans, etc., by planning for students to engage in enjoyable independent activities. Some teachers provide a "bag of tricks," a special box or folder of work, games, or projects. These activities also can be used if unforeseen "blank spots" occur in the day.

d. Feedback.
   (1) Feedback forms for daily reports to students and parents.
   (2) Feedback forms for recognition of special behaviors displayed by students.
   (3) Feedback forms for objective and subjective comments by the substitute to the absentee teacher regarding the day's events and the students' progress. Forms should have space for listing special problems encountered by the substitute.

279

       (4) Forms for the substitute's evaluation of the lesson plan left by the special education teacher.

       (5) Provide a tape recorder, if available, should the substitute prefer giving feedback on a tape.

    e. Volunteers and aides.

       (1) Names of volunteers and aides. An aide is a partner in the classroom organization and can be of immeasurable help to the substitute.

       (2) Schedule of their times in the room.

       (3) Description of aide's responsibilities such as lunch supervision, grading papers, dispensing tokens, making materials, or individual tutoring.

3. Miscellaneous techniques.

    a. A special education teacher can prepare students for a substitute teacher by doing some of the following:

       (1) Have discussions or role-playing activities.

       (2) Discuss reasons for needing a substitute teacher.

       (3) Invite other adults to visit the room so the students can become acquainted with strangers in their classroom; occasionally, the teacher should step out of the class while the other adult is present.

       (4) Familiarize the students with some recess activities that can be done indoors in case of unfavorable weather on substitute's day.

       (5) Involve the students in some of the routine jobs.

       (6) Invite the substitute to visit the class if the upcoming absence is known in advance.

    b. A teacher may need to reassess a day's planned activities if a substitute is known to be coming to the class. These are some "don'ts":

       (1) Discussions or lectures that are too specific in detail and content — such activities may be difficult for the substitute to do without considerable advance planning.

       (2) Group projects that have potential for negative contagion.

       (3) Introduction of new curriculum materials, especially if advance preparation is needed for their introduction.

       (4) Movies, if a darkened room will invite problems.

       (5) Visitors or observers. Reschedule their visitation dates.

(6) Planning the use of audio-visual materials if they are not accompanied by operating instructions.

(7) Demonstrations, especially if a substitute is not familiar with the needed materials.

Items (6) or (7) could be included in a substitute's day if a student is capable of assuming a leadership role in the activity.

After substitutes have been in the classroom, the special education teacher should provide feedback to the building principal and/or designated staff member responsible for hiring substitutes. If special feedback forms are not used for this purpose, the special education teacher should make a personal contact with the designated personnel regarding the physical order in which the class was left, the degree to which the plans were followed, reliable student reactions, and reactions of the aide or other staff members.

PARENT COMMUNICATIONS

Special class placement is not a panacea — it is a part of the services a disturbed youth can receive. The youth alternately may need placement in a 24-hour-a-day residential setting, psychiatric treatment, or support and guidance from counselors and social workers. Since a student's enrollment in a special educational environment is limited to five or six hours a day, many teachers are involved in communications with parents for purposes of extending the supportive milieu as much as possible. Cooperation between home and school is considered vital to sustained improvements in students' behavior.

This important communication link with the adults associated with the youth is highly developed in some residential settings where a team of staff members is in frequent and close communication. In some residential settings, child care workers are parent substitutes; therefore, they are contacted by the teachers for the "home"-school interaction. For parents of students attending special classes in public schools, strong efforts should be exerted by the teachers to develop a communication network to maximize students' growth potential. The network may involve teacher-parent conferences, group meetings, phone calls, and visitations.

Group Meetings

A group parent meeting is one technique for facilitating communications on a topic of common interest to the group. These meetings may be prearranged for specific times throughout the school year or scheduled aperiodically. All meetings must be planned in advance with a special goal in mind. The program for the meetings may focus on problem solving topics, information gathering, training, or be designed to have therapeutic outcomes.

A problem solving meeting may include topics on conflict between siblings, acceptance of responsibilities, shoplifting, resentment of authority, bedwetting, and runaways. Topics in information sessions may include availability of community services to the youth and family such as mental health clinics, guidance centers, and youth groups, and school services such as speech therapy, vocational guidance, and career planning. At some meetings parents may be involved in learning child rearing, management, or listening techniques. Individuals with a working knowledge of the topics and who can empathetically relate to parents should conduct the meetings. Discussion leaders could include psychologists, social workers, counselors, speech clinicians, psychiatrists, special education directors, school nurses, building principals, and teachers. Only qualified personnel should be asked to lead the discussions, especially the ones designed with therapeutic goals.

Teachers should conduct the meetings which describe classroom activities. During the first weeks of a school year, most teachers have an orientation group meeting to describe the organization of the school day, some of the activities, the grading system, feedback, evaluation and schedule forms, program goals. Subsequent meetings can encompass general progress descriptions of class events, class interests, and major organization program changes since the last meeting.

Teachers could use slide presentations to illustrate the class activities. Pictures are more graphic, especially for parents who do not have the opportunity to observe the class in session. Teachers do not need to have photographic skills to give a slide presentation. Most "instamatic" type cameras can use slide as well as print film. Portions of the slide presentation could be accompanied by audio recordings of and by the students. One special education class video-taped classroom activities. The initial presentation was so enthusiastically received that parents requested more video tapes. Another room had a Saturday morning class session in the late fall to encourage the attendance of male family members. Fathers, uncles, and grandfathers were invited to observe class activities.

Group parent meetings can be advantageous because individual parents can share solutions to problems; more parents can be reached at one time; parents can be supportive of each another outside of the meetings through phone contacts; others feel comforted in the realization that they are not the only ones having problems. For some parents, communication achieved in group meetings is the means of improving personal interactions with their children.

Individual Conferences

Conferences with parents should concentrate on a topic as it directly relates to their child. The student should be informed when a conference is scheduled and should know the nature of the conference. Sometimes, specific pieces of information are shared with the student before or after the conference. It is important for a student to realize that parent conferences are an established and vital part of the program; therefore, the first parent conferences and group parent meetings should be non-threatening. This approach is especially important for students and parents whose prior experiences with teachers' conferences have been debilitating, demeaning, or negative. If the parent contact begins with casual introductions during the pre-academic year planning week, and is followed by a group meeting orienting parents to the education program and a detailed get-acquainted conference on their child's individual education program, the foundation is formed for potential cooperative communication rather than a combatant one. Topics for the teacher-parent conferences include the following:

Get Acquainted

Get acquainted overtures could be directed toward parents being introduced to the student's daily schedule of activities as it is currently integrated with overall goals of the program; or it could be a get acquainted conference directed toward the teacher becoming acquainted with students' lives outside of school, such as their likes and dislikes, relationship with siblings and friends, and leisure time activities. Sometimes a conference is held in the home, where parents might feel more comfortable.

283

Home visits can provide clues to enhance a teacher's understanding of the youth; however, teachers should try to avoid making subjective judgments.

In a conference with parents of primary aged students, one teacher included a description of the daily assignment sheet and the evaluation system. The teacher marked the sheet for the parents with the points they received during the conference, and stars for their "work." Parents were encouraged to show their sheets to their children as one technique to encourage school work. Another teacher and the students prepared a scrapbook of room activities, continually adding to the book over time. The scrapbook was shared with parents and also with new students and their parents prior to the students' entering the special class.

Sharing

This type of conference focuses on objective observations of the student's performance in class. The teacher could share tangible evidence of student accomplishments including worksheets, writing samples, pages in a text on which the student currently is working, results of a product, the student's participation in verbal discussion, charts or graphs, drawings and photographs of the student engaged in various activities.

Teachers should initiate the conference with evidence of the student's positive growth efforts. Weaknesses can be discussed specifically using terminology such as, "Vince needs strengthening in . . ." or, "Linda needs to improve in the . . .." Teachers also could describe meaningful incidents such as a withdrawn student's first verbal contact with a peer; or a student's refusal to play ball. The latter student's cherished activity was ball throwing, but he became embarrassed when his teacher encouraged him to play ball with several visitors. The embarrassment and refusal were the first signs of self awareness and autonomy shown by the child.

Parents could share items indicating students' growth by verbally describing incidents and/or bringing in tangible products from home. Some students do school-oriented activities at home such as calculating the car mileage for the family vacation, doubling a cookie recipe, or writing the grocery list. Students sometimes do activities at home that indicate abilities not observed in the classroom. For example, one seven-year-old was an excellent card player and was able to play games calling for detailed observational skills, mental addition with sums up to 31, waiting for turns, and attending to games for long periods of time. Another student was able to disassemble and assemble a variety of motors.

Planning

Some conferences involve planning activities for a home-school program relating to consistency in management techniques for identified, inappropriate behaviors. Parents and teachers also can plan intervention techniques designed to recognize danger signals, such as signs of anger that lead to verbal or violent outbreaks, moods that precede depressions, and so forth. Plans for phasing out a student to classes within the building or home-school involve joint efforts. Additional personnel may be involved in planning conferences; for example, the building principal and regular teacher may be involved in the phasing out conference, or a psychologist may be involved in the management conference.

Teaching

If a cooperative home-school program has been planned, the teacher may find that teaching or demonstrating a lesson is useful before the parents initiate the activity at home. If a student were involved in a sequential language program, the teacher, possibly aided by a speech clinician, could demonstrate how to elicit, stimulate, and reinforce language. In some situations parents have observed teachers, co-taught with the teachers, then proceeded with some coaching, if needed. Thus, the parents receive supervision and support until they feel comfortable about proceeding with the activity. Parents, too, can ask teachers to follow through with a home initiated activity such as having a language-deficient child practice using new words in the classroom.

Crises

Among the wide variety of incidents that can elicit conferences are fights involving objects thrown on the bus, students not coming home at night, parents upset about their child receiving a tangible reinforcer, or students appearing in class with bruises on the face. Strong feelings can be transmitted in these unanticipated conferences. Therefore, the teacher should proceed calmly before initiating crisis conferences, and should be a sympathetic listener if the parent or other personnel initiate the conference as a result of some emotionally upsetting experience.

285

Problem Solving

This type of conference usually centers on a chronic problem, whereas the crisis conference focuses on a situational problem. Other professionals may be available to share knowledge with the teacher and parents as they attempt to find solutions to a problem. For instance, the school nurse or family physician might be involved in a conference based on a health related problem with a diabetic child who will not follow the doctor's prescribed eating plan.

Telephone Contacts

Many special education teachers encourage parents to use the telephone as part of the cooperative communication effort. Phone calls to the teacher can be valuable and should be received with an attitude of concern and responsive listening. Some teachers make weekly or bi-monthly calls to parents to elaborate on daily reports and discuss special situations. Certain types of concerns are best conveyed through calls, as in those requiring immediate attention. Phone calls also are made to provide feedback on a home-school plan, to reinforce parents for responding to a request, to report an exceptionally good day, or to share appreciation for efforts by the parents; in other words, the parents should not receive only negative information that may lead them to dread teacher phone calls.

Conference Techniques

Some techniques that teachers can use to enhance an open communication network during classroom conferences are:

1. Provide adult-sized chairs.
2. Arrange chairs informally.
3. Provide ashtrays.
4. Have coffee and tea available.
5. Serve refreshments at group meetings.
6. Offer several appointment options for conferences, including evening and before-school hours.
7. Be prepared for students and siblings who may accompany parents to the conferences. Arrange for activities the children can do indepen-

dently while the adults are engaged in the discussion. Supervision of younger children also may need to be considered.

8. In teacher-initiated conferences, prepare an outline of the discussion topics.

9. Develop a parent conference form to record conference dates, names of individuals attending the conference, major topics covered, and plans, if any, that are to be followed through.

10. Be an active and responsive listener.

11. Assume a partnership role.

12. Be cognizant that as the teacher and parents discuss a student's behavior, the student is being described according to two different environments. The student may be responding differently in these environments so, in a sense, you are talking about two different children. Some teachers and parents have a tendency to mistrust each other's behavioral descriptions, especially if discrepancies arise. For example, a student could be extremely quiet in a family setting and yet be an acting-out child in the classroom.

13. Keep the student in mind during the conference, as the focus of the meeting.

14. Be positive in the discussions. If the student's weaknesses are part of the discussion, make the wording positive, such as, "Susan needs to grow in . . ." rather than, "Susan has weakness in . . ."

15. Be honest, but use tact and diplomacy.

16. Remember that a teacher is not a therapist, although a conference could have therapeutic effects. If the student's parents need counseling, consider including carefully chosen additional staff personnel in a conference.

17. Have parents leave a note on their child's desk regarding something positive that occurred during the conference (for example, "Your teacher said you have tried hard in math," "I saw your neat science essay," "Your graph on sharing shows a lot of progress."

18. Compliment the parents for their efforts.

19. Encourage parents, guardians, or involved child care workers to attend all conferences. If only one member attends a conference, do not assume that information emerging during the conference is shared with the absent persons.

20. Be sure to follow through on ideas, communication gains, goals, and plans evolving from the conferences.

21. Invite parents to observe their child's class in session.

Group parent meetings, individual parent conferences, telephone calls, and feedback notes (discussed in other chapters) are some of the techniques for establishing and maintaining a communication system among the home, special class, and other personnel associated with the class. Development of trusting and cooperative home-school relationships may be a slow process. If the desired cooperation and communication with some parents do not develop maximally even after concentrated and concerted efforts by school personnel, the teacher should remember that many variables can exert stronger influences than that of the teacher and school. The teacher can at least have satisfaction in doing everything possible to further home-school communication.

PHASING OUT

Phasing out is a procedure by which students in the special class gradually are integrated into the mainstream of school activities. Frequently, this procedure is followed as an intermediate step before returning a student to the home school because, initially, phasing out may begin in a regular classroom in the building where the special classroom is located, in a classroom in a neighboring school near the residential setting. Before phasing out begins, the student should be engaged in many activities that occur near the end of the continua of the scheduling guidelines. This means that the student has been using regular textbooks and materials, is involved in group work and cooperative activities, has made the adjustment from tangible to natural reinforcers, and is making decisions appropriate for the age group. The phasing out procedure attempts to support the student making a transition into a regular classroom environment, and the responsibilities of the special class teacher begin to change. The teacher's role as the student's primary source of instruction and guidance shifts to one of resource.

A single set of phasing out steps cannot be developed to encompass all disturbed youth because different variables are associated with each student's return to the mainstream of school life. The climates of school environments differ because of variations in administrative organization and style, teachers' attitudes, and the schools' relationships with parents and community. The number of persons involved in implementing the phasing out procedure ranges from two to a group consisting of any or all of the following personnel: special education teacher, building principal, therapist, social worker, psychiatrist, psychologist, parents,

288

child care worker, regular class teacher, special education director, and parents.

The three known persons involved in a student's departure from a special class are the student, the receiving teacher, and sending teacher. The following list of techniques is offered primarily for these three individuals, but any of the ideas can be adapted and embellished to accommodate the phasing out procedure for a specific student in a specific situation.

Preliminary Activities between Special and Regular Class Teachers

Frequently, teachers of students having behavioral disorders are misunderstood because they enjoy working with the "mentals." Thus, a special education teacher should be consciously involved in the use of public relations skills. A little thing such as making the student look good may well lead to the teacher's being cast in the role of a winner. Such "promotion" efforts should lay some groundwork before a student is phased out to a regular classroom. A teacher can select preliminary techniques for phasing out from among the following suggestions:

1. Share materials with other teachers. Sometimes special classrooms have better budgets, more materials, and materials different from those in regular classes but which can be used advantageously by other teachers.
2. Accent the positive abilities of students by displaying individual student's worksheets, science projects, creative and academic papers, or results of class activities, such as a mural, quilt, or flag.
3. Arrange a sharing time with interested students from regular classes, especially if a student has a special skill such as guitar playing, weaving, or motor repair.
4. Co-plan a field trip with a regular class or invite members to join the special class on a field trip.
5. Exchange talents with a regular class teacher by teaching each other's class an academic subject or leisure time skill such as terrarium making, macrame, model building, or photography.
6. Keep the classroom door open as much as possible — open doors invite drop-ins and lessen feelings of isolation of the special class.

289

7. Be genuinely interested in searching for new ideas and curriculum input from other teachers.
8. Be available if other teachers want to chat about materials, new ideas, or a student's problems. A pot of coffee in the classroom may tempt other teachers to stop in for a visit.

Activities between Special and Regular Class Teachers before Phasing Begins

After the receiving teacher has been identified, communication channels must be developed for the benefit of the student. Special education teachers have used the following communication techniques, among others:

1. Discuss with the receiving teacher the tentative plan for phasing out. The discussion can give each teacher an opportunity to share thoughts and reactions. The special education teacher may need to explain the terms *mainstreaming, phasing out, emotional disturbance,* and *behavioral disorders.* Ramifications of the label *emotional disturbance* for the student being phased out may need additional explanation. During this conference or in a subsequent one, the receiving teacher should be asked to anticipate possible problems that might occur when the special student is in the regular class. Both teachers could formulate plans for managing potential problems.
2. Describe students' progress by comparing their current work with earlier work. Graphs, charts, actual papers, materials, and photographs can be used to illustrate the comparisons. Share the information accrued from daily observations and contacts.
3. Relate positive attributes about the student to the receiving teacher.
4. If a student has a mannerism such as continuous eye-blinking under tension or other behavioral idiosyncracies such as having an imagined green mold allergy, explain these.
5. Together as teachers, select the initial activities for the student's participation in the regular classroom.
6. Ask the regular teacher for any suggestions on times that may be most appropriate for the special student's entrance into the class. One teacher suggested a day when a new instructional unit was to begin.
7. Tell the receiving teacher why you think a student will benefit from placement in that class.

8. Describe any special or unusual techniques that have been useful in teaching the student to establish work habits, to approach a task, or to manage a behavior. Include a description of limits and controls if they are needed by the student.

9. Be candid in discussing failures so that your communications don't suggest infallibility.

10. Ask to visit the regular class to observe the teacher's instruction style and approach, evaluation, discipline, and reinforcement systems, for purposes of acquainting the student with these variables before entrance into the class.

11. A special education teacher and regular class teacher in one instance conducted a mini-project: They asked a student teaching supervisor to assist in this project because of her time schedule, which had greater flexibility in arranging to be in either of the rooms. The regular class teacher was asked to identify two or three students who could be described as typical students. Then, some of the behavior — being on task, daydreaming, out-of-seat behavior — were observed and recorded by the supervisor during specific intervals. When the special student was integrated into the regular class, the supervisor continued the recording. Results indicated that the special student's behavior had improved in all of the observed areas, significantly on some behaviors. A six-week followup check indicated that the special student's behavior continued to improve, approaching that of his peers in the new setting. These recordings supported the decision regarding the special student's placement into the regular classroom. Furthermore, the regular teacher was pleased to learn the observation and recording techniques used by the supervisor.

Activities between Receiving Teacher and Students before Phasing Out Begins

Some regular class teachers have initiated or incorporated special topics in affective activities to promote peer acceptance of new pupils, such as:

1. A series of activities focusing on feelings for persons who are different can be conducted in a regular class. One awareness activity calls for a week of discriminations. Each day a different set of students is discriminated against through planned ignoring, talking, or segregation,

because of the color of eyes or hair or the dominant use of right or left hand. These activities are followed by a group discussion on "What happened when discrimination occurred?" "How did it feel?" "What should you do if you observe discrimination against another student in the future?"

Another awareness activity is done as follows: The students sit in a circle, each taking turns to do a common simple activity. The other students are asked to comment in a negative manner regardless of the individual student's performance. After each student has experienced the adverse reaction and failure of acceptance, each in turn performs another simple task. This time the other students respond in a positive way and offer encouragement. After all the students have experienced the positive reactions and feelings of approval and acceptance, an active discussion ensues, comparing feelings during the two incidents and effects of peer approval and disapproval.

2. Results of a sociogram can be used to help determine regular students who will be asked to be the incoming special student's buddy or be seated at an adjacent desk. Their accepting manner and positive behavior are criteria and attributes that can serve as models of performance for other students.

Activities between Receiving Teacher and Special Teacher during Phasing Out Process

Special teachers have continued communications with the receiving teacher by engaging in some of the following activities:

1. Be available and offer assistance, reassurance, and support if needed by the regular teacher.
2. Offer to teach regular students who may be experiencing academic difficulties. Special education teachers have so many different individual programs occurring concurrently that sometimes they can include another student in their program with few modifications.
3. Be complimentary about admirable materials and activities in the regular classroom. Ask to use observed ideas that can enhance the special students' program, and offer to share materials and ideas.
4. Develop a feedback sheet to facilitate ongoing communication. Daily personal conferences are seldom possible, so many teachers prefer a checklist form with space for comments.

292

5. Keep lines of communication open, and be honest in contacts.
6. Compliment the regular teacher on the special students' progress.
7. Pass along students' comments to the teacher, building principal, and parents.
8. Keep parents informed of students' progress.
9. Keep the principal informed of students' progress.

Phasing Out Activities for the Special Student

Many students with behavioral disorders are placed in self-contained classrooms as part of a continuum of services they receive until they are able to perform adequately in regular classes. Thus, their entrance into a special class is accompanied by the goal that they also will leave. Some teachers candidly discuss this goal with the student during the educational diagnostic session. Throughout the student's enrollment in the special class, the goal is again restated in casual ways. When a student has acquired a skill, the teacher might say, "That's just the way you'll do it when you're in the _____ class," If a student has learned to put a heading on a notebook paper, the teacher might say, "Did you know that most teachers ask their students to put headings on their papers, but each teacher has different requirements on how to do this?" After the student has acquired the necessary behaviors to leave the special class and the receiving teacher has been identified, the student should engage in some orientation activities. Techniques which special education teachers have used are included in the following suggestions:

1. Introduce the student to the receiving teacher and allow the two of them time to get acquainted.
2. Ask the receiving teacher to visit the student informally in the special classroom during a high interest time.
3. Suggest that the regular teacher work with the student in a certain subject area in a special class and that the special education teacher instruct the regular class during that time.
4. Invite the teacher and the new class to visit the special class for an activity such as watching a film and having popcorn or participating in a special visit with guest speakers.
5. Give the special student the opportunity to explore the new classroom when it is empty.
6. Have the student go on errands to the future new classroom.

7. Engage in a private discussion with the student about the impending phase-out. Encourage the student to ex,press concerns or fears. Be sure that the student is led to perceive the move as progress.

8. Keep the student informed of the phasing out arrangements.

9. Set up a conference with the student and receiving teacher to decide on the first phase-out activity. A student's obvious area of strength may be a logical choice. The conference also reveals information that may have slipped the mind, such as materials needed by the student; for example, students phased into math may need special equipment such as metric conversion table, compass, 12-inch ruler also marked in centimeters, and 1/4-inch graph paper.

10. Acquaint the student with the school routine by presenting opportunities for getting library and hall passes, learning how to locate a locker, how to use a combination lock, or how to change classes within the required time limit.

11. Acquaint the student with the routine of the new class, its rules and regulations.

12. Use the same grading system as the receiving teacher uses. This may mean that the student receives checkmarks for incorrect responses, no marks for correct responses, and the number wrong at the top of worksheets.

13. Plan a special event if a student is involved in a phase-out done by half-days. If a special class were located in a residential setting or in a special school building, the student may leave for half days rather than by single classes. One class in a special school planned a farewell party and sent invitations to staff members involved with the student. All the students were involved in the party activities which included decorating the room, serving refreshments, and conversing with the guests. The departing student was the party's host.

Another teacher made a game for a student who was to return home, thousands of miles from the residential setting. The teacher made a game board identifying major geographic settings in the boy's current environment (the town where the residential setting was lo-cated, the nearby shopping center, his favorite "hangout," the airline ticket office, airport, etc.). Game markers were silhouettes of baseball players, each with a student's photo replacing the players' faces. The markers were moved around the board through use of chance cards associated with the student's move. Through this game, the departing student became thoroughly acquainted with events surrounding his departure.

14. If students are leaving the special class for a half day, parents may need to be more involved in the phase-out procedure because of additional transportation arrangements, enrollment processes, and similar considerations.

    One teacher from a special school was able to do many of the previously described activities in regular junior high schools when students were phased out by half days because they always had been required to attend the last class session at their home schools. The students were involved in classes where they could participate adequately. The special education teacher often went to the buildings to establish and maintain communications with the regular teachers and principal.

15. Young students could prepare a scrapbook to introduce themselves to the new group. They could write a short biography and include interests, likes, and dislikes. Snapshots of the student participating in various activities could be included in the scrapbook. Some teachers, however, disagree with this activity because it calls undue attention to a new student.

16. Listen to the student during the phasing out days for any signs of feelings about success or failure, interest, and concern.

SUMMARY

The maintenance procedure cannot exist until teacher and students interact with the special environment. Thus, this procedure depends to a large extent on the other procedures of the structured approach. The importance of structure cannot be overemphasized because, without its techniques, planning for a substitute teacher, parent communications, and other techniques such as shifts in the scheduling continua and ongoing diagnosis could not be carried out. Maintenance is not stagnation; it is the continuance and extension of a special environment. Thus, it is an ongoing procedure.

The phasing-out procedure begins in small ways during the student's initial days in a special class, and continues to be integrated into the student's program. It becomes prominent when the student accrues more appropriate behaviors. The procedure is integrated with the other procedures, but it is emphasized near the end of a student's enrollment in a special class.

BIBLIOGRAPHY

Bakwin, Harry, and Bakwin, Ruth. *Clinical Management of Behavioral Disorders in children.* Philadelphia: W. D. Saunders Company, 1960, pp. 192-210.

Baratta, Mary Lorton. *Actively Centered Learning in the Home for Parents.* Menlo Park, CA: Addison Wesley, 1975.

Buscaglia, Leo. *The Disabled and Their Parents: A Counseling Challenge.* Charles B. Slack, Inc., 6900 Grove Rd., Thorofare, NJ, 08086.

Gronlund, Norman. *Sociometry in the Classroom.* New York: Harper, 1959.

Kroth, Roger. *Communicating with Parents of Exceptional Children: Improving Parent Teacher Relationships.* Denver: Love Publishing Co., 1975.

Kvaraceus, William, and Hayes, E. Nelson. *If Your Child is Handicapped.* Boston: Porter Sargent, Publisher, 1969.

McKee, Paul. *Primer for Parents: How Your Child Learns to Read.* Palo Alto, CA: Houghton Mifflin.

SUGGESTED RESOURCES

Closer Look. A project of the U.S. Department of Health, Education & Welfare, established for parents to gain practical advice on how to locate educational programs and special services. Box 1492, Washington, DC 20013.

Exceptional Parent. A bi-monthly magazine with practical emphasis; has articles dealing with the kinds of problems faced by parents of handicapped children; features a forum for exchange of parents' ideas and experiences. P.O. Box 964, Manchester, NH 03105.

Parenting Materials Information Center. A project cataloging materials about parenting; for parents, teachers, and paraprofessionals. Request "PMIC User's Handbook," Southwest Educational Development Laboratory, 211 E. 7th St., Austin, TX 78701.

APPENDIX TO CHAPTER EIGHT

BOOKS ABOUT THE LIVES OF
EMOTIONALLY DISTURBED CHILDREN

Axline, Virginia M. *Dibs in Search of Self*. New York: Ballantine, 1969,
  Dell, 1971.

Baruch, Dorothy. *One Little Boy*. New York: Dell, 1964.

D'Ambrosio, Richard. *No Language But a Cry*. New York: Doubleday,
  1970, Dell, 1971.

Elliott, David. *Listen to the Silence*. New York: New American Library,
  1971.

Green, Hannah. *I Never Promised You a Rose Garden*. New York: Holt,
  Rinehart & Winston, 1964.

Greenfield, Josh. *A Child Called Noah*. New York: Warner Paperback
  Library, 1973.

MacCracken, Mary. *A Circle of Children*. New York: J. B. Lippincott,
  1973.

Neufeld, John. *Lisa, Bright and Dark*. New York: S. G. Phillips, 1969.

Park, Clara. *The Siege: The First Eight Years of an Autistic Child*. Boston:
  Little, Brown, 1972.

Platt, Kin. *The Boy Who Could Make Himself Disappear*. New York:
  Dell, 1971.

Rothman, Esther. *Angel Inside Went Sour*. New York: Bantam, 1972.

Wilson, Louise. *This Stranger, My Son*. New York: New American
  Library, 1971.

INDEX